Diagnosis
and
Treatment
of the
Disabled Reader

Homer L. J. Carter
WESTERN MICHIGAN UNIVERSITY

Dorothy J. McGinnis
WESTERN MICHIGAN UNIVERSITY

Diagnosis

and

Treatment

of the

Disabled Reader

THE MACMILLAN COMPANY
COLLIER-MACMILLAN LIMITED, LONDON

Second Printing, 1971

Library of Congress catalog card number: 78–85792

THE MACMILLAN COMPANY
866 THIRD AVENUE, NEW YORK, NEW YORK 10022
COLLIER-MACMILLAN CANADA, LTD., TORONTO, ONTARIO

Printed in the United States of America

Preface

Diagnosis and Treatment of the Disabled Reader has been written for all those who wish to understand *why* children are having difficulty in learning to read and what can be done about it. These individuals will need to identify factors affecting reading performance. In order to accomplish this goal they must focus their attention upon the child and interpret physiological, psychological, sociological, and educational factors affecting his learning and adjustment. Such individuals, it is assumed, are not well prepared in all of these disciplines. Nevertheless, they wish to determine conditions which adversely affect achievement in reading and, as far as possible, mitigate or remove them. This book can help classroom teachers contribute more effectively to the total reading program by showing them how to meet the needs of children experiencing difficulty in reading. Not all classroom teachers can be expected, because of lack of preparation, laboratory facilities, and time, to make detailed clinical studies of their children. They can, however, identify, interpret, and fulfill the reading needs of their pupils. They want to do more than developmental teaching.

This book has been designed to help principals and teachers identify and select children with reading difficulties who can profit from instruction in the classroom, those who require temporary treatment by the reading therapist, and those in need of clinical study. It will also prove helpful to those teachers who wish to acquire through graduate study a practical point of view concerning a clinical approach to reading disabilities. *Diagnosis and Treatment of the Disabled Reader* can be used as a resource text in college clinics and by remedial teachers or clinicians in training. The book will be of value to school psychologists and guidance counselors who are frequently required to deal with problems of reading maladjustment. The text emphasizes an integration of facts resulting from interviews, observations, and informal inventories as well as from objective tests. The professional worker is shown not only how to interpret the child's

v

present adjustment in relation to his past, but how to evaluate him in terms of his experiential background, his immediate goals, and his way of life. The teacher learns to profit from a moving picture of the child over a period of time as well as from a snapshot of him at the moment of examination. Remediation in the case of the disabled reader involves diagnosis and treatment, and the latter consists of both instruction and therapy. In the opinion of the writers, the two should be carried on simultaneously. In this book the emphasis has been placed upon practical approaches for the professional worker. Brevity is an outstanding characteristic.

The Guided Activities accompanying each chapter provide an opportunity to apply in actual situations many of the ideas presented in the chapter. Questions and parallel references stimulate the student to extend and deepen his background by reading materials contributed by contemporary writers.

H. L. J. C.

D. J. McG.

Contents

Diagnosis
and
Treatment
of the
Disabled Reader

Chapter 1

Philosophy Underlying the Study and Treatment of Disabled Readers

It is the purpose of this chapter to present an overview of the reading situation as it exists today and to suggest an all-school attack on the problem. It is also our intention to set forth a point of view concerning reading and the diagnosis and treatment of the disabled reader. In essence, this chapter contains an educational philosophy and is a delineation of the horizons to be broadened in the text.

A PROBLEM

Steve is nineteen years old and a nonreader. He is a youth of average intelligence who, despite fourteen years of attendance in the public schools, has not learned to read. He works for his father as a construction worker and, until recently, was engaged to be married. Perhaps we should permit Steve to tell his own story.

From the very beginning I had trouble with reading. I repeated first grade but that didn't help. I was big for my age so I was never held back except for that one time in first grade. Each year I was passed to the next grade even though I couldn't read a word. No one seemed to care except my mother. She tried to teach me at home but that was awful! I don't even want to talk about it; it was that bad. There was just one person at school

1

who ever tried to help me, and that was my eleventh-grade art teacher. But she didn't know how to teach reading and so that was another failure. Finally everyone gave up, and they handed me my diploma.

I'm ashamed of my inability to read, and I manage to hide it from most people. But recently my reading problem blew all my plans for the future sky-high. Joan and I had been engaged for several months. She knew I didn't read much and couldn't read very well, but I guess she hadn't realized how bad my reading really was. Well, on my last birthday my friends had a party for me. After everyone left, I asked Joan to read the birthday cards to me. What a mistake that was because it really hit her then that I couldn't read. For several months she tried to teach me to read, but I couldn't learn a thing. Finally she broke off the engagement, convinced that I was dumb and would make a poor husband.

There are many "Steves" in our world today who are severely penalized because of their inability to read. Most of them, however, can overcome their handicap if given the right kind of help at the right time by the right person. Every elementary and secondary teacher has had the experience of having students who, like Steve, are severely retarded in reading. The number of pupils needing special help is so great that administrative adjustments must be made to remedy the problem of the disabled reader.

SOME PROBLEMS CONFRONTING THE CLASSROOM TEACHER

Miss Clair is a sixth-grade teacher who has thirty-six boys and girls in her room. In keeping with the policy of her school, the Iowa Silent Reading Test, Elementary Battery, was administered to her group during the second week of the semester. The distribution of grade scores made by her students is shown in Table 1-1. Observations of the children's reading ability and skills made over a two-week period showed that several pupils needed to learn to identify main ideas, to read for a specific purpose, and to make ideas their own. Ten of the group needed to learn to read for the purpose of drawing conclusions from facts stated in a social science text. Eight needed to learn how to build up reading and spelling vocabularies from their textbooks in reading. The two pupils reading at the second-grade level were both boys, and one was found by the school psychologist to have an IQ on the Stanford Binet of 136. All the children in the class were reported by their former teachers to be of average intelligence or better. Six boys and girls in the group came from culturally de-

**TABLE 1-1 Distribution of Grade Scores on
Iowa Silent Reading Test, Sixth-Grade Class**

Grade Score	Frequency
9.0	2
8.0	4
7.0	5
6.0	6
5.0	7
4.0	5
3.0	5
2.0	2
Total	36

prived homes. The school histories indicated that several students
had visual, auditory, and other physical disabilities.

Miss Clair's problems are similar to those experienced by teachers
throughout our country. In order to meet effectively the needs of
students, teachers must determine for themselves answers to the
following questions.

How can the teacher deal with so great a range of achievement
within a class?

Can any one approach to the teaching of reading be adequate?

Should children be grouped according to grade levels in reading
or according to certain specific objectives to be accomplished?

Should children be told of their achievement in reading?

Should parents of children who are reading far below the expected
level be acquainted with this fact?

What children should the teacher refer to the reading therapist?

What children should the teacher recommend for study by a group
of clinical workers?

What factors contribute to the reading performance of pupils in
a class?

How can the teacher do corrective work in reading?

Can the teacher be expected to raise the achievement level of all
the children to that of their grade placement?

How can teachers prevent reading maladjustment among their
children?

AN ALL-SCHOOL APPROACH TO THE PROBLEM

A thoroughgoing developmental program can meet the reading needs of approximately 92 per cent of the total school population. Most classroom teachers in grades one to six are well aware of the aims to be accomplished. They have many well-chosen materials with which to work, and they are acquainted with approaches, methods, and techniques for the effective teaching of reading. The wide range of reading levels within a class can be dealt with successfully by utilizing a flexible-grouping plan. Students can be grouped temporarily in order to accomplish specific purposes. When these goals have been achieved, new groups can be arranged to attain still other reading objectives. This approach should not be confused with grouping according to grade equivalents in reading or with multiple-track plans. Flexible grouping is based on the immediate reading needs of pupils, and each group functions as an integral part of the class for only a few days.

It is the consensus of many teachers of reading that a flexible-grouping plan is a satisfactory solution to the problem of variability of grade levels and needs within a class. In fact, corrective reading can be provided by the classroom teacher as she utilizes a flexible grouping plan. The teacher will be primarily concerned with meeting the reading needs of her children by furnishing specific instruction within the various groups, irrespective of their reading levels. Materials can be selected not only on the basis of what they are to accomplish, but according to the interest and reading levels of the children involved. Flexible grouping can make clear to the child that other children have reading needs similar to his own. This understanding and the progress which the child makes from day to day can contribute to his self-concept and feeling of security. In this manner the classroom teacher can conduct a thorough developmental program in reading and at the same time meet some of the needs of the disabled reader.

In many junior and senior high schools, classes in adult reading are being organized to show the student how to improve certain reading skills as he does his regular academic work. The student is shown, for example, how to acquire the following skills.

- Identifying main ideas.

- Reading for a purpose.
- Making ideas his own.
- Making the most of words.
- Learning what to accept and what to reject.
- Skimming a textbook effectively.
- Developing rate and flexibility.
- Concentrating.
- Reading different kinds of literature.
- Reading in the field of mathematics.
- Reading in the field of science.
- Reading in the social studies.
- Reading creatively.

The instruction in the course is generally goal oriented and is designed to aid the student achieve *his* objectives. Enrollment is voluntary; however, students planning to attend college are advised to enter these classes.

The classroom teacher in grades one to twelve is well aware of his responsibility for the teaching of reading. He is extending his preparation by graduate courses in psychology, sociology, and education. He is a member of professional groups and subscribes to professional journals. He should be recognized for his efforts in the first line of defense against maladjustment in reading.

The improvement of reading ability is an educational objective to which all instructional and supervisory staff members should contribute. School administrators, however, have assigned to certain members of their faculty specific areas of responsibility.

The Reading Consultant

The reading consultant, having an educational background of teaching methods, especially in the field of reading, is expected to guide both elementary and secondary teachers as they attempt to develop the reading skills of their students. The reading consultant should be able to do at any level that which he expects others to do. Experiential background is a requisite, as is a knowledge of contemporary research in the language arts. The ability to evaluate reading materials effectively and to suggest reliable sources of information is a necessary attainment. The chief responsibilities of the reading consultant are to *stimulate, inform,* and *guide* teachers who request or need assistance. Leadership is essential.

The Reading Clinician

The reading clinician has an adequate background in physiology, psychology, sociology, and education. This reading specialist is primarily concerned with identifying and interpreting causal factors underlying disabilities in reading. The clinician studies the child in his environment and cooperates with specialists in other disciplines. In treatment, the reading clinician utilizes instructional procedures and psychotherapy. In general, the reading clinician should aspire to meet the requirements of a consulting psychologist.

The Reading Therapist

A background of education and psychology is essential to the preparation of the reading therapist. This specialist provides instruction and psychotherapy for individuals and small groups generally in cooperation with the reading clinician or school psychologist. A reading laboratory adequately equipped with reading materials at all levels is her place of operation. Students who remain with their peers and home-room teachers come to the reading laboratory for short periods of guidance and specific instruction. The reading therapist emphasizes specific aims, well-selected materials, and carefully designed procedures. With these concepts in mind let us ask an important question.

WHAT IS READING?

Reading is a function of the total organism. It is more than a stimulus-response dictum, for meaning is obtained from the organism and not from the printed page. Reading is a purposeful process of identifying, interpreting, and evaluating ideas in terms of the mental content of the reader. This theory of reading developed by the writers from the psychological contributions of Witasek, Wertheimer, and John Stuart Mill[1] is expressed in the following manner.

[1] See item 9 of Questions and References at the end of this chapter.

Reading is a function of

$$\left(\frac{S}{M} \cdot \frac{S}{M^2} \cdot \frac{S}{M^3}\right)$$

In the formula S represents any symbol expressing an idea and M designates mental content which is the total awareness of the individual at any one moment. The three aspects of reading are expressed as Gestalts. They are operational in nature and are not to be considered as mathematical models to be proved or disproved.

Identification is expressed as:

$$\frac{S}{M}$$

Interpretation is expressed as:

$$\frac{\frac{S}{M}}{M} \quad \text{or} \quad \frac{S}{M^2}$$

Evaluation is expressed as:

$$\frac{\frac{S}{M^2}}{M} \quad \text{or} \quad \frac{S}{M^3}$$

In each of the three configurations mental content is a crucial factor, for it is the *ground* which provides meaning for each *figure*. For example, the reader *identifies* the word *sine* in terms of either trigonometry or Latin, depending on his mental content. He *interprets* that which he has identified as "a function of an angle" or as "without" depending on his mental content. In any case, it is obvious that more mental content, M^2, is required for interpretation than for identification. In a similar manner, the reader evaluates that which he has interpreted in terms of his mental content. Sine, depending on his background, becomes useful to him as he reads the sentence, "The meeting was adjourned *sine die*," or as he attempts to solve a trigonometric problem. Again it is apparent that more mental content, M^3, is required for evaluation than for interpretation. Reading can be expressed as a function of

$$\left(\frac{S}{M} \cdot \frac{S}{M^2} \cdot \frac{S}{M^3}\right)$$

These configurations lose their identities and emerge as reading. Reading, then, is an integration of skills rather than an accumulation.

This concept of reading is broad in its implications; however, it can be applied more specifically by limiting it to the identification, interpretation, and evaluation of visual stimuli which appear as written or printed characters. Words are signs and symbols of thought which are rich in meaning to the informed. The word *villain,* for example, meant originally the dweller in a villa or small town. Later the word grew to mean, for various reasons, a scoundrel.

Speaking, writing, listening, and reading are closely related. When the individual speaks or writes, he builds up and creates. When the individual listens or reads, he first analyzes the communication and then creates his own concept of it. In all these forms of communication the total organism responds, and this response is manifested by both implicit and explicit behavior. Reading is, in part, the process of transferring meaning from visual signs to well-known auditory symbols. In the act of reading, implicit speech is a concomitant of this transfer as the whole organism reacts to the visual stimuli. Linguistics and reading are related, and some authorities stress the importance of this relationship.

The concept of reading suggested here emphasizes the participation of the whole organism in the reading process. Nearly all modalities are activated—for example, visual, auditory, kinesthetic, and tactual. The whole individual reacts in the quest for meaning, and this meaning is dependent on mental content. Let us now consider the importance of this definition of reading and its relation to the study of the disabled reader.

Importance of the Reading Definition

The theory of reading presented here stresses the importance of the organism in the act of securing meaning. It implies that the individual in his environment is the chief object of study in the clinical investigation of reading disabilities. If this concept of reading is accepted, the teacher or clinician will investigate the individual in *his* environment. She will consider the individual's maturation and his experiential background, which may or may not have contributed to his readiness for reading. She will be concerned not only with what the individual knows but what he feels. The emphasis of the teacher and therapist will be on the individual, and not solely on the subject matter or the reading skills which the individual may need to acquire. In the application of treatment, the therapist will stress the teaching of fundamental skills in a goal-oriented process, and not as separate entities. The teacher will understand that the reader must utilize what he knows and feels to profit from the act of reading. She will understand that the reader must contribute in order to receive, because meaning comes from the reader and not from the printed page. This concept of reading, if accepted, will determine how the teacher and therapist study the child and guide him as he achieves his goal. Strang[2] has also pointed out that techniques of diagnosis will vary with theories of reading. She shows how each of the following concepts would necessitate a separate approach to the study of reading disability.

- Reading is a visual task.
- Reading is primarily word recognition.
- Reading is a process of securing meaning.
- Reading is interpretation of author's ideas.
- Reading necessitates use of material read.
- Reading necessitates change of reader's ideas, feelings, attitudes, and behavior.

Relation of the Concept of Reading to Study of Individual in His Environment

One's concept of reading determines how he studies the disabled reader. If the diagnostician accepts the concept of reading set forth in this chapter, he will understand that:

- He must focus attention on the individual in his environment.
- Reading is an act of the whole organism.
- Degrees of mental content determine degrees of readiness for reading.
- In any act of reading, mental content determines what the individual is to see, hear, and feel.
- Both interest and emotional states are resultants of mental content.

[2] Ruth Strang, *Diagnostic Teaching of Reading* (New York: McGraw-Hill Book Company, 1964), pp. 6–7.

In the study of the disabled reader the teacher and clinician are concerned with the *causes* that precede what we shall call the *effect*. It may not be an invariable sequence but a probability of a specified occurrence. In general, causation is multiple—no one cause is the only determiner of an event. In the case of an individual, however, a single factor can trigger a series of reactions in which several factors are involved. Many contributing factors interact and present a pattern producing an effect. Causes may be classified as primary, constitutional, exciting, predisposing, and secondary. There is, of course, much overlapping.

In the investigation of causes all data are not of equal importance. Some facts are *relevant*, for they are related to the cause of the reading disability. Some facts fit together into a configuration and tentatively point to a specific conclusion. These facts are said to be *material* because they are essential to the interpretation of the immediate problem. The term *consequential* is used to describe a fact or condition which through a sequence of events leads to an effect. In all instances the value of the judgment is dependent on the intelligence, training, and experience of the evaluator. In every reading case some facts will be rejected because they are *irrelevant, immaterial,* and *inconsequential*.

Sources of data cannot be used to determine relevance. Even routine testing and history taking do not always furnish facts that fit together into a well-integrated design of causal factors. When this impasse occurs, the diagnostician knows that his problem has become acute. More facts are needed. More tests must be administered. More interviews must be conducted. More observations must be made. New sources of information must be found. After additional study, facts may be discovered which make up configurations of factors that are relevant, material, and consequential to the problem under consideration.

Constellations of relevant data which require interpretation and evaluation can be gathered from many sources. In the study of human behavior and especially reading, a prime area of investigation is the *physical* organism. Vision, audition, and neurological factors will need investigation. Other factors that may be considered are motor coordination, dominance, and general health. *Psychological* factors such as mental maturity, emotional maturity, mental content, emotional stability, and self-concept will require detailed and systematic study.

Educational factors generally identified in the school and classroom environment are essential to an understanding of the individual's reading performance. Knowledge of the school's educational philosophy, the materials, and methods employed is required if the reading clinician is to comprehend the effect of the school environment on the individual and his ability to learn. No pattern of factors should be ignored. *Sociological* constituents require an investigation if the individual is to be studied in his relations to others making up his everyday world. Parents, the home, the church, and the neighborhood can provide data that are necessary for an understanding of the individual and may suggest causes underlying the individual's inability to read at the expected level.

SOME CONCEPTS OF DIAGNOSIS

Diagnosis, as defined in this chapter, is an explanation of an individual's maladjustment. It can be made at several levels and with varying degrees of competence. As observed in Figure 1-1, identification of a disability is the lowest form. At this level, it is only pointed out that the individual's difficulty in the classroom is due to the fact that he cannot read. He is merely identified as a nonreader. At the second level, the problem is described in some

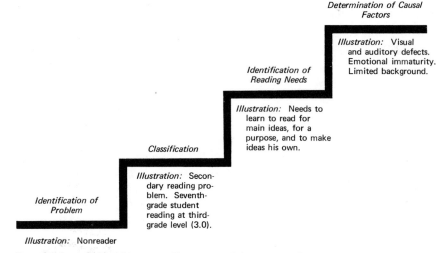

Figure 1-1   Levels of Diagnosis Shown on a Schematic Scale

detail, for it is pointed out that a seventh-grade student is reading at the third-grade level (3.0) and is classified as a secondary reading problem who is penalized because of his disability. The chief characteristics of this level are measurement, classification, and description. At the third level of diagnosis, the reading needs of the individual are identified. It is shown, for example, that the person needs to learn how to read for main ideas, how to read for a purpose, and how to make ideas his own. These inferences may be based upon the use of tests, observational procedures, informal inventories, and interviewing techniques. The value of these procedures is dependent on the relevant information they furnish concerning the individual being studied. These procedures are merely tools utilized in obtaining facts pertinent to diagnosis and treatment. The fourth and highest level of diagnosis involves the determination of causal factors. The chief objective is to determine *why* the individual does what he does. In the diagnosis of an individual at this level there frequently is need for cooperation with others trained in such fields as pediatrics, ophthalmology, otology, neurology, psychology, and sociology. It is the responsibility of the reading clinician to arrange for referrals or cooperative study. He should not attempt to muddle through alone.

At level four the problem is carefully identified. Hypotheses as to probable cause are set up. Investigations in many areas are made to determine relevant facts. On the basis of these facts, hypotheses are rejected until finally one is found and accepted because it represents a configuration of consequential facts which adequately explains the fundamental difficulty. The effectiveness of diagnosis depends on an interpretation of the individual's performance rather than merely an evaluation of his achievement. The proof of this diagnosis is based upon prediction and later verification.

Diagnosticians at all levels use a variety of approaches, numerous techniques, and wisely chosen procedures. They appreciate the fact that no single routine can be satisfactory with all individuals. Inventories, clinical tests, and instruments of precision are chosen with well-defined objectives in mind. The effective clinician works systematically, methodically, and objectively, combining the interests of a parent for his child and the point of view of the laboratory technician as he examines a piece of tissue under a lens. He believes that reading, a form of human behavior, depends on the organism as a whole rather than upon particular parts. He refuses to accept the concept that "brain damage," "perceptual difficulties," and "inadequate neurological organizations" alone are responsible for reading disabilities. The diagnostician must be aware of the ever-changing organism. As one causal factor is mitigated or removed, another factor may operate in such a manner as to contribute to the disability. Diagnosis is not static but ongoing in its nature. The clinician is aware of the uniqueness of the individual and his needs and does not assign a ready-made diagnosis to all of his clients. In all instances, the effectiveness of diagnosis is dependent upon the experience and mental content of the clinician involved in the study. He understands the responsibilities of privileged communications and the various situations constituting malpractice. Furthermore, the clinician maintains high ethical standards in his professional practice. He is thoroughly acquainted with the Code of Ethics set forth by the International Reading Association and with the Ethical Standards of Psychologists established by the American Psychological Association.

A diagnosis at any level should lead directly to treatment and the improvement of the individual's ability to read effectively. In fact, treatment cannot accomplish its purpose unless the diagnosis is correct, valid, and specific. A cure is seldom, if ever, the result of accident.

SOME FACTORS TO BE CONSIDERED IN TREATMENT

Treatment may be *specific* or *palliative*. Specific treatment prevents or cures a disorder, whereas palliative treatment merely eases or mitigates a disability without curing it. Palliative measures may be applied at any level. In general, specific treatment is instigated only after causal factors have been identified and diagnosed at the fourth level. Specific treatment generally results in the removal of causal factors and the restoration of normal growth and development. In providing treatment of reading disabilities, the therapist selects adequate materials in terms of the needs, interests, and reading level of the individual. He accepts the individual as he is, without disapproval, and helps him to realize his potential. The therapist understands that each individual is seeking satisfaction, security, and recognition. He realizes that frustration and a feeling of inadequacy can seriously interfere with the individual's self-concept and the success of the instruction. To be effective, learning must be goal oriented. Instruction and treatment must aid the disabled reader to accomplish his goals and achieve his purposes. He must secure his satisfaction, his security, and his recognition.

Palliative measures and specific treatment may be applied simultaneously or in a sequence depending on the factors involved and the urgency of the situation. Generally, in treating reading disabilities, palliative measures designed to alleviate serious maladjustment are most frequently applied. In fact, there are only a few specifics for the treatment of reading disabilities.

Remediation in reading does not occur immediately, in a few days, in a few weeks, or even in a few months. It results in growth which cannot always be evaluated reliably over short periods of time. Exaggerated claims of marked growth in reading achievement are fairly common and should be considered with caution.

Time and place of treatment are always important issues which must be resolved in terms of the individual and his welfare. In some instances, regular classroom instruction will suffice. In others, treatment in a reading laboratory is essential. Decisions must be made in consultation with the child, his parents, and school authorities. The welfare of the child should be the first consideration.

Personnel providing treatment can generally determine its success or failure. Some teachers do excellent work with a group of children but fail to meet the needs of some individuals. Many parents lack the patience to deal adequately with their own boys and girls, and consequently corrective work in reading should not be entrusted to them. Treatment, following diagnosis, should be assigned to well-trained therapists with a clinical background in dealing with the individual who has a serious reading problem. Certification should be a requirement for these reading specialists.

SUMMARY

In this chapter attention has been directed to the retarded reader in his class and school. A concept of reading has been related to the diagnosis and treatment of the maladjusted reader. The authors' philosophy underlying the study of the disabled reader is briefly summarized as follows:

- The clinician's definition of reading determines how he will study the disabled reader.
- The good diagnostician uses a variety of approaches, numerous techniques, and wisely chosen procedures and is aware of the uniqueness of the individual and his needs. He does not assign a ready-made diagnosis to all his clients.
- Diagnosis of reading disability is based on interpretation of a child's performance rather than merely on an evaluation of his achievement.
- The diagnostician is aware of the ever-changing organism. He understands that diagnosis is not static, but ongoing.
- In diagnosis and treatment there is need for cooperation with others trained in such fields as pediatrics, ophthalmology, otology, neurology, psychology, and sociology.
- The clinician combines the interest of a parent for his child and the point of view of a laboratory technician.
- Diagnosis is dependent on the experience and mental content of the clinician.
- The clinician understands that each individual is seeking *satisfaction, security,* and *recognition.*
- The clinician accepts the individual as he is without disapproval and helps him to realize his potential.
- Remediation is the result of growth and is most effective when related to the purposes and goals of the individual.
- The clinician understands the responsibilities of privileged communications and maintains high ethical standards in his professional practice.
- A clinical study of a minor should not be made without permission from the parent or guardian.

GUIDED ACTIVITY 1

Aim

To evaluate a point of view concerning diagnosis and treatment of reading disabilities.

Materials

1. Chapter 1, *Diagnosis and Treatment of the Disabled Reader.*
2. Reference materials suggested at the end of this chapter.

Procedure

1. Show how teachers of reading and clinicians differ in their approach to a study of the individual.
2. What points of view do they have in common?
3. How do the preparation and academic background of clinicians differ from those of teachers of reading?
4. How can a teacher's definition of reading affect her teaching of reading?
5. How can a clinician's definition of reading affect his approach to a study of an individual with a reading difficulty?
6. Show how instruction in reading and treatment of a reading disability may differ.
7. Explain why, in your opinion, a good teacher can or cannot be a good clinician.
8. How do teachers and clinicians differ in their basic philosophy?
9. Clinical work and teaching are essential vocations. State the area in which you wish to participate and give your reasons.

QUESTIONS AND REFERENCES

Questions

1. How do the points of view expressed in Chapter 1 of this book differ from those expressed in Chapter 1 of *Diagnostic Teaching of Reading* by Strang?

2. How should teachers be prepared to teach reading?

3. What are some contributions to the diagnosis and treatment of reading disabilities?

4. How can teachers and clinicians cooperate?

References

1. Ruth Strang, *Diagnostic Teaching of Reading* (New York: McGraw-Hill Book Company, 1964), Chap. 1.

2. Mary C. Austin and others, *The Torch Lighters: Tomorrow's Teachers of Reading* (Cambridge, Mass.: Harvard University Press, 1961).

3. "Contributions to the Diagnosis and Remedial Treatment of Reading Difficulties: Symposium," *British Journal of Educational Psychology*, 30:146–179 (June, 1960) and 31:79–105 (February, 1961).

4. Homer L. J. Carter, "Cooperative Study, the Clinic and the Class-

Questions	References
	room Teacher," *Reading and Inquiry* (Newark, Delaware: International Reading Association Conference Proceedings, 1965), pp. 212–214.
5. What is an interdisciplinary approach to diagnosis?	**5.** Roy Kress, "Diagnosis: An Interdisciplinary Approach," *Reading and Inquiry* (Newark, Delaware: International Reading Association Conference Proceedings, 1965), pp. 195–197.
6. What ethical standards should the psychologist maintain?	**6.** Anne Anastasi, *Psychological Testing*, 3rd ed. (New York: The Macmillan Company, 1968), Appendix A.
7. What ethical standards should the reading specialist maintain?	**7.** "Code of Ethics," *Journal of Reading*, **10:**4 (October, 1966).
8. How do the definitions of primary and secondary reading disabilities provided in this book differ from those set forth by Rabinovitch?	**8.** Ralph D. Rabinovitch, "Dyslexia: Psychiatric Considerations," in John Money, ed., *Reading Disability* (Baltimore: The Johns Hopkins Press, 1962), p. 74.
9. What are the theories of Witasek, Wertheimer, and J. S. Mill in relation to meaning?	**9.** Robert D. Williams and Roger M. Bellows, *Background of Contemporary Psychology* (Columbus, Ohio: Harold L. Hedrick, Publisher, 1935), pp. 102–104 and 219–221.

Chapter 2

Identification and Selection of Individuals Requiring Diagnosis and Treatment

It is the purpose of this chapter to define reading disability, to outline means of identifying the disabled reader, and to stress the importance of early identification. Two approaches to the problem of the retarded reader are presented, and suggestions are given for selecting individuals requiring clinical service as opposed to those who can profit from corrective instruction.

DEFINITION OF READING DISABILITY

The retarded reader is generally an individual who has been unable to learn to read effectively when taught by regular classroom procedures. Frequently, his deficiency is observable in his whole environment. It may, and usually does, affect his educational, psychological, and vocational adjustment. He can be found at all levels of mental maturity and is not performing as well as his physical and mental maturation would suggest. Some readers are not aware of their inadequate reading skills. These individuals are characterized as people showing *primary* reading disabilities. Other individuals who are aware of their reading disability and are severely penalized academically, socially, or vocationally because of their problem are described as people with *secondary* reading disabilities.

Such terms as the *retarded reader,* the *disabled reader,* and the *maladjusted reader* need clarification. There is one factor common to all three terms and that is the inability to read effectively in various situations. In general, the expressions are synonymous and have the same connotation, if not the same denotation. In this book these terms will be used interchangeably. The retarded reader may be

- One whose scores on a reading test are two or more years below his grade placement.
- One who is reading significantly below his expected level as determined by an individual test of intelligence, such as the Stanford-Binet Intelligence Scale or the Wechsler Intelligence Scale for Children.
- One who scores well on a survey test of reading ability but whose achievement in certain reading skills is quite inadequate and imposes a penalty.
- One who shows average or better than average performance on a reading test and yet, because of tension, anxiety, frustration, or personality defects, is unable to utilize the reading skills he possesses.
- One who is a nonreader with causal factors known or unknown.

Money[1] differentiates five types of reading disorders: The first is caused by sensory handicaps, the second by mental defect, the third by improper or insufficient instruction, the fourth by inadequate home environment, and the fifth by unknown causes which he labels *specific dyslexia.* Furthermore, he describes dyslexia as resulting from developmental and traumatic causes.

IDENTIFICATION OF DISABLED READERS

Children who are having difficulty in learning to read can be identified by a careful consideration of their *academic history,* by *observations* of them in the classroom, by data from *informal reading inventories,* and by *objective tests.* Each of these approaches to the problem of identification will be briefly discussed.

[1] John Money, *Reading Disability* (Baltimore: The Johns Hopkins Press, 1962), pp. 3–4.

The Academic History

The school history of a child can provide a means of evaluating his progress and in many instances can explain his performance in the classroom. The past can be a preparation for the present and a prediction of the future. Some questions involving the school history which can aid in the identification of the disabled reader are:

In what grade is he now enrolled?

How long has he attended school?

Did he ever fail to be promoted?

Why did he fail?

What grades did he receive last year in each of the following subjects: reading, spelling, language, social studies, mathematics?

Have teachers reported that the child's progress in any subject is due to difficulties in reading?

Has a former teacher pointed out that the child is in need of reading therapy?

Has the child ever been referred to a reading therapist?

Has the child, for one reason or another, been neglected by his teachers?

Have the parents of the child ever come to school to discuss his reading problem?

What academic goals have the parents set up for the child?

In the student's academic history not all facts are of equal significance. Some are relevant, a few are material, and a lesser number are consequential. Those engaged in the study of the child must evaluate and interpret these facts in terms of the child in his environment. A single fact may be consequential for one child and only relevant or perhaps insignificant for another.

Observations

The classroom teacher has many opportunities to observe her students as she conducts her daily classes. She can readily identify the student who cannot read. His acts and words can show the perceptive teacher that he fails to grasp the meaning of words, that he is unable to blend words into meaningful phrases and sentences, that he is unable to select essential ideas, that he cannot organize information, and that he is unable to summarize facts and answer questions based on what he has read. The teacher, however, does not see the child's total behavior. She may not be familiar with his performance in his other classes and with his other teachers. Her limited information may be modified by subsequent observations and other means of verification. The teacher must not become a biased witness unduly influenced by her associates and previously prepared checklists. She must make observations and prepare her own inferences.

Disabled readers frequently show many of the following characteristics:

- Inability to identify words.
- Inability to interpret words in terms of ideas.
- Inability to evaluate ideas.
- Guessing and bluffing in reading situations.
- Alphabet confusion.
- Inability to do satisfactory academic work.
- Marked reversal tendencies.
- Limited rate of reading.
- Inability to identify main ideas.
- Failure to enjoy reading activities.
- Inadequate means of attacking unknown words.
- Manifestation of emotional reactions in reading situations.
- Comparatively low independent-reading level in relation to capacity level.
- Lack of interest in books.
- Application in learning situations other than reading.
- Good verbal ability, yet inability to read effectively.
- Infrequent use of the library.

The Informal Reading Inventory

The classroom teacher can gain valuable information from informal reading inventories designed to determine the independent-reading level, the instructional level, the frustration level, and the capacity level of the individual. For more detailed information on these levels of attainment, it is suggested that the reader turn to Chapter 8. Informal reading inventories can aid the teacher in securing on-the-spot information on the child's reading status. Data resulting from their use can be surprisingly valid and reliable because materials utilized are similar to materials actually used in the classroom. Clinical workers frequently report that scores provided by standardized tests resemble closely the frustration levels of students as determined by informal reading inventories. These inventories can be employed to identify quickly and effectively the individual who shows evidence of reading maladjustment.

The discrepancy between the child's capacity and independent-reading levels suggests the seriousness of the reading difficulty. A boy, for example, may have the capacity level of an individual in the seventh grade and an independent-reading level of a child in the second grade. This disparity of five years suggests that the student is a disabled reader. Inferences resulting from informal reading inventories should be substantiated by data from other sources. Some questions which an informal reading inventory can be of value in answering are as follows:

- What is the child's independent-reading level?
- What is the child's instructional level?
- What is his frustration level?
- What is his capacity level?
- Is there a disparity of two or more years between the independent-reading level and the capacity level?
- After observing the child's performance, do you believe that he is in need of special instruction in reading?

Standardized Tests

Tests are systematic procedures for comparing the performance of individuals in terms of a particular point of reference. Carefully selected tests of reading ability are of value in the identification of children with reading disabilities. They provide a general estimate of the reading attainment and the range of reading performance within a class. The teacher, however, should understand that group scores are more reliable and valid than a single score of an individual. In spite of this fact, children scoring two or more years below their grade placement should be identified and made the object of further investigation. Table 2-1 shows how this has been accomplished with John, Lee, Stephen, and Carl. Their reading scores converted into reading ages have called attention to their achievement. Data from Stanford-Binet tests, observations, school histories, and informal reading inventories have been utilized in determining whether or not the children have reading problems. It is obvious, then, that test scores in reading can alert the classroom teacher to the possible needs of her pupils who score two or more years below their expected level on survey tests of reading achievement.

Individual measures of mental maturity can be of value in determining the intellectual level at which the individual is functioning at the time of the examination. The mental age on the Stanford-Binet and the IQ on the Wechsler suggest the level at which the individual can be expected to perform. The child's achievement in reading can be compared with this level, for it furnishes a point of reference. Group tests of intelligence, however, should not be used for this purpose. In general, these tests involve reading ability, and consequently the disabled reader will make low scores which are inadequate measures of his mental status. The Stanford-Binet and the Wechsler tests are individual measures of mental maturity which should be administered by qualified examiners. These tests are useful in determining the potential of the individual. Measures of reading ability indicate the degree to which this potential has been attained. Information resulting from standardized tests should be integrated with and interpreted in terms of all the facts derived from all the sources. Emphasis should not be given to any one area of information. The disabled reader should not be identified solely on the basis of test scores. Instead, consideration should be given to his academic history, to facts observed in the classroom, and to data resulting from informal reading inventories. Facts from all sources must be recapitulated and valid conclusions drawn.

Some questions which standardized tests can be of value in answering are as follows:

• Do test scores of mental maturity indicate a high, average, or low potential?
• Do test scores in reading indicate a high, average, or low achievement level?

- Is the child's performance in reading significantly below his potential?
- Is the child's performance in reading below his grade placement level?
- Do standardized-test scores suggest that the child is a disabled reader?

EXAMPLES OF DISABLED READERS

Table 2-1 shows some, but not all, of the factors to be considered in determining whether or not an individual has a reading problem. These factors are chronological age, mental age, reading-age equivalent, and independent, instructional, frustration and capacity levels, along with observations and school history. All children shown in Table 2-1 were ten years of age and had the same grade placement, yet their ability to read varied greatly.

John is an intelligent boy who apparently is not reading at his expected level even though he is performing at approximately his chronological age level. John and children like him often are not identified as underachievers, for frequently they may be doing average or better work in the classroom and the teacher has no means of determining their expected levels. These boys and girls, when wisely treated, can become leaders.

Most clinicians would regard *Lee* as a child requiring clinical study and treatment. He is a boy of average mental maturity whose performance in reading is significantly below his chronological and intellectual expectations. Boys similar to Lee frequently try to conceal their disability in reading by aggressive behavior or by other forms of compensation.

Stephen may be doing all that can be expected of him. Data from informal reading inventories reinforce the assumption that although Stephen is reading below his grade placement, he is not to be identified as a disabled reader because he is doing all that he is capable of doing. In other words, his performance in reading is in keeping with his total growth and development.

Carl, like John, is probably not achieving at his expected level, and an effort should be made to determine and mitigate the causal factors involved in his reading maladjustment.

In brief, it may be pointed out that no child should be identified

TABLE 2-1 Four Children Frequently Identified as Having Reading Problems

Child	Observations	Mental Age	Reading Age	Independent Level	Instructional Level	Frustration Level	Capacity Level	School History
John	Wide range of reading interest	13-3	10-0	4.0	5.0	6.0	8.0	Normal progress
Lee	Frequently in trouble	10-1	8-0	1.0	2.0	3.0	5.0	Academic and disciplinary problem
Stephen	Asks for help	8-4	8-2	1.0	2.0	3.0	3.0	Poor grades
Carl	Does not contribute to class discussion	8-6	7-4	Primer	1.0	2.0	4.0	Culturally deprived

as possessing a reading disability solely on evidence presented by test scores or any other single factor. His complete history along with observations of him in his environment should be carefully evaluated.

EARLY IDENTIFICATION ESSENTIAL

Many reading consultants believe that the retarded reader is not identified and referred for help early enough. In the typical school approximately 8 per cent of the student body can be classified as disabled readers. In order to help these individuals, we must know who they are and be able to provide aid as soon as possible. It has been estimated that if the school can identify and provide adequate treatment for these children no later than the third grade, there is a 70 to 80 per cent chance of success. If the treatment is delayed until the seventh grade, the chance of success drops to 30 per cent, and if put off until grades nine to twelve success is more difficult to attain, because by this time the clinician has to deal not only with the reading problem but with the student's intense feelings of failure and inadequacy.

TWO APPROACHES TO THE PROBLEM

In dealing with the disabled reader both corrective and clinical approaches are utilized. The corrective approach is chiefly concerned with the determination of reading needs, or, in other words, with diagnosis at the third level. The emphasis is on instruction and educational techniques and not on therapeutic procedures designed to mitigate personality disorders. The clinical approach, on the other hand, is primarily concerned with the study of the disabled reader so as to identify causal factors affecting or contributing to his maladjustment. The clinician diagnoses at the fourth level and becomes involved in the investigation of the individual in his environment. He suggests both instructional and therapeutic treatment which can be applied by the teacher or the reading therapist.

The well-prepared teacher in the classroom can meet the reading needs of approximately 92 per cent of her children by means of developmental instruction. Her greatest difficulty is in dealing with the wide range of reading ability within her class. If she is a sixth-grade teacher, this range of reading levels may extend from second to ninth grade. The teacher in the classroom can diagnose the reading attainment of her children at the first, second, and third levels. She can then provide developmental instruction as she groups her pupils tentatively to accomplish specific objectives. This flexible grouping based on the reading needs of her students can be modified as her goals are attained. Corrective work with individuals can grow out of this plan.

Approximately 8 per cent of the school population may be considered as seriously retarded readers. Most of these individuals, or approximately 5 per cent of the total school population, can be successfully treated by the reading therapist in a reading laboratory. The remaining 3 per cent are generally assumed to be in need of careful clinical study. These data are based on a consensus provided by several investigators.

SELECTION OF INDIVIDUALS FOR CORRECTIVE READING

Developmental and corrective reading have much in common, for seldom does any individual learn completely at the first presentation. In general, corrective reading is designed for those individuals who have not profited from regular classroom instruction. Consequently, in many school systems corrective or therapeutic treatment is provided by reading specialists in reading laboratories especially designed and adequately furnished. The therapist attempts to meet the reading needs of the students assigned to her individually or in small groups.

The selection of students for corrective reading should be made on the basis of (1) degree of reading difficulty, (2) emotional and mental maturity, (3) absence of emotional and social maladjustment, and (4) extent to which the student can probably benefit from individual or group instruction without clinical study.

In general, corrective treatment should be recommended for individuals in the third grade and above who are reading two years below their grade level, who are mentally and emotionally mature, who are fairly well adjusted emotionally and socially, and who can profit from individual or group instruction. These students, so selected for instruction for short intervals of time, can benefit by treatment and at the same time continue in their regular classes. Their reading disabilities would probably not warrant study by a clinical team. Children in the first and second grade who are failing to make satisfactory progress in learning to read and who are of average intelligence or better are in need of special consideration by the home-room teacher. If progress is not made during a three-month period following identification, the child should be referred for clinical study.

The reading laboratory under the direction of the reading therapist should at no time become a dumping ground for the mentally, emotionally, and socially unfit who are troublesome to the classroom teacher. Candidates for corrective reading should be selected primarily because of their ability to benefit from the temporary treatment of the reading therapist.

SELECTION OF INDIVIDUALS REQUIRING CLINICAL SERVICE

Teachers are frequently asked to recommend students for special treatment in reading. This responsibility involves the consideration of many factors and is not an easy one to assume. Obviously, not all individuals who have difficulty in learning to read should be referred to a reading clinic or to a team of clinical workers. Most children can receive adequate aid through developmental instruction in the classroom. Many school systems, as previously pointed out, are adding to their teaching staff *reading consultants* who work with teachers, *reading clinicians* who are in charge of clinical services, and *reading therapists* who provide corrective instruction and therapy both individually and in small groups. In most communities less than 3 per cent of the students need to be referred for clinical study and treatment. This number, however, causes the teacher and school administration great concern. It is not always easy to choose wisely individuals who can and should be referred to a team of clinical workers. Several factors should be given careful consideration.

- In general, individuals of average intelligence or better who have a history of reading disability extending over a two-year period of classroom instruction and whose performance in reading is three years or more below their grade level should be referred for clinical study.

- Individuals two years or more retarded in reading who are seriously penalized academically, socially, and emotionally and who, in the opinion of the teacher and principal, are mentally capable should be recommended for clinical study.
- Clinical service should be considered for disabled readers who appear to be mentally retarded but show marked ability in two or more subject-matter areas other than the language arts.
- Children in grades two to four reading one or more years below grade level, demonstrating better than average intelligence, and showing evidence of emotional and social maladjustment should be considered for clinical study.

In determining whether or not an individual should be referred to a team of clinical workers, representatives of the school should consider the following questions carefully.

Do the parents and teachers want psychological service for the child?

Are they willing to be present and cooperate in interviews?

If necessary, are they willing to make adjustments in the home and school in order to help?

Are the parents "shopping around" so as to obtain diagnosis and treatment according to their liking?

Are the parents willing to cooperate with the school and with other agencies making the referral?

Are the parents or guardians willing to sign an agreement permitting the examinations, interviews, and discussions of clinical data to be observed by teachers within the school system?

Does the individual really want to improve his ability to read? (A yes or no response may be equally significant.)

Does he have the ability to profit from treatment?

Can clinical studies of the individual be of profit to in-service training of teachers in the school system?

Does the family physician recommend or concur in the referral to the clinic team?

Will the team have an opportunity to cooperate with civic and social agencies in the study of the child?

Is the individual under the care and treatment of an agency or professional worker?

SUMMARY

In this chapter an attempt has been made to delineate the factors used in the identification and selection of individuals who can profit from *corrective instruction* in the classroom and from *clinical service* made available by a team of professional workers. Most individuals can improve their reading skills and make normal academic progress as a result of adequate developmental instruction provided by the alert and well-prepared classroom teacher.

GUIDED ACTIVITY 2

Aim

To see more clearly some of the factors considered in the identification and selection of individuals for clinical study.

Materials

1. Table 2-1, *Diagnosis and Treatment of the Disabled Reader.*
2. Table 2-2, Distribution of Grade Equivalent Scores Resulting from the Administration of the Iowa Silent Reading Test in a Fifth-Grade Class, p. 32.

Procedure

1. Show why you can or cannot accept the inferences given in the text concerning the children shown in Table 2-1.
2. The boys described in Table 2-1 are members of the class shown in Table 2-2. With this information in mind, what problems occur to you as you study the distribution?
3. In dealing with Lee's reading problem, outline some reasons for recommending clinical service which can be discussed with his parents.
4. If you were a reading consultant, what suggestions would you make for meeting the reading needs of this fifth-grade class of thirty-six pupils?
5. Prepare an outline which may be used for showing Stephen's parents why he should not be selected for clinical study.
6. In many schools teachers are asked to recommend students for clinical service. What criteria would you set up in your school system to help teachers select students who could really profit from this service?

TABLE 2-2   Distribution of Grade Equivalent Scores Resulting from the Administration of the Iowa Silent Reading Test* in a Fifth-Grade Class

Grade Equivalents	Frequency
8.0	2
7.0	5
6.0	7
5.0	9
4.0	6
3.0	4
2.0	3
Total	36

* Iowa Silent Reading Test, New Edition, by H. A. Greene and V. H. Kelley. Harcourt, Brace and World, Inc., New York, 1943.

7. In the typical school situation there are not enough special reading teachers to work with all the children who need this service. Work out a plan which, in your opinion, will alleviate this situation.

8. Present arguments, pro and con, about whether first- and second-grade children who are experiencing difficulty in learning to read should be referred for clinical diagnosis and treatment?

QUESTIONS AND REFERENCES

Questions

1. How is the disabled reader described?

2. How can the disabled reader be identified?

3. What is retardation in reading?

References

1. Guy L. Bond and Miles A. Tinker, *Reading Difficulties, Their Diagnosis and Correction* 2nd ed. (New York: Appleton-Century-Crofts, 1967), pp. 82–83.

2. *Ibid.*, pp. 83–95.

3. Ruth Strang, *Diagnostic Teaching of Reading* (New York:

Questions	References
	McGraw-Hill Book Company, 1964), p. vi.
4. How can poor readers in college be identified?	**4.** Paul D. Leedy, "Discovering Those Who Need Individual Help in College," *Reading and Inquiry* (Newark, Delaware: International Reading Association Conference Proceedings, 1965), pp. 166–168.
5. How can potential dropouts in high school be identified early?	**5.** Ruth C. Penty, *Reading Ability and High School Drop-Outs* (New York: Bureau of Publications, Teachers College, Columbia University, 1956), Chap. 3.
6. What are some ethical standards in client relationships?	**6.** *Ethical Standards of Psychologists* (Washington: American Psychological Association, 1953), pp. 37–87.
7. How can a clinical team cooperate with parents?	**7.** Homer L. J. Carter, "Parents, Teachers and Clinic Personnel Can Cooperate in Solving Reading Problems," in Ralph Staiger and David A. Sohn, eds., *New Directions in Reading* (New York: Bantam Books, 1967), pp. 213–215.

Chapter 3

Two Major Approaches: Clinical and Corrective

The individual with a reading disability presents a challenge to both teacher and clinician. This chapter shows how a crucial problem can be resolved from two points of view. The clinical approach in the field of reading is defined, outlined, and illustrated. Utilizing the background information and the academic history of the same individual, the corrective approach by the classroom teacher is illustrated.

CLINICAL APPROACH

The term *clinical* characterizes a method of studying the individual as a whole. In order to understand and aid the person, his specific behaviors are observed, and causal factors may be inferred. Stress is placed on the intuitive judgment of the clinician as well as on measurement and observation. There is an integration of data from several fields of investigation in determining causal factors requiring remediation. A clinic provides a team of several individuals who, because of their background in various disciplines, are able to study the child as a whole. In every clinical study the purpose is to determine why the individual is disabled and what can be done about it.

Sequence of Acts in Clinical Study

The procedures to be followed in making an individual study are

- Recognition of the problem. In dealing with an apparent problem of reading maladjustment, it is not always possible to recognize immediately the real or basic problem. Frequently a child referred to a clinic as a reading problem may be one in whom emotional or personality deviations are chiefly significant.
- Accumulation and summary of subjective data resulting from interviews, observations, and informal inventories.
- Preparation and summary of data from tests and other objective measures.
- Diagnosis or interpretation of the factors underlying the difficulty.
- Treatment or suggestion of remedial measures.
- Evaluation of treatment and summary of results.

Illustration of a Clinical Approach

An application of the clinical method may help the reader identify the sequential acts and evaluate the importance of each in the study of reading disability.

PROBLEM

John, a fourteen-year-old youth, is enrolled in the seventh grade. He has been in the public schools nine years and according to his teacher is reading at the second-grade level. The immediate problem is, "Why is John such a poor reader?"

HOME CONDITIONS

John's father is an automobile mechanic who operates a small fruit farm. He reports that he too "had trouble with reading but have more money in the bank than most of my neighbors." There are four children in the family, three girls in addition to John. All are enrolled in the public schools, and each of John's three sisters—ages thirteen, eleven, and eight— is making satisfactory progress in all classes. John's mother works thirty hours each week in a restaurant. She says she has had little time for reading. John and the oldest sister assume many responsibilities in the home, and all the children are expected to make their own beds and keep their rooms in order. The parents subscribe to several magazines; however, there are few books in the home of interest to growing children. Both radio and television are in operation throughout a greater part of the day and evening. The family does not attend church nor are they members of any religious group. John has an allowance of two dollars each week, and from this he is able to purchase some of his clothing and to save some for his bank account. His favorite sports are football and baseball. John likes to hunt and fish. He has several staunch friends who are younger than he. The following statements on a Reading Attitude Inventory[1] were answered in the affirmative by John's parents.

Most children ask too many questions.
Most children ask questions merely for the purpose of having something to say.
There is a lot of sense to the old adage, "Children should be seen and not heard."
Since many children have to be encouraged to eat at mealtime, the wise mother will discourage her children from talking while eating. Children will monopolize the conversation if they are permitted to do so.

DEVELOPMENTAL HISTORY

John's birth was reported as normal. Breast feeding was later supplemented by bottle feeding. John acquired his first tooth at four months and was creeping at eight months. He sat alone at six months and was walking at twelve months. He said several words at ten months. There were no physical deformities, and muscular coordination was excellent. John's right hand was dominant. The only illnesses reported were whooping cough and measles. John, as a young child, was well nourished and was accepted by his peers.

SCHOOL HISTORY

John entered kindergarten at the age of five years and first grade at the age of six. He repeated the second grade and entered the third grade at the age of nine. School reports show that he was shy and unwilling to answer questions. As he was promoted from grade to grade, success in all subjects except art and music was difficult to attain. His poorest achievement was in the language arts. His teachers reported that he was a "slow learner" and that they "did not have time for individualized instruction." The school history indicated that "later he gave up trying to succeed." Actually, in the

---

[1] A description of the Reading Attitude Inventory can be found in *A Comparative Study of the Attitudes of Parents of Superior and Inferior Readers Toward Certain Child Rearing Practices, the Value of Reading, and the Development of Language Skills and Experiential Background Related to Reading,* an unpublished doctoral dissertation by Dorothy J. McGinnis, Michigan State University, East Lansing, Michigan, 1963.

classroom John was neglected. Until he was referred for clinical study, his teachers expected him to read the textbooks of his grade. He was regarded as mentally incapable and merely permitted "to sit" in the various classes. When referred to a reading tutor, he was required to read from a first-grade basal text which he found boring. He became more certain that he was a "can't reader" and that he should go to work as soon as the law would permit. When John was in the sixth and seventh grades, his mother asked that he be placed in a room for retarded children. Several former teachers agreed with the mother's suggestion. Psychological tests were administered, and later his mother was informed that this transfer was unwise because John was of average intelligence. John was reading at approximately the second-grade level at this time. In writing he employed only e, r, s, t, l, and m to form words. His teacher reported that he liked to look through science books with illustrations. In the sixth grade it was discovered that John needed glasses.

MEDICAL REPORT

The report of the family physician showed that John was underweight with no physical abnormalities of growth, development, or function except possible visual and auditory losses. The physician suggested the possibility of mental retardation and recommended that John be referred to a reading clinic for study and to an otologist for examination.

DATA FROM OBSERVATIONS AND INFORMAL INVENTORIES

Observers reported that "John's voice lacked animation and that he seemed discouraged and dull." Tests of dominance indicated that he was right-handed and right-eyed, a pure dextral. An Informal Reading Inventory showed reading levels as follows:

Capacity level	4
Frustration level	3
Instructional level	2
Independent level	1

John's responses were made slowly and at times were inaudible. He observed the speaker's lips closely. When asked, "Who is President of the United States?" he made no response. To the question, "Where are you?" he replied, "I do not know." He did not recall the kind of car his mother drove or the kind of gas she used.

OBJECTIVE MEASURES

John's performance on the Wechsler Intelligence Scale for Children indicated that he was functioning within the average range of intelligence. His IQs on the verbal, performance, and full scales were 90, 104, and 96, respectively. His lowest scores were on tests of information, vocabulary, and arithmetic. His responses to questions involving time concepts and literary knowledge were poor. He performed well on all tests involving psychomotor skill.

On the Healy Pictorial his performance was equivalent to the 95th percentile for individuals of fourteen years. Consequently, it may be inferred that John has superior ability to identify, interpret, and evaluate situations in a nonlanguage background.

Measures of personality showed marked feelings of inadequacy, a lack of self-confidence, and a tendency to experience rejection.

The audiometric examination revealed a total loss in the right ear and a moderate loss in the left ear for frequencies involving the critical speech range. These results were confirmed later by an otologist who reported "a permanent and total sensorineural hearing loss on the right side probably of viral origin."

The visual examination with correction revealed normal visual acuity. There was, however, evidence of lateral imbalance and faulty fusion at both far and near points.

Grade scores in reading, spelling, and arithmetic were 2.8, 2.1, and 4.8, respectively.

DIAGNOSIS

Table 3-1 summarizes and shows the basis of observation of relevant factors which may be material and consequential in the diagnosis of John's disabilities. They are derived from several sources of information such as histories, observations, objective testing, and informal inventories. Several disciplines are represented, such as psychology, sociology, medicine, education, otology, and applied optics. The clinical worker had at his disposal known factors, and he had to determine those that were *relevant, material,* and *consequential* in the solution of the problem.

The diagnosis may be briefly stated as follows: John, who is functioning within the average range of intelligence, has failed to make anticipated achievement in the language arts, especially reading and spelling, chiefly because of a deficiency in experiential background resulting from a marked hearing loss. The problem is further complicated by a feeling of inadequacy and a lack of effective instruction.

TREATMENT

1. The staff recommends that John, through his family physician, be referred to an otologist.

2. It is suggested that careful observations be made from time to time of John's visual adjustment.

3. It is important that both the home and the school consider John as a boy of average intelligence who because of physical handicaps appears

TABLE 3-1 Summary of Relevant Causal Factors

Disabilities	Basis of Observation	Treatment
Visual defect	Keystone Visual Survey Test. Report of physician.	None required at present.
Auditory defect	Report of physician. Audiogram.	Refer to otologist.
Inadequate mental content	Home environment. Wechsler Intelligence Scale for Children. Limited general knowledge.	Use Visual-Visual-Auditory approach. Extend range of experience.
Poor self-concept	Observation. Statements of John. Report of teachers. Personality measures.	Give praise and commendation whenever deserved. Provide John with explanation of his difficulty and with proof of his intelligence.
Limited reading and spelling vocabularies	Informal reading inventories. Measures of reading and spelling.	Make use of VAKT and use words in context.
Cannot identify and interpret ideas in textbooks now being used	Required to use books far too difficult. Report of teachers.	Select materials of real interest at second-grade level. Ask questions and have John read for answers. Stress *why* and *how* questions.

to be functioning at a low average level. John should understand that he can make a satisfactory academic, vocational, and social adjustment in his world.

4. It is recommended that the public schools make some adjustment so that John can receive corrective instruction in reading. He should be given an opportunity to select material of high interest to him and of a difficulty level of approximately the first or second grade. In providing instruction, the use of *why* and *how* questions should be emphasized. It is recommended that the Visual, Auditory, Kinesthetic, and Tactual (VAKT)

approach which was demonstrated in the clinic be used to develop simultaneously both a reading and spelling vocabulary. Words taught in this manner should be used in context as demonstrated. Flashcards made up of these words should be filed and reviewed from time to time.

5. It is recommended that the Visual-Visual-Auditory approach to the teaching of words and the construction of experience charts be utilized in working with John. This approach will give John an opportunity to associate a word with an object in a picture projected upon a chalkboard. This procedure is

 a. Project picture of interest to John on the chalkboard.
 b. Encourage him to discuss the picture.
 c. Label objects in the picture.
 d. Ask for recognition of these words while the picture is exposed.
 e. Turn off switch, thereby eliminating the picture.
 f. Ask John to identify again these words and if difficulty is experienced, turn on the switch and restore the picture.
 g. Have John tell a story concerning the picture.
 h. Write the story on the chalkboard and have John read it.
 i. Emphasize phrase and sentence reading and use of words in other sentences.

6. It is suggested that John's parents create in the home an intellectual climate by placing a greater emphasis upon current events, state and national issues, and problems of interest to the family. John should be encouraged to express his ideas and to seek information which would substantiate or disprove his opinions. Furthermore, John should be permitted to have experiences that will broaden and deepen his knowledge of the world about him.

7. It is recommended that after an interval of six months John return to the clinic for an evaluation of his reading and spelling achievement.

EVALUATION OF TREATMENT

Five months after the initiation of remedial measures, John was reported to be reading as well as an individual eight months in the fourth grade (4.8). This was a significant gain of two years. His teacher reported that he asked for more books in his field of interest and that he was improving his ability to spell and his ability to write paragraphs. She added, however, that he did not participate in class discussion and that he was reluctant to enter some of his classes.

CORRECTIVE APPROACH

Now we shall examine the approach a classroom teacher or reading therapist might use in attacking John's problem from the viewpoint of his reading needs, rather than from the standpoint of causal factors contributing to his reading maladjustment.

John, as the reader will recall, is enrolled in the seventh grade. His home-room teacher could have referred him to a reading therapist who worked with small groups of students for short periods of time. The therapist could have made use of data from informal reading inventories to determine independent, instructional, frustration, and capacity levels. These informal inventories along with her observations could have demonstrated his reading needs. Relevant factors are summarized in Table 3-2.

TABLE 3-2   Summary of Relevant Factors in Determination of Needs

Disabilities	Basis of Observation	Treatment
Does not react to words as a whole, i.e., families, blends, word analysis.	Informal reading inventories. Observations.	Make use of VAKT. Use words in context.
Cannot identify and interpret ideas in textbooks.	Report of teachers. Observations in classroom.	Select materials of interest at second-grade level. Ask questions and read for answers. Emphasize *why* and *how* questions.
Inadequate mental content.	Limited general information shown in interviews.	Use Visual-Visual-Auditory approach. Group discussions and trips.

Materials of interest to John which were designed for students reading at second-grade level could have been selected. Words unknown to John could have been developed, and he could have been shown how to build up both reading and spelling vocabularies simultaneously. Words taught in this manner could have been employed and reviewed in context by means of flashcards. In working with John at this stage, silent reading, not oral, could have been motivated by questions requiring him to read for definite answers. Questions involving *who, what, where,* and *when* could have been asked and later followed by those requiring *why* and *how* responses. John's experiential background and mental content could have been developed by use of the Visual-Visual-Auditory approach described earlier in this chapter. Group discussions and well-planned trips to centers of interest could have added much to his background.

These instructional procedures, however, are not sufficient. They have not been designed to alleviate the chief cause of John's disability in reading, his marked and significant hearing loss and his consequent lack of information. These instructional approaches have not explained to John why he has had difficulty in learning to read. He has erroneously assumed that he was "dumb." Furthermore, his previous teachers made the same error. The discovery and explanation of the basic causal factors were essential for John's welfare. Merely meeting his reading needs could not have been sufficient.

SUMMARY

A clinical approach to the study of the individual has been presented. A sequence of acts in the investigation has been illustrated as a global attack upon the problem has been made. Causal factors have been identified and procedures set forth for treatment after the individual was studied *in* his environment. Differences between the clinical approach and the corrective approach have been illustrated. Furthermore, this chapter contrasts the differences between diagnosis at the third and fourth levels. Each has its place.

GUIDED ACTIVITY 3

Aim

To develop a comprehensive point of view concerning a clinical and corrective approach to the study of an individual with a reading disability.

Materials

1. Chapter 3, *Diagnosis and Treatment of the Disabled Reader.*

Procedure

1. Show how a definition of reading will influence the clinician in his investigation of the disabled reader. See Chapter 1.
2. Tell why you would or would not accept a multidisciplinary approach to the study of the disabled reader.
3. Tell why a reading problem may grow worse with the passing of time.
4. List areas of information that may be essential to the study of a reading problem and tell why.
5. What are the advantages and disadvantages of diagnosis at the third level? (See Figure 1-1, Chapter 1.)
6. Tell why, in your opinion, home background was or was not a relevant factor in John's disability.
7. Discuss factors that determine the nature of treatment.
8. Discuss factors that determine the evaluation of treatment.
9. List the contributions of each of the following specialists in a clinical study of a disabled reader.
   a. Psychologist.
   b. Sociologist.
   c. Educator.
10. If possible, visit a reading clinic and observe the work being done with a child.
    a. Summarize your observations.
    b. Report your reactions.

QUESTIONS AND REFERENCES

Questions

1. What are some general principles of diagnosis?

2. What factors make up an analysis of reading difficulties?

3. What are some specific approaches to diagnosis?

4. What are some causes and treatment of reading disabilities?

References

1. Guy L. Bond and Miles A. Tinker, *Reading Difficulties, Their Diagnosis and Correction,* 2nd ed. (New York: Appleton-Century-Crofts, 1967), Chap. 7.

2. *Ibid.,* Chap. 8.

3. *Ibid.,* Chap. 9.

4. Florence Roswell and Gladys Natchez, *Reading Disability,*

Questions	References
	Diagnosis and Treatment (New York: Basic Books, Inc., 1964).
5. What factors are to be considered in dealing with the retarded reader?	**5.** Paul A. Witty, Alma Moore Freeland, and Edith H. Grotberg, *The Teaching of Reading* (Boston: D. C. Heath and Company, 1966), pp. 290–317.
6. Can teachers make case studies?	**6.** *Ibid.*, pp. 393–395.

Chapter 4

Some Causes of
Disabilities in Reading

In this chapter we shall define and discuss briefly the nature of cause and summarize and interpret significant research findings and opinions of authorities concerning factors affecting reading performance. No attempt will be made to evaluate the opinions of specialists or the findings of research workers in the field.

THE NATURE OF CAUSE

Cause shall be taken here to mean a factor or configuration of factors responsible for part or all of a disability, so that when the factor or configuration of factors is removed or mitigated through treatment or instruction, improvement occurs. Many theories have been set forth to explain reading disabilities. No single causal factor has ever been identified which accounts for all reading disorders. Consequently, it is the consensus that causation is multiple and that maladjustment in reading is the result of a sequence of several contributing factors. Witty and Kopel[1] express two concepts which are essential to the understanding and treatment of the disabled reader.

Poor reading may well be considered in most instances a retarded or inhibited developmental condition, which reflects the reciprocal interaction, over a period of time, of physical, mental, emotional, social, and educa-

---

[1] Paul Witty and David Kopel, *Reading and the Educative Process* (Boston: Ginn and Company, 1939), p. 205.

tional factors. Hence the problem of diagnosing reading disability necessitates identifying not specific minutiae but rather patterns of growth and development.

In general, assumed causes of reading disability can be grouped under one or more of the following headings: physical, psychological, sociological, and educational. Summaries of points of view and research in each of these areas will be set forth.

PHYSICAL FACTORS AND READING PERFORMANCE

The individual's achievement in reading may be affected by vision, audition, general health, neurological organization, cerebral dominance, and the functioning of the endocrine glands. We shall discuss each in turn.

Visual Factors and Reading

Learning to read requires visual readiness. Several investigators have found a high percentage of first-grade children to be far-sighted. They report that the visual mechanism at six years of age is unstable and that many children have difficulty in fixating at definite points and in keeping their place in reading. Children at this age make many regressive movements and are inaccurate in moving from one line of print to the next. At seven, most children have made marked improvement in visual acuity. They can fixate their eyes at certain points on the page and can move from line to line quite readily. Gray and Reese[2] point out that some children are unable to fixate on objects at close range until they are seven or eight years old. Cole[3] reinforces this judgment by showing that the eyes of young children are generally not mature enough to read printed symbols before the age of eight. Some children who cannot adjust to the difficulties of near vision find reading so uncomfortable that they give up trying to learn.

Many research workers have attempted to determine whether or not visual deficiencies cause reading disability. In general, these investigators do not agree on the amount of importance to be attached to visual difficulties as a cause of reading retardation. Some show that

[2] Lillian Gray and Dora Reese, *Teaching Children to Read* (New York: The Ronald Press, 1957), p. 99.

[3] Luella Cole, *The Improvement of Reading with Special Reference to Remedial Instruction* (New York: Farrar and Rinehart, Inc., 1938), p. 282.

visual disturbances are largely responsible for reading maladjustment. Some state that there is little relationship between visual disturbance and inability to read. Some believe that visual defects and limited ability to read have a common causal factor. Gesell[4] and his associates take the position that vision involves the body as a whole. They stress the organismic nature of vision and urge that one should not focus too much attention upon the eyes. Nevertheless, nearly all students of the subject insist that visual factors should be considered and that each child experiencing difficulty in reading should have an eye examination.

It is generally agreed that two major visual defects can be responsible for retardation in reading. Refractive dysfunction is one of these and binocular difficulties is the other. Individuals with the former problem have refractive errors in one or both eyes. Individuals with binocular difficulties show an inability of the two eyes to perform successfully together.

The following terms, which are defined in the glossary, should be thoroughly understood by the clinician who wishes to identify and evaluate visual disorders.

Accommodation	Lateral and
Aniseikonia	vertical imbalance
Astigmatism	Mixed dextral
Binocular	Mixed sinistral
coordination	Myopia
Convergence	Phoria
Dextral	Sinistral
Fusion at near	Stereopsis level
and far points	Suppression
Hyperopia	Visual acuity
Image	

Research workers such as Piaget,[5] Cruickshank,[6] Wedell,[7] and

[4] Arnold Gesell, Francis L. Ilg, and Glenna E. Bullis, *Vision: Its Development in Infant and Child* (New York: Paul B. Hoeber, Inc., 1949), p. 14.

[5] Jean Piaget, *Les Mécanismes Perceptifs* (Paris: Presses Universitaires de France, 1961).

[6] William M. Cruickshank et al., *A Teaching Method for Brain-Injured and Hyperactive Children* (Syracuse, N.Y.: Syracuse University Press, 1961).

[7] K. Wedell, "Variations in Perceptual Ability Among Types of Cerebral Palsy," *Cerebral Palsy Bulletin*, **2** (1960), 149–157.

Thurstone[8] have found that several visual perceptual abilities are involved in the process of recognizing and discriminating stimuli. Maslow and others,[9] in reporting on their work with children referred to the Marianne Frostig School of Educational Therapy, indicate that disturbances of visual perception were frequent symptoms which appeared to contribute to learning disabilities. Children who had difficulty in writing seemed to be handicapped by poor eye-hand coordination. Children who could not recognize words seemed to have disturbances in figure-ground perception. Children who were unable to recognize a letter or word when it was printed in different sizes or colors apparently had poor form constancy. Children who reversed or rotated letters or words seemed to have difficulty in perceiving position in space. Children who interchanged the order of letters in a word also appeared to have difficulty in analyzing spatial relationships. Scott[10] too has shown that there is a relationship between young children's perceptual skills and their later success in reading. His findings appear to support the position that compensatory programs which emphasize oral language without giving adequate attention to perceptual learnings may not provide the necessary experiential foundation for later reading success.

Eye Movement and Reading

In reading there is a sequence of movements of the eyes across the page. The movements are quick, short, and interspersed with pauses. There are regressive movements and a return sweep of the eyes to the following line. At the moment of fixation, the eyes pause so that the individual can react to the stimuli. During these pauses or fixations the individual identifies and interprets letters, words, and phrases. This "eyeful" is sometimes called the *span of recognition,* and its length depends on the effectiveness with which the individual functions. Buswell[11] has photographed the eye movements of in-

[8] L. L. Thurstone, "A Factorial Study of Perception," *Psychometric Monographs,* 4 (Chicago: University of Chicago Press, 1944).

[9] Phyllis Maslow et al., "The Marianne Frostig Developmental Test of Visual Perception," *Perceptual and Motor Skills,* 19 (1964), 463–499.

[10] Ralph Scott, "Perceptual Readiness as a Predictor of Success in Reading," *The Reading Teacher,* 22 (October, 1968), 36–39.

[11] Guy Thomas Buswell, *Fundamental Reading Habits: A Study of Their Development,* Supplementary Educational Monographs, No. 21 (Chicago: University of Chicago Press, 1922).

dividuals ranging from first grade to the college level. From his data he draws the conclusion that eye movement skills develop rapidly in the first four grades and after this little change occurs. Spache[12] has pointed out that frequency of fixation is not necessarily related to reading rate. Tinker[13] has questioned the desirability of attempting to improve reading skills through exercises calculated to correct faulty eye movement. Spache[14] points out that it is actually undesirable to try to limit regressive movements. Furthermore, he suggests that there is little reason to believe that irregular eye movement causes poor reading. It is the consensus of several research workers in the field that exercises designed to improve eye movements are of little value in the improvement of reading skills.

Auditory Factors

According to Monroe,[15] defects in auditory acuity and auditory discrimination are related to reading disability. She suggests that auditory memory is probably a significant factor in learning to read. Monroe[16] explains that sounds differ from one another in *intensity, pitch, timbre, duration,* and *sequence* and that all children can profit from training in auditory skills. She points out that children should develop sensitivity to nonvocal sounds, vocal sounds, and sounds in words. Dahl[17] shows that on a verbal test such as the Binet the IQ is about seven points lower for hard-of-hearing children than for children of normal hearing. On nonlanguage tests, however, there is no significant difference. Strang[18] points out that four factors affect

[12] George D. Spache, "A Rationale for Mechanical Methods for Improving Reading," *Significant Elements in College and Adult Reading Improvement.* Seventh Yearbook of the National Reading Conference for Colleges and Adults (Fort Worth: Texas Christian University Press, 1958), pp. 115–132.

[13] Miles A. Tinker, "The Role of Eye Movements in Diagnostic and Remedial Reading," *School and Society,* 39 (February, 1934), 147–148.

[14] Spache, *op. cit.*

[15] Marion Monroe, *Children Who Cannot Read* (Chicago: University of Chicago Press, 1932).

[16] Marion Monroe, *Growing into Reading* (Chicago: Scott, Foresman and Company, 1951).

[17] L. A. Dahl, *Public School Audiometry: Principles and Methods* (Danville, Ill.: The Interstate Printers and Publishers, 1949).

[18] Ruth Strang, *Diagnostic Teaching of Reading* (New York: McGraw-Hill Book Company, 1964), p. 181.

success in reading in the first grade. They are auditory discrimination, visual discrimination, range of information, and mental age. Of all these, auditory discrimination has been ranked first in importance by several investigators. Auditory discrimination is the ability to differentiate between closely related speech sounds. According to Wepman,[19] there is a constant increase in sound discrimination ability with age; children vary in the rate of development of both auditory discrimination and auditory memory (the ability to retain and recall speech sounds); and auditory discrimination and auditory memory are not well developed in some children until the age of nine. Wepman contends that those who have inadequate auditory discrimination are most likely to experience difficulty in learning to read and that the presence of poor auditory perception provides the therapist with clues for remediation. Olson[20] in a study of 1,172 first-grade children states that "September tests which measure knowledge of letter names provide the best predictions of February success in reading." Strang[21] adds that children with auditory defects tend to learn better by visual methods than by auditory or phonic methods.

General Health

Reading is the act of identifying, interpreting, and evaluating ideas in terms of the mental content of the reader. Mental content is based on the experiential background of the individual. Physical defects, poor health, and inadequate nutrition tend to restrict activities and consequently retard the development of the mental content required for effective reading. Any condition that hinders activity can affect reading growth and development. Johnson[22] has reported that 65 per cent of the reading cases referred to her for clinical study had re-

[19] Joseph M. Wepman, "The Modality Concept—Including a Statement of the Perceptual and Conceptual Levels of Learning," in *Perception and Reading*, Conference Proceedings of the International Reading Association, Vol. 12, Part 4 (1968), 1–6.

[20] Arthur V. Olson, "Growth in Word Perception Abilities as It Relates to Success in Beginning Reading," *Journal of Education*, Boston University, **140** (February, 1958), 25–36.

[21] Strang, *op. cit.*, p. 181.

[22] Marjorie S. Johnson, "A Study of Diagnostic and Remedial Procedures in a Reading Clinic Laboratory School," *Journal of Educational Research*, **48** (April, 1955), 565–578.

current illnesses. Mateer[23] has shown that pituitary dysfunction may cause mental retardation, visual disturbances, reversal tendencies, and motor incoordination. Furthermore, she has shown that vitamin deficiencies may be related to reading difficulties. Smith[24] states that treatment at the endocrine level has yielded results ranging from promising to dramatic. Cavanaugh[25] shows that 18 per cent of 660 children participating in a study conducted by him had thyroid deficiencies severe enough to cause them to be retarded two or more years in physical maturity. In these studies many variables have not been controlled. Consequently, we cannot infer that a causal relationship has been established between these physical conditions and ability to read. In the study of an individual health factors are certainly worthy of consideration.

Neurological Factors

From a neurological point of view the ability to speak and the ability to read are closely related. The speech center and the center of other motor processes involved in reading are usually located in the language center on the left side of the brain. Vernon[26] provides evidence that the speech center of left-handed persons usually will be in the right hemisphere. After reviewing twenty-four studies, Eames[27] concludes that neurological lesions in the language center may retard both the ability to speak and read.

Like any other organ, the brain is subject to injuries and to certain internal changes that may interfere with its proper functioning. A common abnormality is the inadequate or faulty development of brain tissue. Infections such as encephalitis and paresis may damage neural tissue and consequently interfere with normal activities.

[23] Florence Mateer, "A First Study of Pituitary Dysfunction in Cases of Reading Difficulty," *Psychological Bulletin,* 32 (1935), 736.

[24] Donald E. P. Smith, "A New Theory of Physiological Basis of Reading Disability," *Reading for Effective Living,* Conference Proceedings of International Reading Association, 3 (1958), 119–121.

[25] Lyman A. Cavanaugh, "Reading Behavior with Regard for Endocrine Imbalances," *Implementing the Process of Reading,* Thirteenth Yearbook of the Claremont College Reading Conference, Claremont, 1948, pp. 95–102.

[26] M. D. Vernon, *Backwardness in Reading* (Cambridge, England: The University Press, 1957).

[27] Thomas H. Eames, "The Relationship of Reading and Speech Difficulties," *Journal of Educational Psychology,* 41 (January, 1950), 51–55.

Arteriosclerosis and other degenerative diseases can lead to faulty functioning. It is assumed that the brain can be damaged by vitamin deficiencies. Endocrine disturbances and toxins can bring injury that results in aphasia and can interfere with and destroy the ability to read. A loss of speech is sometimes associated with brain damage.

Delacato[28] has proposed the concept of neurological organization and has stressed its relation to reading. He emphasizes inadequate neurological organization as an etiological factor in the development of both language and reading skills. He accentuates the relationship between laterality and neurological disorganization. Robbins[29] assessed the influence of a program advocated by Delacato on the reading and lateral development of second graders and tested certain relationships between neurological organization and reading as postulated by Delacato. The results of his investigation failed to support the validity and practicality of Delacato's theory.

During recent years there has been a tendency to place more and more emphasis on brain injury and cerebral dysfunction in the diagnosis of reading disability. The overactivity and distractibility of many brain-damaged children make it difficult for them to focus attention on any learning task and consequently may result in difficulty in learning to read. Brain damage, however, is difficult even for the well-trained neurologist to diagnose accurately. In many instances injury is inferred from symptomatic behavior and even from the interpretation of Wechsler findings, rather than from neurological examinations. In the opinion of many neurologists and psychologists, brain damage is a relatively rare cause of reading disability.

Cerebral Dominance and Reading

Lateral dominance is the preference for and consistent use of the eye, hand, and muscles of one side of the body. *Mixed dominance* is a state of control in which the dominant hand and dominant eye are on opposite sides. The dominant cerebral hemisphere is the one on the opposite side from the dominant hand, eye, or foot. For example, the left hemisphere is dominant in a right-handed individual. In-

[28] Carl E. Delacato, *The Treatment and Prevention of Reading Problems* (Springfield, Ill.: Charles C Thomas, 1963).

[29] Melvyn Paul Robbins, "The Delacato Interpretation of Neurological Organization," *Reading Research Quarterly*, 1 (Spring, 1966), 57–78.

dividuals who are both right-handed and right-eyed are spoken of as *pure dextrals*. Individuals who are left-handed and left-eyed are called *pure sinistrals*. Individuals who are left-handed and right-eyed are called *mixed sinistrals*. Those who are right-handed and left-eyed are called *mixed dextrals*.

Selzer[30] and others have contended that *cross dominance*, that is, mixed dextral or mixed sinistral control, is an important factor in learning to read. Fernald[31] adds that many good readers have mixed dominance. She also reports that a kinesthetic method is of value in working with nonreaders regardless of handedness. Several theories of dominance have been set forth to explain reading disabilities. None of them have been proved. Orton[32] has suggested that if cerebral dominance is well developed when the child begins to read, difficulty in reading is not apt to occur. Harris[33] has suggested that directional confusion in reading is much more important than the child's pattern of lateral dominance. Studies of children with reading disabilities have provided some evidence of a relationship between poor reading and lack of dominance. Both Eames[34] and Monroe[35] have found that poor readers show a greater frequency of cross dominance than children without reading disabilities. Hildreth[36,37] in summarizing research found no evidence for a causal relation between handedness and success in reading. Obviously, there is a lack of agreement on

[30] Charles A. Selzer, *Lateral Dominance and Visual Fusion: Their Application to Difficulties in Reading, Writing, Spelling and Speech*, Harvard Monographs in Education, No. 12 (Cambridge: Harvard University Press, 1933), p. 85.

[31] Grace Fernald, *Remedial Techniques in Basic School Subjects* (New York: McGraw-Hill Book Company, 1943), p. 161.

[32] Samuel T. Orton, "An Impediment to Learning to Read—A Neurological Explanation of the Reading Disability," *School and Society*, **28** (September, 1928), 286–290.

[33] Albert J. Harris, *How to Increase Reading Ability* (New York: Longmans, Green and Company, 1956).

[34] Thomas H. Eames, "The Anatomical Basis of Lateral Dominance Anomalies," *American Journal of Orthopsychiatry*, 4 (October, 1934), 524–528.

[35] Marion Monroe, *Children Who Cannot Read* (Chicago: University of Chicago Press, 1932).

[36] Gertrude Hildreth, "The Development and Training of Hand Dominance: I. Characteristics of Handedness; II. Developmental Tendencies in Handedness; III. Origins of Handedness and Lateral Dominance," *Journal of Genetic Psychology*, 75 (December, 1949), 197–220, 221–254, 255–275.

[37] Gertrude Hildreth, "The Development and Training of Hand Dominance: IV. Developmental Problems Associated with Handedness; V. Training of Handedness," *Journal of Genetic Psychology*, 76 (March, 1950), 39–100, 101–144.

the relationship between dominance and reading disability. Because so little agreement exists, it may be assumed that dominance is only one of the possible factors to be considered in a study of reading disability.

Some individuals, and especially young children, frequently reverse letters, parts of words, or even whole words. Sometimes d is called b, and p is confused with q. *No* may be called *on* and *saw* may be called *was*. Orton[38] reports that some children have a tendency to make reversals and that this confusion or tendency to read from right to left is probably due to delayed cerebral development. This may explain why children with a marked tendency to make reversals frequently recover on becoming more mature. Orton implies that reversal tendencies result from cross dominance. Spache,[39] however, disagrees very emphatically on the meaning of reversals. He says, "Reversals are not related to handedness or eyedness or cerebral dominance, nor are they indicative of laterality or visual handicaps." In the opinion of many reading specialists, reversals are quite normal during childhood. Apparently, they become a reading problem only when they continue beyond the elementary grades. Monroe,[40] however, found reversal tendencies occurring more frequently among children with reading disabilities than among normal readers.

In the act of reading, the individual learns to proceed from left to right. This is true not only in reading a line of type but also in identifying a word. Teachers who show young children how to print, write, or type a word call attention to the sequence and direction of letters in words and of words in lines. Bond and Tinker[41] have pointed out that reversals may be due to the emphasis the teacher may have placed on phonics and word analysis techniques. Fernald[42] has recommended a sounding-tracing method for the teaching of

[38] Samuel T. Orton, "Word Blindness in School Children," *Archives of Neurology and Psychiatry,* 14 (1925), 581–615.

[39] George D. Spache, "Factors Which Produce Defective Reading," *Corrective Reading in Classroom and Clinic.* Supplementary Educational Monographs, No. 79 (Chicago: University of Chicago Press, 1953), pp. 49–57.

[40] Marion Monroe, *Children Who Cannot Read* (Chicago: University of Chicago Press, 1932).

[41] Guy L. Bond and Miles A. Tinker, *Reading Difficulties: Their Diagnosis and Correction,* 2nd ed. (New York: Appleton-Century-Crofts, 1967).

[42] Grace Fernald, *Remedial Techniques in Basic School Subjects* (New York: McGraw-Hill Book Company, 1943).

reading. A Visual-Auditory-Kinesthetic-Tactual approach to word study is recommended by many clinicians and teachers. This approach is sometimes called VAKT. Reversal tendencies that persist beyond the second grade are generally associated with poor reading ability. They can be symptoms of underlying difficulties which may require interpretation and treatment.

PSYCHOLOGICAL FACTORS AND READING PERFORMANCE

Mental maturity, emotional maturity, mental content, and the individual's concept of himself are psychological factors which should be considered in the study of the disabled reader.

Mental Maturity

Mental maturity is the level at which the individual can interpret actual sensory perceptions. For example, a six-year-old child generally possesses the following characteristics. He is alert. He notices likenesses and differences. He can tell of his experiences. He pays attention for longer periods of time. He makes use of language. He tells and recites stories and poems. He understands that symbols may represent pictures or things. He memorizes easily. He can generalize and make inferences.

Mental maturity implies the ability to learn and apply what is learned. It suggests a readiness to make a conscious adjustment to a new situation. It has many dimensions and is best evaluated by individual measures such as the Revised Stanford Binet Intelligence Scale and the Wechsler Intelligence Scale for Children. Both of these instruments should be administered, scored, and interpreted only by a well-trained examiner.

Strang[43] states, "Mental age as measured by tests is not an adequate guide to an individual's reading potential." Studies show a positive correlation between mental maturity and performances in reading. This relation, however, is not high enough to predict one score from another. Research shows that some severely retarded readers have IQs ranging between 90 and 110. This, of course, is well

[43] Ruth Strang, *Diagnostic Teaching of Reading* (New York: McGraw-Hill Book Company, 1964), p. 214.

ithin the normal range. Monroe[44] and Dean,[45] as early as 1932 and
939, suggested that a child should be mentally at least six years and
_ix months old before success in reading can be expected. Research
and opinions recently publicized show that some children can learn
to read at a much earlier age. It is reasonable to assume, however,
that it is not possible to set a definite minimum mental age for learning to read because too many other factors are involved.

Individual measures of mental maturity can help to provide an
adequate understanding of the disabled reader. Observation of the
behavior of the disabled reader as he responds to the examiner who
administers the Stanford Binet or Wechsler can provide cues or
"hunches" as to why the individual is maladjusted in reading. How
the child reacts is much more important to the clinician than a mental
age or IQ. As he observes the child in a highly structured situation,
the observer is concerned with the quality of the responses, the items
completed successfully, and the items completed unsuccessfully. As
he administers the test he looks for "hunches" which may explain the
child's difficulty in reading. He concerns himself with why some items
were failed and other items were passed. This testing situation can
provide the keen observer with information that is much more significant in many instances than are mental ages and IQs.

Emotional Maturity

Emotional maturity, as the term suggests, means that an individual
has grown up emotionally; that is, he has learned to do the thing
that needs to be done when it needs to be done whether he wants
to do it or not. It implies the capacity for self-direction and social
responsibility, and the will to become involved in tasks essential to
the welfare of the individual himself or the good of others. Specialists[46]
in the area of human growth and development have discussed the
nature of maturity, and they present six characteristics considered to
be indicative of a mature, responsible person: feelings of security and

---

[44] Marion Monroe, *Children Who Cannot Read* (Chicago: University of
Chicago Press, 1932).

[45] C. D. Dean, "Predicting First-Grade Reading Achievement," *Elementary
School Journal,* 39 (April, 1939), 609–616.

[46] William S. Gray and Bernice Rogers, *Maturity in Reading* (Chicago: The
University of Chicago Press, 1956), p. 49.

adequacy; understanding of self and others; recognition of democratic values and goals; problem-solving attitudes and methods; self-discipline, responsibility, and freedom; and constructive attitudes toward change.

Some characteristics of the emotionally mature child may be briefly listed.

- Can easily make home-to-school adjustments.
- Can accept changes in routine quickly and calmly.
- Can accept opposition and defeat without being emotionally upset.
- Assumes responsibilities.
- Plans and does things on time.
- Meets and talks to strangers without shyness or undue boldness.
- Takes care of equipment and materials.

Overprotection and domination of the child by his parents can lead to dependence on others, unwillingness to assume responsibility, infantile behavior, and general immaturity. Studies by McGinnis[47] in 1963 show that fathers and mothers of inferior readers express attitudes that contribute to a greater degree of dependence of their children on them than fathers and mothers of superior readers. All her findings leading to this conclusion were significant at the 0.01 per cent level. As early as 1937 Monroe and Backus[48] in their study of retarded readers reported evidence of emotional immaturity as a causal factor in reading disability. Clinical experience and research findings suggest that some children fail to make satisfactory progress in reading chiefly because of emotional immaturity. This factor requires consideration in any study of the disabled reader.

Mental Content

In the act of reading one is chiefly concerned with meaning. In order to identify, interpret, and evaluate the ideas of the writer expressed in visual symbols, the reader must utilize his total awareness

[47] Dorothy J. McGinnis, *A Comparative Study of the Attitudes of Parents of Superior and Inferior Readers Toward Certain Child Rearing Practices, the Value of Reading, and the Development of Language Skills and Experiential Background Related to Reading.* Unpublished doctoral dissertation, Michigan State University, 1963.

[48] Marion Monroe and Bertie Backus, *Remedial Reading: A Monograph in Character Education* (Boston: Houghton Mifflin Company, 1937).

at the moment. This total awareness has been called *mental content* by some psychologists such as Brentano, Witasek, Ward, Wertheimer, Wundt, and John Stuart Mill. Mental content has affective as well as cognitive characteristics. It is a crucial factor in reading, because the individual sees with what he has seen and he experiences with what he has experienced. High degrees of mental content lead to high degrees of meaning. Mental content can be useful in explaining why some reading disabilities occur and why some individuals make rapid progress in learning to read and others little, if any. Hilliard and Troxell[49] in a study of kindergarten and first-grade children found that boys and girls coming from homes of limited educational and cultural advantages did not make as rapid progress in reading as those from a more fortunate environment. Psychologists and educators such as Dewey, Bode, and Zerbes, who are pragmatists and who stress the experiential background of the child in the learning process, have made use of this concept. The term *mental content* is ignored by neobehaviorists. In determining causal factors, the background and mental content of the disabled reader should be investigated.

Self-Concept

An inadequate self-concept is frequently associated with a reading disability. It can be either *cause* or *effect*. The child who is unable to read at his expected level usually becomes frustrated and conspicuous in his class. He is hurt, ashamed, and learns to dislike reading. His lack of success and his feelings of inadequacy may contribute to emotional and social maladjustment. He fails to get satisfaction, security, and recognition in a manner pleasing to himself and at the same time acceptable to his group. In this state of mind, he may become aggressive, put on a bold front, and assume the role of a cruel and destructive bully. On the other hand, he may become timid and withdrawn. He may feel inferior and show a lack of confidence. In both instances, his self-concept has been reduced.

An inadequate concept of self, along with other factors, can be a cause of reading disability. Snygg and Combs believe that behavior

[49] George H. Hilliard and Eleanor Troxell, "Informational Background as a Factor in Reading Readiness and Reading Progress," *Elementary School Journal,* 38 (December, 1937), 255–263.

is determined by all the experiences and feelings of which the individual is aware at the instant of action.[50] This awareness can determine success or failure, because what a person thinks and feels determines what he will do. An idea clearly entertained in the mind works itself out in action. Reading, like all human behavior, is a function of the total personality. When the child reads, he *identifies, interprets,* and *evaluates* in accordance with his needs, goals, wishes, defenses, and values. He perceives meaning that will satisfy his needs and rejects meaning that threatens and belittles his self-concept. In other words, what he has experienced and felt determines what he perceives in a book. Furthermore, his willingness to put forth effort will be proportionate to his desires, goals, and needs. The clinician, in observing disabled readers, should identify individuals with feelings of worthlessness and hopelessness concerning their inability to read. On the other hand, they will observe persons who have feelings of optimism and hope. These concepts of self are important in the learning process.

SOCIOLOGICAL FACTORS AND READING PERFORMANCE

The interests, attitudes, and points of view of the individual have their origin in the environment. Consequently, students of human growth and development agree that sociological factors, and especially those centered in the home and community, can affect the reading performance of the growing child.

Home Environment

Published research seems to support the thesis that parental attitudes affect the child's academic progress. Kurtz and Swenson[51] employed a series of interviews with parents, teachers, and children to study the home backgrounds of forty underachievers and forty overachievers in academic work. In general, marked differences were found between the two groups. Pride, confidence, affection, and interest of parents in their children as shown by instances in which parents read to their children, played with them, or attended school with them

[50] Donald Snygg and Arthur W. Combs, *Individual Behavior* (New York: Harper & Row, 1949).

[51] John J. Kurtz and Esther J. Swenson, "Factors Related to Overachievement and Underachievement in School," *School Review,* **59** (November, 1951), 472–480.

appear to be in greater evidence for overachievers than for underachievers.

Shaw and Dutton,[52] in their attempt to determine whether or not differences exist between the parents of achievers and the parents of underachievers with respect to their attitudes toward children, compared responses to the Parental Attitude Research Instrument of parents of bright academic achievers to the responses of parents of bright academic underachievers. Parents of underachievers had significantly stronger negative attitudes toward their underachieving children.

Only a few investigations have been made of the relationship between parental attitudes and the child's reading achievement. Preston[53] investigated the attitudes of parents after reading problems had developed and found that parents indulged their children until the reading problem arose and then suddenly changed to impatience and scolding. A child who failed to read was considered by his parents to be "abnormal, queer, not quite right."

Mothers of retarded readers were found by Stewart[54] to have strong ambivalent feelings toward their children. The mothers were somewhat hostile to their children and experienced guilt feelings which made them generally overindulgent or overprotective.

Missildine,[55] in his eight-year study of the home and family relationships of thirty retarded readers, describes one third of the mothers as "overtly hostile" and still another one third as "markedly tense, criticizing, and coercive." These maternal attitudes were judged to be conducive to reading failure.

Seigler and Gynther's study[56] shows that parents of poor readers use critical or derogatory descriptive terms more frequently than parents of good readers. They more frequently describe their children as aggressive, distrustful, or dependent and devaluate their children's

[52] Merville C. Shaw and Bert E. Dutton, "The Use of the Parent Attitude Research Inventory with the Parents of Bright Academic Underachievers," *Journal of Educational Psychology,* **53** (October, 1962), 203–208.

[53] Mary I. Preston, "The Reaction of Parents to Reading Failure," *Child Development,* **10** (September, 1939), 173–179.

[54] Robert S. Stewart, "Personality Maladjustment and Reading Achievement," *American Journal of Orthopsychiatry,* **20** (1950), p. 415.

[55] Whitney H. Missildine, "The Emotional Background of 30 Children with Reading Disabilities with Emphasis Upon Its Coercive Elements," *The Nervous Child,* **5** (July, 1946), p. 271.

[56] Hazel G. Seigler and Malcolm D. Gynther, "Reading Ability of Children and Family Harmony," *Journal of Developmental Reading,* **4** (Autumn, 1960), 17–24.

personalities more often than parents of good readers. Parents of poor readers were less frequently identified with their spouses and with their children than parents of good readers. These findings were interpreted as supporting the hypothesis that family conflict is greater in the home of a poor reader than it is in homes in which no child has a reading deficiency.

Vickery[57] found that parents of children in a "high" reading group had significantly different child-rearing attitudes from parents of children in a "low" reading group. Parents of the better readers favored to a high degree attitudes which reflected permissive child-rearing practices.

McKinley[58] attempted to determine if certain aspects of the home environment, in their influences upon the child's emotional development, were determining factors in success or failure in reading. Maternal personality, maternal child-rearing attitudes, and maternal sensitivity to the child's emotions were the specific variables considered. Three groups of thirty mothers each, selected on the basis of their children's reading ability, were studied with regard to these factors. Results of the statistical treatment of data disclosed significant differences among mother groups only with regard to their sensitivity to their child's emotions or feelings. No appreciable differences in personality or child-rearing attitudes among the groups studied were found.

A number of investigators have studied the relationship between other home factors and reading achievement. Parr,[59] in his study of college students who were poor readers, found a lack of reading material in the home, lack of interest in reading, and little or no recreational reading in childhood.

Almy,[60] in her study of children's experiences and their success in

[57] Verna L. Vickery, "A Study of the Relationship of Certain Parental Attitudes and Personality Characteristics to the Reading Achievement of Children in the First Grade," *University Bulletin, Louisiana State University: Abstracts of Dissertations, Titles of Theses,* XLVII (2), (1955), 56–57.

[58] Douglas P. McKinley, *A Study of Certain Relationships of Maternal Personality and Child-Rearing Attitudes to Children's Reading Performances.* Unpublished doctoral dissertation, University of Florida, 1958.

[59] Frank W. Parr, "Factors Associated with Poor Reading Ability of Adults," *School and Society,* 35 (May 7, 1932), p. 626.

[60] Millie Corinne Almy, *Children's Experiences Prior to First Grade and Success in Beginning Reading* (New York: Bureau of Publications, Teachers College, Columbia University, 1949).

beginning reading, found a significant relationship between success in reading and such experiences as looking at books and magazines, having someone read to them, and taking interest in words, letters, and numbers. Ladd,[61] in her study of the home environment of retarded readers, found that homes of lower socioeconomic status and a foreign language background were associated with poor reading. Jackson's investigation of 600 good and poor readers yielded similar findings.[62] He found socioeconomic status, family size, and parental educational level to be distinguishing factors between retarded and nonretarded readers. Increase in family size favored the retarded reader, whereas higher socioeconomic status and parental educational level favored the good reader. A more recent study by Sheldon and Carrillo[63] revealed that retarded readers generally come from large families of lower socioeconomic status, have fewer books available, and have parents who left school sooner than the parents of advanced readers.

A study by McGinnis[64] shows that parents of superior readers express attitudes that are less dictatorial and more democratic than do parents of inferior readers. Mothers and fathers of superior readers manifest attitudes that foster independence rather than dependence, include outside influences rather than exclude outside influences, place less emphasis on the deification of parents and more on group thinking and group participation. Parents of superior readers convey attitudes that encourage their children to voice their ideas and points of view rather than attitudes that discourage freedom of discussion. Attitudes of these parents suggest that their children can discuss any topic with them without shame, ridicule, or reproach.

Furthermore, the McGinnis study indicates that parents of superior

[61] Margaret R. Ladd, *The Relation of Social, Economic, and Personal Characteristics to Reading Disability* (New York: Bureau of Publications, Teachers College, Columbia University, 1933), p. 81.

[62] Joseph Jackson, "A Survey of Psychological, Social and Environmental Differences Between Advanced and Retarded Readers," *Pedagogical Seminary and Journal of Genetic Psychology,* **65** (1944), 113–131.

[63] William D. Sheldon and Lawrence W. Carrillo, "Relation of Parents, Home, and Certain Developmental Characteristics to Children's Reading Ability," *Elementary School Journal,* **52** (January, 1952), 262–270.

[64] Dorothy J. McGinnis, *A Comparative Study of the Attitudes of Parents of Superior and Inferior Readers Toward Certain Child Rearing Practices, the Value of Reading, and the Development of Language Skills and Experiential Background Related to Reading.* Unpublished doctoral dissertation, Michigan State University, 1963.

readers manifest attitudes suggesting that they refrain from attempting to hurry the growth and development of their children. Instead, the attitudes of these parents suggest that they appreciate the concept of readiness. Attitudes of parents of superior readers emphasize the value of communication and the development of language skills. This study also shows that the parents of superior readers and the parents of inferior readers differ significantly in their attitudes toward the importance of reading, the value of language development, and the importance of experiential background. These differences in attitudes suggest differences in kind and degree of mental content which children have an opportunity to acquire.

A study by Carter[65] shows that differences in attitudes exist between parents of superior and inferior readers at the college level. He found that parents of superior college readers, to a significant degree, placed a higher value on reading, the development of language skills, and the building of experiential background than did parents of inferior readers at the college level.

In general, research seems to substantiate the inference that there are differences between the parents and home environments of superior and inferior readers.

The Community

The community from which a child enters the classroom can adversely affect his reading achievement. Families making up the various economic and social classes tend, for various reasons, to seek their own kind. Consequently, the community reflects the characteristics of its predominant economic-social groups. The depressed areas produce many disadvantaged and culturally deprived children who are adversely affected by the social and educational climate of the neighborhood.

Barton[66] shows that "the most important single factor in progress

[65] Homer L. J. Carter, "A Study of Attitudes Toward Certain Aspects of Reading Expressed by Parents of Inferior and Superior College Readers," *The Philosophical and Sociological Bases of Reading,* Fourteenth Yearbook of the National Reading Conference (Milwaukee: The National Reading Conference, Inc., 1965), pp. 188–194.

[66] Allen H. Barton, "Social Class and Instructional Procedures in the Process of Learning to Read," *New Developments in Programs and Procedures for*

in reading in school is socio-economic class." He has shown that in the first six grades children who come from working-class families were generally reading below their actual grade levels. The difference was even greater for children from the lower-skilled, lower-paid levels of the working classes. Deutsch[67] explains that a lack of effective language stimulation early in life in the neighborhood and school can make success in reading and the language arts progressively more difficult to attain. Loban,[68] who found writing ability related to socioeconomic position, has pointed out that individuals who were low in general language ability were also low in reading achievement. In a study of the reading performance of white and Negro children in Georgia, Cooper[69] observed a decrease in rate of growth in both vocabulary and comprehension. She points out that this was more marked for Negro than for white subjects, particularly at the upper grade levels.

There are within our society large numbers of people who live in subcultures which do not prepare them adequately to adjust to academic requirements or to the demands of the world at large. Edwards[70] states, "Our American society has allowed many millions of its members to remain culturally isolated, locked in their own cultural cocoons, as it were, either by design or neglect." He points out that as a result of this segregation from contact with the predominant culture, they grow up culturally different. There is a tendency for them to feel inferior, rejected, and without a significant place in our society. Their experiences are limited. They speak a divergent dialect of American English or a different language. Their concepts are highly specialized and limited. Furthermore, their value systems differ from and fre-

---

College-Adult Reading, Twelfth Yearbook of the National Reading Conference (Milwaukee: The National Reading Conference, Inc., 1963), pp. 167–174.

[67] Martin Deutsch, "The Role of Social Class in Language Development and Cognition," *American Journal of Orthopsychiatry,* **35** (January, 1965).

[68] Walter D. Loban, *The Language of Elementary School Children,* National Council of Teachers of English, Research Report No. 1 (Champaign, Ill.: National Council of Teachers of English, 1963).

[69] Bernice Cooper, "An Analysis of the Reading Achievement of White and Negro Pupils in Certain Public Schools in Georgia," *School Review,* **LXXII** (Winter, 1964), 462–471.

[70] Thomas J. Edwards, "Cultural Deprivation: Ideas for Action" in *Forging Ahead in Reading,* Conference Proceedings of the International Reading Association, Vol. 12, Part 1 (1968), 357–363.

quently conflict with those of the dominant culture. The Ausubels[71] report that the problem is even greater for the Negro child because he "perceives himself as an object of derision and disparagement."

Cheyney[72] summarizes the problem effectively by explaining, "Culturally disadvantaged children lack facility in oral expression, both in vocabulary and in correct speech patterns." He shows that low self-concepts, personality disorders, and a high delinquency rate are common among those who suffer from poverty and that inadequate diet compounds the problem. It appears from these studies that children who come from a poor environment and who represent minority groups are less apt to make normal progress in the language arts and especially reading.

EDUCATIONAL FACTORS AND READING ACHIEVEMENT

Bond and Tinker[73] have pointed out that "among all the factors that are considered possible causes of reading disability the group of conditions classed as educational stand out as tremendously important." The school, even with its professionally prepared teachers and supervisory personnel, can contribute to the child's inability to learn to read. Some conclusions based on research in this area are briefly summarized here.

Educational Philosophy and Policy

Many school systems lack a unified educational philosophy. For example, as Dolch[74] has pointed out, many school systems disagree about whether child development or learning to read during the early years should be of primary concern to the school. Some teachers have believed that the chief goal of the school should be the happy, well-balanced, and socially competent individual, whereas others stress the

[71] David P. Ausubel and Pearl Ausubel, "Ego Development Among Segregated Negro Children," A. Harry Passow, ed., *Education in Depressed Areas* (New York: Teachers College Press, Columbia University, 1963), 109–141.

[72] Arnold B. Cheyney, *Teaching Culturally Disadvantaged in the Elementary School* (Charles E. Merrill Books, Inc., Columbus, Ohio, 1967), p. 20.

[73] Guy L. Bond and Miles A. Tinker, *Reading Difficulties: Their Diagnosis and Correction,* 2nd ed. (New York: Appleton-Century-Crofts, 1967), p. 138.

[74] E. W. Dolch, *Problems in Reading* (Champaign, Ill.: Garrard Press, 1948).

idea that learning to read is the major objective of education in the early grades. Here there is a conflict of purpose. Austin,[75] in pointing out another conflict in educational philosophy, has explained that "while it has been recommended that no one method of word attack, in particular phonetic analysis, be used to the exclusion of all others, it is assumed that phonetic and structural analysis will be included in any list of techniques of word recognition. Unfortunately, many prospective teachers themselves do not know these techniques."

As early as 1938 Luella Cole[76] stated that the chief cause for the prevalence of corrective reading classes was the failure of the school to modify the curriculum in accordance with the current promotion policy. At that time, and today, children were promoted on the basis of seniority rather than achievement with no lowering of curriculum requirements. Consequently, as poor readers were "promoted" from grade to grade, they became frustrated and were unable to keep up with their group. Eventually their reading disability led to emotional and social maladjustment. Furthermore, until very recently, developmental instruction in reading was provided only for elementary school children. Obviously, both the school and the community have failed to regard reading as a continuous process, having its beginning in the home and continuing throughout the elementary grades, junior high school, and the secondary schools.

Selection and Preparation of Teachers

The Austin[77] study indicates that all too frequently students are admitted to an educational major without effective screening. She explains that throughout the country many senior faculty members, prominent in the field of reading, rarely teach undergraduate courses in reading instruction. Rather, they devote their time to graduate courses, research projects, and counseling services. This situation does not produce enthusiastic and well-prepared teachers for the area of reading. Austin[78] adds that despite its importance in relation to all

[75] Mary Austin et al., *The Torch Lighters* (Cambridge, Mass.: Harvard University Press, 1961), p. 146.

[76] Luella Cole, *The Improvement of Reading* (New York: Holt, Rinehart and Winston, 1938).

[77] Mary Austin et al., *The Torch Lighters* (Cambridge, Mass.: Harvard University Press, 1961).

[78] *Ibid.*

other areas in the elementary curriculum, reading is frequently not given enough emphasis in the training of teachers. Prospective teachers are now receiving little more than minimal training in the teaching of reading during their undergraduate years, and they should receive further training and effective guidance as beginning teachers. She shows that the student entering secondary school needs to expand his reading skills for future scholastic success, but few prospective secondary school teachers receive any instruction in the teaching of reading that will enable them to provide adequate guidance for their pupils.

McGinnis[79] found in a study of the preparation and responsibility of secondary teachers in the field of reading that 70 per cent were expected to provide some reading instruction and that 90 per cent had not been enrolled in classes where the teaching of reading had been emphasized. Austin[80] and her associates add that one of the major problems faced by college instructors is that of relating the theory of reading instruction to its practical application in the elementary school classroom and of developing within students the necessary competencies for dealing with teaching problems they may encounter as beginning teachers.

Inadequate Teaching Methods

Austin[81] reports that classroom teachers are handicapped by inadequate understanding of research related to instructional techniques in teaching reading. Many teachers have assumed that if a method is new it is good and that if it is old it is to be disregarded. Choice of teaching methods has not been based on well-designed and well-controlled research. The studies by Austin[82] indicate that in many instances a dichotomy exists between the theory of reading advocated at the college level and the practices involved in the teaching of reading in the elementary classroom where prospective teachers re-

[79] Dorothy J. McGinnis, "The Preparation and Responsibility of Secondary Teachers in the Field of Reading," *The Reading Teacher,* **15** (November, 1961), 92–97.

[80] Austin, *op. cit.*

[81] Mary Austin et al., *The Torch Lighters* (Cambridge, Mass.: Harvard University Press, 1961).

[82] *Ibid.*

ceive their professional training. Obviously, in many instances, there is a wide gulf between the theory advocated in the college classroom and the problems actually found in the elementary and secondary schools. Apparently, teachers have not been made aware of the fact that they should focus their attention upon the child and adjust aims, materials, and procedures to his needs and way of learning. They should know that no one method works equally well for all children.

SUMMARY

This chapter has discussed briefly the nature of cause and its relation to reading. Research findings and opinions of leaders have been set forth without comment and evaluation. Physical, psychological, sociological, and educational factors have served as a basis of classification. It is the consensus that no single factor or pattern of factors can explain and account for all maladjustment in reading. Attention must be focused on the individual, and many factors must be considered before an adequate explanation can be made of the individual's inability to read effectively.

GUIDED ACTIVITY 4

Aim

To review and evaluate causal factors of reading disabilities as reported by workers in the field.

Materials

1. References provided in Chapter 4.
2. 5- by 8-in. cards.
3. *Reader's Guide to Periodical Literature.*
4. Card catalogue.
5. *Psychological Abstracts.*
6. *Educational Index.*

Procedure

1. Prepare a card index which can be helpful to you in clinical practice. Summarize briefly inferences and opinions of investigators of physical factors affecting reading achievement. State author, title of article, date,

publisher, and page numbers so that you can easily refer to original sources. Classify cards under headings such as vision, audition, nutrition, glandular dysfunction, and neurological factors.

2. Prepare a card index which can be helpful to you in clinical practice. Summarize briefly inferences and opinions of investigators of psychological factors affecting reading achievement. State author, title of article, date of publication, publisher, and page numbers so that you can easily refer to original sources. Classify cards under headings such as mental maturity, mental content, self-concept, emotional stability, and personality factors.

3. Prepare a card index which can be helpful to you in clinical practice. Summarize briefly inferences and opinions of investigators of sociological factors affecting reading achievement. State author, title of article, date of publication, publishers, and page numbers so that you can easily refer to original sources. Classify under headings such as home background, parents, neighborhood, recreation, school, and church.

4. Show how Orton and Delacato are similar and dissimilar in their points of view.

5. Show how Kephart and Money are similar and dissimilar in their points of view.

6. Explain why well-known investigators differ radically in their opinions concerning the causes of reading disabilities.

7. After your study of causal factors affecting reading achievement, what are your general conclusions?

QUESTIONS AND REFERENCES

Questions

1. How is perception related to seeing and believing?

2. What factors are involved in working with problem readers?

3. What are some thinking disorders in brain-injured children?

References

1. Richard S. Lewis, Alfred A. Strauss, and Laura E. Lehtinen, *The Other Child* (New York: Grune and Stratton, 1960), Chap. 2.

2. Robert M. Wilson, *Diagnostic and Remedial Reading* (Columbus, Ohio: Charles E. Merrill Books, Inc., 1967), Chap. 1.

3. Alfred A. Strauss and Laura E. Lehtinen, *Psychopathology and Education of the Brain-Injured Child* (New York: Grune and Stratton, 1947), Chap. 4.

Questions	References
4. What is the anatomy of acquired disorders of reading?	**4.** John Money, ed., *Reading Disability, Progress and Research Needs in Dyslexia* (Baltimore: The Johns Hopkins Press, 1962), Chap. 8.
5. What are some preliminary conclusions affecting education of brain-injured children?	**5.** Alfred A. Strauss and Newell C. Kephart, *Psychopathology and Education of the Brain-Injured Child* (New York: Grune and Stratton, 1955), Chap. 8.
6. What are some causes of difficulties in learning to read?	**6.** Marion Monroe and Bernice Rogers, *Foundations for Reading* (Chicago: Scott, Foresman and Company, 1964), Chap. 7. Helen M. Robinson, *Why Pupils Fail in Reading* (Chicago: The University of Chicago Press, 1946), pp. 7–102.
7. What is the nature of reading growth?	**7.** Guy L. Bond and Miles A. Tinker, *Reading Difficulties: Their Diagnosis and Correction* 2nd ed. (New York: Appleton-Century-Crofts, 1967), Chap. 2.
8. What are some learning principles and the reading process?	**8.** Henry P. Smith and Emerald V. Dechant, *Psychology in Teaching Reading* (Englewood Cliffs, N.J.: Prentice-Hall, Inc., 1961), Chap. 3.

Chapter 5

Observation: A Means of Studying the Individual

The perceptive observer sensitive to the child and his needs can acquire an understanding of him that supplements, and in some instances surpasses, information resulting from other means of investigation. In this chapter the nature of observation, some difficulties encountered in its use, and some means of improving its effectiveness will be discussed, with emphasis on applications to the study of the disabled reader.

THE NATURE OF OBSERVATION

Effective observation is an interaction between the examiner and the individual under investigation. Every act of the observed is a projection of the inner self and is worthy of consideration. Observation is not a passive process of merely looking on. Instead it is more like a chess game between two individuals. It is a purposeful act and involves a plan for action which can be modified instantly in order to capitalize on an opening or "hunch." The ability to observe, like the ability to play chess, can be developed by study, supervision, and practice.

Some observations are general and *free-ranging*. The observer, for example, in an informal situation sees, hears, and experiences a sequence of acts which he interprets and evaluates in terms of his own background. He builds up his inferences without previous intent and gradually becomes aware of a problem. On the other hand, the observer may be cognizant of a maladjustment that demands his attention. His observation will then be *analytical*, for he attempts to identify and interpret specific aspects of behavior in order to evaluate causal factors contributing to an effect. Both free-ranging and analytical observations are worthy tools for teacher and clinician.

MENTAL CONTENT IN OBSERVATION

In the act of observing, the examiner is influenced by his past. His experiential background provides information, attitudes, and points of view for the identification, interpretation, and evaluation of that which is observed. The good observer "reads" the individual and makes effective use of the data so acquired. In order to accomplish this objective, the observer must know not only what to look for but its significance as well. He must be well acquainted with his field of specialization and be able to determine which of his observations are *relevant, material,* and *consequential* to the situation under investigation. In the field of reading, for example, some understanding of physiology, pediatrics, ophthalmology, otology, psychology, and education is essential. Furthermore, the observer must be interested in the total personality of the child and be willing to accept him as he is without disapproval. He must see and hear the observed with the human interest of the parent for his child and at the same time with the objective attitude of the laboratory technician.

SOME DIFFICULTIES ENCOUNTERED BY OBSERVERS

Observations produce facts that become the basis for inferences concerning the student and his needs. Inferences based on observations may be untrustworthy because of both *sampling errors* and *observer errors*. Conditions and situations change from day to day, and consequently the observer must be certain he has an adequate sampling of the examinee's total behavior. This can only be accomplished by observing specific behavior on many occasions and requires time and careful planning.

Frequently, teachers, observing a child as he is administered an informal reading inventory vary greatly in their report of observed facts. Some overemphasize certain types of responses and fail utterly to report others. Obviously, they find that for which they are looking. Their errors are systematic and not random. In other words, they are biased observers utilizing their preconceived ideas and are considering only that which they believe to be significant.

Sampling and observer errors can be negated and made less damaging if the observer refrains from making fixed inferences and generalizations. Instead, he can set up hypotheses which are tentative and subject to acceptance or rejection when more facts in the total situation are available. The observer must strive for objectivity and find means of minimizing subjective errors.

DIFFERENTIATION OF FACTS AND INFERENCES

A single observation can lead to a variety of inferences. For example, forty-five students saw their teacher stop his lecture, sit down, and put his head on the desk. Everyone present agreed as to the accuracy of the observation. When asked to explain what they had observed, nine different explanations were made by the forty-five students. Each explanation was an *inference* and was obtained *subjectively*. It may be stated then that an observation is a statement of a fact and an inference is an interpretation of a fact.

Inferences are hazardous at any time and should be plainly labeled so that the observer will not accept them at face value. After an inference has been made, it is frequently judged to be true or false, and consequently an end is made of further investigation. This, too, is dangerous. When the critical observer seeks information, he wants facts, not fantasies disguised as facts. It is hazardous, indeed, to confuse the two.

An incident occurring at the student center of a Midwestern University was observed and reported by a counselor. In Table 5-1 the facts are shown in the left-hand column and the inferences in the column at the right.

During an interview with this young girl it was learned that both of her parents were opposed to cigarette smoking and that her mother, the dominant member of the family, gave her little opportunity to solve her own problems and to make her own choices of clothing, friends, and subjects elected in the university. It can be assumed that the girl was in conflict between two ways of life. Her act with the cigarettes was an innovation of which her mother would not approve.

TABLE 5-1 Free-Ranging Observation

Facts	Inferences
A girl wearing a freshman sweater seated herself at a table in the student center. She looked about.	
She pulled her skirt down.	
She took a package of cigarettes from her purse.	1. She wants to attract attention.
She adjusted her skirt.	2. Her skirt adjustment is a manifestation of her early home background and upbringing.
She tore the whole top from the pack of cigarettes.	
She adjusted her skirt and looked about smiling.	
In getting a cigarette from the pack she tore off its end. This act was repeated with a second cigarette.	
She looked about the room and smiled.	3. She does not know how to smoke.
She adjusted her skirt.	4. She wants those about her to think that she is a sophisticated woman on campus.
After securing a cigarette from the pack, she pounded one end on the table.	
She then put into her mouth the end that she had not tapped on the table.	
She adjusted her skirt and looked about.	
She made three attempts to light the cigarette.	5. There is a conflict between two goals. She wants to maintain

TABLE 5-1 (Continued)

Facts	Inferences
After succeeding, she tossed back her head and inhaled.	the traditions of her home and to secure at the same time the acceptance of her peers.
After coughing, she adjusted her skirt.	

Her total behavior was an expression of her inner self and to the perceptive observer had meaning.

OBSERVATION OF CHILD WITH READING DISABILITY

Dick is seven years old and is in the first grade. He was asked to read silently the following sentences.

John has a cat.
Its name is Spot.
Spot has five kittens.
They are black and white.
Spot drinks milk.
The kittens are learning to drink milk.

The observed facts are shown in the left-hand column of Table 5-2 and the inferences are listed in the column at the right.

TABLE 5-2 Analytical Observation

Facts	Inferences
Dick pointed to each word, and lip movement was evident.	
He asked help with the word five.	

TABLE 5-2 (Continued)

Facts	Inferences
He reported that he had a cat named Tops.	1. Habit of reading lines of print from left to right is well established.
He required aid with the word *black* but not with *white*.	2. Habit of reading word by word has been acquired.
He hesitated with the sentence, "Spot drinks milk," but finally said, "Tops likes milk."	3. Tendency to reversals should be investigated.
	4. Makes use of contextual clues.
Dick asked for help with the word *learning*.	
When asked, "What does John have?" he replied, "A cat."	
When asked, "What is the cat's name?" he replied, "Tops."	
When this error was corrected, he said, "Mother tells me not to turn my letters around."	5. Has not learned to use a sentence in responding to questions.
He was asked, "What colors were the kittens?" and his reply was, "Black and white."	6. Has been taught to read for factual information.
When asked, "Who drinks milk?" his reply was "Spot."	7. Lacks ability to attack unfamiliar words.
He was asked, "Why did the kittens have to learn to drink milk?" His answer was, "They must have been stupid."	8. Has not been taught to respond to "why" questions.

IMPROVING THE RELIABILITY AND VALIDITY OF OBSERVATIONS

The teacher and clinician can improve the reliability and validity of observations by utilizing the following suggestions.

- Read school history, physical records, and reports of former teachers so as to identify gaps in information furnished by tests, family history, academic history, and other clinical data. Such information will suggest what to look for in observing the child.
- Establish rapport with the observed. Be tolerant and sincere and try to have the child enjoy his contact with you. Because of personality differences, you may be unable to observe every child with equal effectiveness.
- Be flexible and original in your approach. Modify your routine from individual to individual so as to adjust to and cooperate with the observed. Each act or question must have a purpose. Avoid preconceived ideas, for some observers see what they want to see.
- Be implicit in developing your hypotheses. Here is where you can use your intuitive powers. These hypotheses, however, must be substantiated by observations of the individual in several situations.
- Be explicit and do not infer too much. Adhere to the facts, for in many instances the simplest interpretation is the best. Make tentative judgments and do not try to be profound and technical.
- Be cognizant of change which can be made by the observed. A new car, for example, may travel down the street at fifteen miles per hour, but it would be naive to assume that this rate of movement is an adequate evaluation of its potential speed. In like manner, the individual's response in one situation is not necessarily his response in another. Consideration must be given to changing physical, psychological, and environmental factors.
- Keep in mind that the reliability and validity of observed facts are, to a considerable degree, dependent on the observer's awareness of his own prejudices, preconceptions, and emotional bias.

RECORDING OBSERVATIONS

Behavior observed in the classroom, laboratory, or clinic should be recorded as soon as possible. If time is permitted to elapse, valuable detail related to events and their sequence may be lost. Detailed writing, however, during the observation should be regarded as malpractice. In recording the behavior of an individual child, the use of anecdotal records is recommended. An anecdote is a short report of a single incident of behavior which suggests a valuable inference or interpretation. An anecdotal record commonly consists of a brief statement of fact, inferences or interpretation of this fact, and a summary of action actually taken in the case. Some suggestions concerning the preparation and use of anecdotal records are:

- Report briefly only facts that seem significant.
- Always differentiate between facts and inferences. For example, it is observed that a second-grade child reads *was* for *saw* and *on* for *no* and that although he is right-handed, his left eye is dominant. These statements are facts that can be observed by anyone. From these facts, it may be inferred that confusion in dominance causes reversals and that a sounding-tracing method should be recommended. These assumptions, of course, may or may not be true.
- Anecdotal records should be made as soon as possible after an observed incident.
- Statements complimentary to the child as well as uncomplimentary incidents should be reported.
- The anecdotal record is of significant value when a series of observations points to the same inference.
- Data resulting from anecdotal records should be interpreted only in terms of all the other known facts.
- Teachers should acquire the habit of recording the significant observations of all their children. This is essential to any scientific study.

ILLUSTRATION OF ANECDOTAL RECORD

Archambault, Joan   6B   March 27, 1968
Observation of Fact
Joan confuses o, c, and e. Reports she cannot see words on board.
Inference
She may have an eye defect.
Summary of Action
As a result of telebinocular test, conference was held with parents and it was suggested that Joan would probably profit from an examination by an ophthalmologist.

USE OF VISUAL AND AUDITORY RECORDINGS

Mechanical devices can record and thereby reduce observer errors, record several events simultaneously, and operate continuously for comparatively long periods of time. A sequence of events which has been recorded can later be studied as to cause and effect. Happenings which at first appear to be of little significance may assume greater importance when viewed in terms of the total situation. The use of visual and auditory modalities reinforces the reliability of the observation. There can be a shift from the act of observing to a greater emphasis on objective interpretation. Recent developments in this field have provided equipment that can be easily operated and that is within the price range of many clinics and reading laboratories. However, mechanical devices can become, for some observers, a "gadget" which they focus more attention on than the object of their investigation.

OBSERVATIONS IN TESTING SITUATIONS

In the administration of any individual test, there is opportunity for observing the individual's ways of reacting. In fact, how the examinee responds can be of greater value to the observer than the actual score. Even with Binet and Wechsler tests, observations can be made incidentally and provide significant clues concerning the child's adjustment in his environment. These by-products of the examination may reveal more concerning the child's interests, his manner of reacting to frustration, and his attitudes than hours of observation in the classroom and on the playground. The examinee's desire, for example, to make a good impression can cause him to show personality traits and individual characteristics that may be related to his immediate problem. Observations based on tests furnish a satisfactory means of evaluating change that may have occurred between the first and second administration of the equivalent forms of the test. The stimulus is a constant factor for each item on these tests. Consequently, changes in the manner of response may be significant. Differences in types of reactions may have more meaning than changes in scores. Inferences, however, must be made with discretion.

OBSERVATION DURING AN INTERVIEW

Observation during an interview with child or parent can be productive of cues that may explain behavior and suggest "hunches" requiring further investigation. Some questions that may tap valuable sources of information are:

Is the individual hostile or belligerent?
Is he eager to make a good impression?
Is he indifferent and passive?
Is there a tendency to avoid certain topics?
Does he exaggerate?
Is he erratic?
Do facial expressions vary during interview?
Is he withdrawn?
Is he overactive and restless?
Are there involuntary movements?
What mannerisms does he show?
Are his responses monosyllabic?
Is it difficult to establish and maintain rapport?
Is he apathetic?
Does he have difficulty in expressing his ideas?
Does pitch of voice vary with topic being discussed?
Is he able to draw adequate inferences and generalizations?
Is he resourceful and creative in his responses?
Is he sensitive?
Is he resentful?
Is he resigned or contented?
Is he emotionally tense?

The observer who focuses attention on the individual will become aware of other facets of his behavior during the interview and will be alerted by what he sees and hears. These questions should not be used as a checklist. They merely furnish loci of valuable information.

OBSERVATION DURING INFORMAL INVENTORIES

The informal inventory provides an opportunity to observe the child in a well-structured situation designed to provide specific information in the field of reading and in such areas as personality and social, economic, and educational adjustment. In fields other than reading, form boards, incomplete sentences, association cards, and parts of psychological tests can be selected for the occasion and utilized as informal inventories designed to accomplish a specific purpose. In this situation the observer is not concerned with the reliability and validity of the instruments but with the clues and "hunches" they may provide to explain the child's behavior. In using these informal inventories, scores have little value in comparison to the "hunches" which the child's responses may suggest. Some typical questions to be considered in observing the examinee are

Can the child sustain effort?
What word attack skills does he show?
Can he read to answer questions?
Does he ask for help with words?
Can he answer why and how questions?
Can he identify, interpret, and evaluate ideas expressed in pictures?
How does he respond with activities involving turning and placing objects on form boards?
How does he respond with activities involving use of tweezers in placing steel pegs in small holes?
Is he able to follow directions?
Which eye is dominant?
Which hand is dominant?
Can he identify main ideas?
Can he identify the topic sentence in a paragraph?
Does he read effectively for detail?
What attitudes toward reading does he display?
Can he organize ideas in order to support a generalization?
In his drawing of a person are there evidences of identification with mother or father?
Does he draw meticulously or in a sloppy manner?
Are the lines heavy or light?
Are his drawings expansive or extremely small and detailed?
As he makes his drawings, does he persist in asking for direction and guidance?
Does he get an idea and carry it through to a logical conclusion?
What does he say about his drawing of a house, a tree, or a person?
Does he give immediate responses to incomplete sentences?
Does he enjoy the activities which have been required of him?

Informal inventories should be selected and designed to secure responses and information that will be relevant to the immediate problem. These tools should be tailored to accomplish a specific purpose. In all instances, observations and their interpretations are more productive than measurement of achievement.

OBSERVING THE ACT OF READING

The teacher of reading in the classroom should know how to observe her pupils, one by one, so as to identify those who are unsuccessful in reading achievement, those who fail to enjoy reading activities, and those who read words instead of ideas. She should be able to detect the child who confuses *o, e, c,* and such words as *bear, hear,* and *near.* She should be able to spot the child who calls *saw, was* and *no, on* and be aware of several possible explanations of why he makes these errors. She can observe the child's manner of holding his book and his frequent loss of place in reading. Watering or inflamed eyes, along with reports of letters blurred or running together, can suggest to the attentive teacher the possibility of a visual difficulty that should be called to the attention of the school physician or nurse. In this situation the teacher does not diagnose a visual defect; she merely reports facts she has observed. It is obvious that she must have mental content and information concerning symptoms of visual defects which are related to reading performance. She also must determine whether facts observed are relevant and material to the child's disability.

An excellent example of observing in a silent reading situation has been provided by a reading therapist.[1] Her facts and inferences have been discretely differentiated as follows.

TABLE 5-3 Observation of Reading Problem

Facts	Inferences
Materials: Science Research Associates Laboratory, Level 2	
Barry came running into room from physical education class. Slid into desk, jumped over seat, and sat down with a bang. Opened desk to get pencil and SRA materials went onto floor. Picked	1. Barry had a good time in the gymnasium and was excited and happy. He appeared far more excited than the other

[1] Loretta Cardno, Kalamazoo Public Schools.

TABLE 5-3 (Continued)

Facts	Inferences
them up. Then went to sharpen pencil. Sat down. Then jumped up and asked to go to bathroom. Was gone 3½ minutes. When he returned, all the rest of class was quietly reading. Barry walked into room slowly. Sat down at desk. Picked up pencil. Opened book. Picked up story card. Held story card with both hands. Laid card down on desk. Used finger to follow words. Another boy coughed. Barry looked around at him, grinned, turned back, and looked down at card. Tapped on desk with pencil while reading. Was told to stop. Looked up, grinned, scratched head with pencil. Looked around room, then back at story. Put both elbows on desk with head between hands. Stayed in this position 3 minutes. Started writing in record book. Erased. Wrote again. Looked at story. Used finger to follow words. Wrote. Another boy went past desk and Barry looked up, squirmed, rubbed ear, and stuck out foot as boy returned. Boy side-stepped and Barry grinned at him. Looked back at story card. Wrote in record book. Did this for 2 minutes. Barry then threw down his pencil, took his record book to its storage place, and asked to go to the bathroom. He had not finished his story.	children. He is, apparently, overly active and stimulated by physical exercise rather than being tired. Could the thyroid gland be involved? 2. The need to use the bathroom could be a delaying tactic to avoid schoolwork or is there a urinary problem? 3. Barry appears to be very easily distracted. He does not concentrate. Noises disturb him. 4. Barry apparently can read this story, as he quietly read for several minutes. 5. Barry likes to be noticed. He wants to be reassured that he is important. He either is the complete center of attention at home or is made to feel unimportant. 6. Barry is irresponsible. He uses each distraction as an excuse to stop working. It is possible that Barry has a urinary infection.

READING SITUATIONS TO BE OBSERVED

In the classroom the teacher and clinician can observe the child in many situations. What the observer sees and hears will depend on the experiential background and mental content he is able to bring to the problem under consideration. No one factor is equally significant for all individuals or for the same individual on different occasions. Some areas to be explored in observing the individual's performance in reading are group instruction, silent reading, and oral reading. The following questions merely suggest fields to be investigated and are not to be considered as items in a checklist. Yes and no answers are of little value.

GROUP INSTRUCTION

To what extent does the child become involved in reading?
How adequately does he express his ideas?
How does he adjust to new situations?
What is his attitude toward reading?
How effectively does he apply himself to the work of the classroom?
What evidence has he shown of creativity?
Can he select main ideas?
Can he follow printed directions?
Can he locate data?
Can he organize data?
Does he ask questions?
Is he a good listener?
To what extent is he accepted by the group?
To what extent does he assume responsibility?
Does he want to read?
Does he ask for help?
Does he possess an adequate experiential background?
Does he make use of the dictionary?
Can he answer "why" and "how" questions?
Are his contributions in class relevant to the topic being discussed?

THE SILENT-READING PERIOD

Does child like books?
Does he select books for himself?

What books does he like best?

Does he use the library effectively?

Does he ask questions and read for answers?

Does he use reference materials?

Does he share his books with others?

While he reads silently, does he make extraneous movements, as of hand, tongue, and foot?

Can he sustain effort?

Does he read to accomplish his purpose?

To what extent does he make ideas his own?

Does he read more than what is expected of him?

Does he vocalize as he reads?

Does he adjust his rate of reading to his purpose and the nature of the material?

Are there physical factors that adversely affect his reading?

What psychological factors retard his achievement?

What environmental factors adversely affect his performance?

ORAL READING

Does child have slow rate of vocalization?

Does he have difficulty with language?

Are there many mispronunciations?

Are repetitions frequently made?

Are ideas inserted?

Are there frequent substitutions of words?

Are ideas omitted?

Is he a "word caller"?

Does he like to read orally?

Does he interpret ideas effectively?

Can he recall what he has read orally?

Do his peers enjoy having him read orally?

Does the child read phrases adequately?

Does punctuation aid him in oral reading?

In observing any reading situation the teacher and clinician are intent on securing hypotheses concerning the quality of the performance and why and how it is achieved. Inferences based on these observations should be substantiated by histories, interviews, informal inventories, and objective tests. In all instances observations should become the basis of hypotheses which should lead immediately to action on the part of the observer.

SUMMARY

Observation is an art essential to the study of the child which can be practiced by the teacher and clinician. It is an interaction between observer and observed and is subject to errors which challenge its reliability and validity. It is suggested that tentative rather than permanent hypotheses be utilized by the observer. Practical suggestions for improving observational techniques are briefly outlined.

GUIDED ACTIVITY 5

Aim

To review the nature of observational procedures and to secure some firsthand experience.

Materials

1. A number of 3- by 5-in. cards.
2. Chapter 6 of *Diagnosis and Treatment of the Disabled Reader.*

Procedure

1. Read Chapter 6 of this text carefully and tell how *observational* and *interviewing* procedures are similar and how they are dissimilar.
2. Observe yourself in a large mirror as you talk to a friend on a topic of mutual interest.
   a. List your physical reactions.
   b. Explain why they occurred.
   c. Explain whether or not your explanations (inferences) are subjective or objective.
   d. Show why it is or why it is not more difficult to observe a child than to observe yourself.
3. If you are a woman, observe a mother and daughter shopping.
   a. Record on a 3- by 5-in. card the behavior and reactions of the mother.
   b. On the reverse side of the card record your inferences.
   c. Explain how it would or would not have been more difficult for you to have observed a father and son.
   d. What generalization would you make?

4. If you are a man, observe a father and son during their discussion of any topic.
   a. Record on a 3- by 5-in. card the behavior and reaction of the father.
   b. On the reverse side of the card record your inferences.
   c. Explain how it would or would not have been more difficult for you to have observed a mother and a daughter.
   d. What generalization would you make?
5. Select from any classroom a child who has difficulty in reading aloud. Observe him *alone* as he attempts to read orally a short selection of several paragraphs.
   a. Record on a 3- by 5-in. card his reactions, behavior, and his reading errors.
   b. On the reverse side of the card record your inferences.
6. Outline your plan for improving your observational techniques in the field of reading.
7. Outline some of the difficulties encountered by you in making reliable and valid inferences based upon observations.

QUESTIONS AND REFERENCES

Questions

1. How can the teacher observe in the classroom?

2. What are the limitations of observations?

3. How does empathy affect observation?

4. What is meant by sensitivity to people?

5. How are clinical sensitivity and hypothesis-making related?

6. How can observations be interpreted effectively?

7. What factors are included in diagnostic reliability and validity?

References

1. Ruth Strang, *Diagnostic Teaching of Reading* (New York: McGraw-Hill Book Company, 1964), Chap. 3.

2. *Ibid.*, pp. 42–43.

3. Henry Clay Smith, *Sensitivity to People* (New York: McGraw-Hill Book Company, 1966), Chap. 6.

4. *Ibid.*, Chap. 1.

5. Richard W. Wallen, *Clinical Psychology* (New York: McGraw-Hill Book Company, 1956), Chap. 3.

6. *Ibid.*, pp. 76–80.

7. Peter E. Nathan, *Cues, Decisions, and Diagnoses: A Systems-*

Questions	References
	Analytic Approach to the Diagnosis of Psychopathology (New York: Academic Press, 1967).
8. What can be learned by observing in the testing situation?	8. Jules C. Abrams, "Observations of the Defense Processes in the Testing Situation," *Reading and Inquiry* (Newark, Del.: International Reading Association Conference Proceedings, 1965), pp. 210–212.
9. What are some unobtrusive measures and why are they utilized?	9. Eugene J. Webb, Donald T. Campbell, Richard D. Schwartz, and Lee Sechrest, *Unobtrusive Measures: Nonreactive Research in the Social Sciences* (Chicago: Rand McNally and Company, 1966), Chaps. 5 and 6.

Chapter 6

Utilizing Interviewing Techniques

The interview can provide immediate information which can aid in the diagnosis and treatment of the disabled reader. In this chapter the interview is defined, some of its advantages and disadvantages are pointed out, some characteristics of the good interviewer are listed, and the procedures generally followed in making an interview are outlined. Several points of view essential to interviewing and some areas to be investigated in the study of the disabled reader are discussed. The intention here is to set forth some major concepts concerning the interview rather than to provide an intensive treatment of the subject.

DEFINITION OF AN INTERVIEW

An interview is a joint quest undertaken by two individuals who are trying to solve a problem. It is a purposeful interaction between the interviewer and the interviewee and is more than a friendly conversation. Ideally, it involves communication between two people who have mutual understanding and respect for each other. Interviews may be fact-finding, exploratory, or therapeutic. The skill of the interviewer is shown by his facility in encouraging the individual to tell his story and by the ease he displays in asking subtle, yet penetrating questions covering all important areas. Each interview with a child or parent concerning a reading problem can have both a diagnostic and a therapeutic function, for the mere expression of anxiety related to the disability can bring relief.

Any interview may tend to be either directive or nondirective depending on the interviewer and the objectives he wishes to accomplish. It may be described as any point on a continuum with two distinct poles, one directive and the other nondirective. Some characteristics of each type are listed. In the directive interview, the interviewer:

- Assumes responsibility for solving the immediate problem.
- Determines the direction of the interview and the areas that will be investigated.
- Assumes an active rather than a passive role.
- Interprets information from various sources.
- Suggests treatment.

In the nondirective interview, the interviewer:

- Expresses a willingness *to help* but rejects the responsibility for solving the problem.
- Encourages the interviewee to express himself freely.
- Accepts, recognizes, clarifies, and objectifies the feelings of the interviewee.
- Aids the interviewee in developing insight concerning the nature of the problem.
- Supplies information on several ways in which the reading difficulty can be overcome.
- Aids but does not direct the interviewee.

The interviewer should focus his attention on the individual and his problem rather than on the ritual of either the directive or nondirective approach.

SOME ADVANTAGES AND DISADVANTAGES OF THE INTERVIEW

The interview is a means of integrating objective data and facts resulting from histories and observations. It yields revealing responses and determines attitudes, points of view, and the reasons for them. One can trace developments quite effectively by its use. The interview is of value in diagnosis, for frequently data from many sources can be interpreted and evaluated without delay. The interviewee can be made to feel that he is important as a person and that what he has to say is of great value to the interviewer. The interview is essential in treatment for it allows a release of anxiety and builds the self-concept of the person being interviewed. It aids in dealing with fears and permits reassurance. In all instances it provides information dealing with the immediate problem and provides a means of determining whether or not facts discovered are relevant, material, and consequential.

The interview has several disadvantages. It is expensive from the standpoint of time. Frequently, the person using it interprets the responses of the interviewee in terms of that which is in his own mind. He finds that for which he is looking. Studies show a low degree of both reliability and validity. The untrained and inexperienced interviewer unconsciously can damage the welfare of his patient and jeopardize his position as an educator or clinician.

SOME CHARACTERISTICS OF THE GOOD INTERVIEWER

Studies in the fields of psychology and sociology show some of the attainments, skills, and characteristics of good interviewers. It is apparent that they are well acquainted with their fields of investigation. They possess background and experiential information which make it possible for them to secure facts relevant to the problem under consideration. They have theoretical and practical training in both directive and nondirective interviewing and are able to select and employ each in its proper place and to the advantage of their client.

The successful interviewer, like the perceptive observer, is able to utilize his understanding of *clinical, educational,* and *abnormal* psychology as he directs his attention to the immediate problem of his client. He can work equally well with both adults and children and is able to win their respect if not their admiration. The good interviewer is sensitive to the feelings of those with whom he works and is able to view them both objectively and subjectively. He is logical and demonstrates a scientific attitude as he differentiates inferences from observed facts. He is well adjusted personally and is tolerant and sincere. The successful interviewer is aware of his own inadequacies and does not attempt to "play God."

THE ART OF ASKING QUESTIONS

Questions may be asked to tap sources of information, to elicit expressions of attitudes, and to determine *how* and *why* the individual attempts to rationalize his behavior. Some questioning techniques are briefly outlined.

- *Leading questions* can be used in areas where generally there is a strong emotional bias which prevents a truthful response. For example, if the interviewer asks, "How frequently do you punish your child?" this question will probably secure more valid information than, "Do you punish your child?"
- The *exploratory question* can tap sources of information which may provide data of great importance. The interviewer may, for example, ask a general question and if the answer is significant he can follow with more detailed questions. He may also proceed from less intimate questions to more intimate ones. For example, when interviewing a mother the therapist may ask, "What help in reading does your son ask of you?" Replies to this question can suggest more specific areas to be investigated.
- The *delayed question* can prevent the development of threatening situations during the interview. The interviewer can encourage the interviewee to talk and freely express himself. As the interview develops, a crucial question such as, "Why was John asked to withdraw from the university?" may occur to the interviewer. If this question is asked immediately, an explosive issue may occur. If delayed, it can be asked in a setting which is less threatening.
- The *hidden question* can reduce anxiety and eliminate undue stress. The significant query can be preceded and followed by a series of routine questions obviously having little importance. The hidden question then appears as only a minor detail to be investigated. For example, the clinician may want to determine if a mother has had a miscarriage. Consequently, he might ask in a routine manner: "How many children do you have?" "Have you had a miscarriage?" "Was any birth difficult?"
- *Projective questions* are employed when the interviewer wishes to determine how the examinee *really* feels. For example, one can ask, "Tell me about the best teacher and the worst teacher your children

have had in the classroom." The response of the interviewee may reveal not only how he reacts to teachers but why he does so.

Questions are tools designed on the spot to accomplish a specific purpose. They should be used with care and responses wisely interpreted. When silences occur, it may be unwise for the interviewer to try to fill the space with rapid-fire questions having little or no significance.

ACTS OF INTERVIEW

The interview is always conducted for a *purpose*. It may be designed for fact-finding, exploratory, and therapeutic situations. In every instance *preparation* is essential. The interviewer should be acquainted with the problem as originally stated, the developmental, family, social, and academic histories. He should be aware of clinical data such as reports of medical specialists, social case workers, and psychologists. While integrating information from all these sources, gaps and inconsistencies will appear. Hunches will be suggested, and many unanswered questions will occur. These gaps, inconsistencies, hunches, and unanswered questions provide purposes to be achieved in the fact-finding and exploratory interview. The interviewer must plan to accomplish specific goals and yet be able to modify his plan as new facts and new needs are determined.

The *approach* to the interview can determine the success of the whole undertaking. Preparation concerning initial contacts and appointments must be made effectively and to the satisfaction of the client. Conditions of interviewing—time, place, and number of persons present—are best determined by the immediate situation. Means of establishing *rapport* should be carefully planned, and the interviewer should not rely too much on the inspiration of the moment. Joint quests do not generally just occur. They are the result of well-designed plans systematically carried out. Rapport can generally be secured by showing one's interest in the problem of the child, parent, or teacher and by putting them at ease. Frequently, the interviewee should be made to feel that he is leading the discussion and that he is the center of attention. The interviewer's vocabulary and language structure, for example, should be adjusted to the social and academic level of his client. He must be ready to put himself in the place of the child or adult and perceive the interviewee as he is in his world. This readiness requires preparation and insight.

After rapport has been established, the *problem* or purpose of the interview should be stated and the interviewee *informed* by the interviewer concerning the nature of the information the interviewer is seeking. Gaps and inconsistencies in the information should be investigated by well-designed questions, and the meaning of all facts should be *clarified* by free discussion. In the fact-finding interview, this level of development becomes the denouement for the interviewer has accomplished his purpose. The clinician, however, as he informs the teacher of his diagnosis and suggested treatment will utilize all the acts outlined in Figure 6-1. The difficulties which develop can fre-

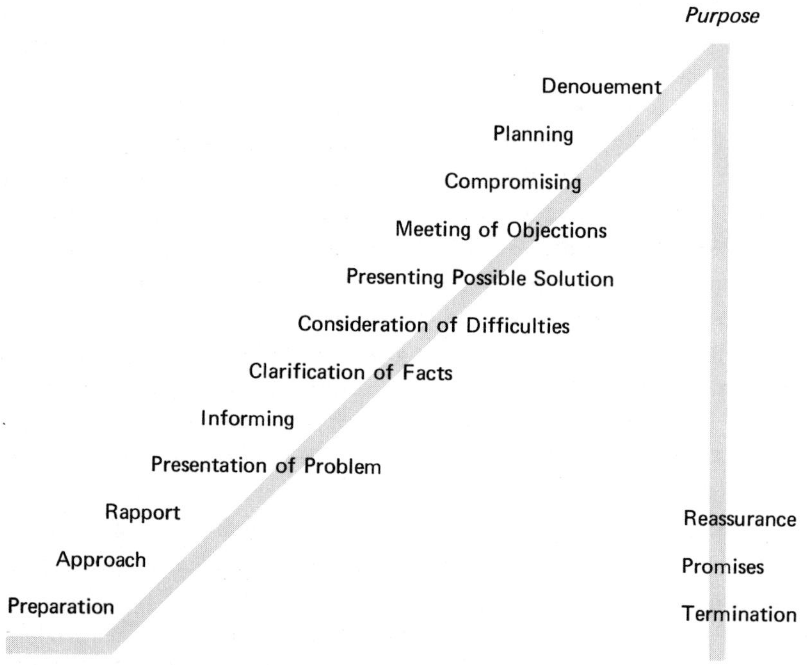

Purpose

Denouement

Planning

Compromising

Meeting of Objections

Presenting Possible Solution

Consideration of Difficulties

Clarification of Facts

Informing

Presentation of Problem

Rapport   Reassurance

Approach   Promises

Preparation   Termination

Figure 6-1   Acts in Interview

quently be resolved by encouraging the interviewee to present his *plan* for a solution. This plan may be modified, if necessary, to meet any *objections* which are encountered. *Compromising* can take place and *planning* can continue until the denouement of the interview is achieved. These related acts are shown graphically in Figure 6-1. These acts with modifications and substitutions can be implemented in fact-finding and exploratory situations dealing with both parents and teachers. Transition from one act to the next should be clearcut and distinct. The movement should be a natural sequence and smoothly executed. After the climax or denouement and after the purpose of the interview has been effectively achieved, *reassurance* and *promises* can be made and the interview quickly brought to the last act or *termination*. The interviewer will rise from his chair and thank the interviewee sincerely for the valuable help and information he has provided in the solution of the problem.

The therapeutic interview usually is conducted by the psychologist or psychiatrist who is supervising the activities of a clinical team of professional workers. This individual must have access to all known facts leading to the diagnosis and have at hand a well-integrated plan for treatment. In general, the therapeutic interview will utilize the activities set forth in Figure 6-1 if a directive approach is employed. In providing assistance to the interviewee, an effort should be made to reassure him concerning his ability to succeed. If this idea is clearly established, it can lead to action. The person's self-concept can be built up by a recounting of his successes. Emphasis must be placed on the positive rather than the negative. As the individual gains in self-confidence, anxiety will be reduced to a minimum. He can understand that with many sources of aid at his disposal, *he* can solve his problems, learn to read effectively, and achieve his goals.

SOME CONCEPTS ESSENTIAL TO INTERVIEWING

In interviewing children, parents, and teachers there are several concepts and points of view which should not be neglected. Some of these briefly stated are the following:

- The interviewer should focus his attention on the interviewee and accept him as he is without preconceived ideas and judgments.
- The interviewer should understand that the first few minutes of the interview can reveal much concerning the interviewee if he is observed in a nonstructured situation free from directives as to where to sit, what to do, and what to talk about.

- Rapport must be established for it is sine qua non.
- Anxiety of child or parent must be eliminated for it contributes to resistance on the part of the interviewee.
- History of disability or situation must become a background for detailed inquiry.
- Hunches must be identified and tested.
- Changes in attitudes must be identified and interpreted.
- New topics should be introduced with "conversational gestures" so as to indicate, "That is complete, and now we begin something new."
- Attention must be given to nonverbal responses of the interviewee, such as rate of speech, changes in intonations, and gestures.
- The interviewer should develop sensitivity to the nuances of behavior so as to combine the advantages of observation with those of the interview.
- The problem should not be oversimplified. This can be brought about by a lack of mental content on the part of the interviewer and by his emotional prejudices of various kinds.
- The interviewer should avoid hasty judgment in assuming that a situation is average or normal and hence requires no further consideration.
- The interviewer must understand the responsibilities of privileged communication and at all times maintain high ethical standards in his professional practice.
- The interview should be creative rather than liturgical.

SOME AREAS TO BE INVESTIGATED

In interviewing parents and teachers, the following items are both significant and suggestive in any investigation of reading maladjustment. The clinician, however, must understand the responsibilities of privileged information and the various situations constituting malpractice.

How long has the child had difficulty in reading, and in what situations did the child find himself when his trouble began? In the investigation of this area, it may be well to determine whether the child has moved from one neighborhood to another. A change of teachers can be significant. The birth of a brother or sister could have been a contributing factor. Marital disturbances in the home or the remarriage of a parent may be a cause of the child's maladjustment.

Were physical and mental abnormalities observed still earlier? The interviewer must be alert for information concerning birth and head injuries, a history of convulsions, premature or instrument birth. Visual and auditory defects must always be considered. Information should be sought concerning congenital mental deficiency, malformations, and nervous diseases. Is there a history of brain injuries, epilepsy, and pluriglandular insufficiency?

How does the child win satisfaction, security, and recognition? This area needs careful investigation by the interviewer. What the child wants and how he obtains his goals are important facts in his study. Is he well nourished, well clothed, and well provided with other essentials? What does he fear? Is he too dependent on his parents? Does he make friends easily? Is he a leader? Does he cry out at night? Is there a history of enuresis? Do his associates tease and laugh at him? How does he gain recognition?

How well adjusted is the child in the classroom? Interviews with the child, his parents, and teachers will aid in the investigation of this area. Does he like to go to school? Is he frequently tardy? Does he avoid reading situations? What books and stories does he prefer? Does he use the school library? Does he waste time? Does he disturb others? Does he have difficulty in concentrating? Does he ask to tell stories which he has read? Is he well liked by his peers? Is he a superior, average, or inferior student? How does he describe his teacher? Does he have a sense of responsibility in the classroom?

What is the child's place in the home? Home should be a place where the family knows all about the child and loves him just the same. Are the child's parents strict or permissive? Is he overprotected or rejected by his parents? Is he adopted, an only child, reared in a foster home or orphanage? Has there been prolonged illness in the home? Is the child subjected to an unfavorable social environment? Is there sibling rivalry? Are activities in the home well organized? Is there excessive parental ambition for the child? Is there an opportunity for the child to acquire an adequate background for reading? Into what position among the brothers and sisters was the child born? Is there dissension in the home?

What are the child's goals? To understand the child one must understand his goals. If left to himself what does the child do? What are his favorite games? What are his favorite television programs? Who are his favorite actors and actresses? Does he daydream and indulge in fantasy? What does he want to do when he becomes an adult? Does he participate in sports? Does he enjoy music? Does he like to work with tools and machines?

What has the child been successful in doing? The individual's successes represent a display of his abilities. The alert interviewer will investigate this area carefully. What does the child think he can do successfully? What do his peers think he can do well? Is he artistic? Is he interested in the outdoors? Does he like science? What drawing or pictures has he produced? What mechanical devices or models has he made? Does he spend his money wisely? Is he successful in dealing with his associates? Can he follow directions? Is he accurate in detailed work? Is he a good worker? Does he express his ideas well?

What are his antisocial attempts to win recognition? Antisocial behavior can be a means of concealing a disability either real or assumed. Such behavior should be interpreted rather than condemned. Why is the child a "smarty"? Why does he annoy the teacher? Why does he try to be "funny" and "wisecrack" before other children? Why does he copy the written responses of other children? Why does he talk so much? Why does he pretend to be stupid?

What are the child's failures and disabilities? The individual's failures and inadequacies need investigation; however, the individual should be accepted as he is. Emphasis should be placed on the positive. Does the child think he is "dumb"? Does he believe that he cannot learn to read? Is he abnormally tall, short, stout, or skinny? Does he have a speech disability? What forms of success does he overvalue? Does he do poorly in sports? Is he unwilling to try something new? Is he a mama's boy? Is the child a poor oral reader? Does he have difficulty in spelling? Does he really want to learn to read?

EXTRACT OF INTERVIEW

Wendy, who is nine years and four months old, is six months in the fourth grade. Wendy's mother insists that her child is a poor reader who really does not like to read. Wendy's father, a physician, refuses to share his wife's anxiety concerning their daughter. When administered an informal reading inventory, Wendy's capacity, frustration, instructional, and independent levels were found to be 7, 6, 5, and 4, respectively.

In an interview with Wendy, which had continued for twenty minutes, she told of her interest in science and especially that dealing with weather. She explained that her greatest problem is to avoid playing football with her brother, who is one year older than she. The interview continued as follows.

THERAPIST: Why don't you like to play football?

WENDY: I do when Jim doesn't get sore at me.

THERAPIST: Go on. Tell me more.

WENDY: Well, when I throw and catch the ball better than Jim, he says I'm too smart for a girl. Sometimes he gets me in wrong with my mother.

THERAPIST: How does Jim do that?

WENDY: Mother spends more time with Jim than she does with me, and he tells mother everything I do. I have one good friend though, and that's my dad.

THERAPIST: Does your father spend lots of time with you?

WENDY: Yes, he does and best of all he says that I am a cute little girl.

THERAPIST: Who does the scolding at your house?

WENDY: Oh, my mother does. She makes me so mad when she tells me that I do not make my bed as well as Jim does his.

THERAPIST: Who are the folks at your house who like to read?

WENDY: My mother reads and reads and reads. Dad says she reads too much. I guess mother and Jim are the folks at our house who do the most reading.

THERAPIST: Does your father read at home?

WENDY: Yes, he reads in his office, but when he has time he talks with me about things.

THERAPIST: What do you and your dad talk about?

WENDY: We talk about why things happen.

THERAPIST: Tell me more.

WENDY: Well, we talk about why it rains and why it snows. My father says I'm a good thinker. We have some science books we talk about.

THERAPIST: Does your mother like science?

WENDY: No, I guess not. She reads literature and books about social justice. My dad says mother is a very brilliant woman.

SUMMARY

The interview, like any tool, has its advantages and disadvantages. It is, however, essential in the process of gathering information concerning the disabled reader. Furthermore, it is necessary to employ the interview in reporting to parents and teachers information that they will require in dealing with the child under consideration. In all instances the interview should involve purposeful communication between individuals each of whom has mutual understanding and respect for the other. The reader should keep in mind that this chapter has provided only a brief introduction to this complex technique.

GUIDED ACTIVITY 6

Aim

To review the process of interviewing and to secure experience in the acts of interviewing.

Materials

1. Chapter 6, *Diagnosis and Treatment of the Disabled Reader.*
2. School History Record generally found in child's folder.
3. Tape recorder.

Procedure

1. Secure from principal of an elementary school the School History Record of a child who needs help in reading. This may require parental permission.
2. Study this school history in detail so as to discover inconsistencies or gaps in the information. List questions which you think are relevant.
3. List in order of significance the reading disabilities which in your opinion the child possesses.
4. Make an appointment for an interview with the child's teacher of reading.
5. At the time of the interview, utilize only the sequential acts of interviewing which are essential to the securing of adequate information.
6. Make a tape of your interview and after you have listened to your recording, give your reactions to the following questions.
   a. Were you adequately prepared for interview?

b. What was your approach?

c. How did you establish rapport?

d. What problem did you present?

e. What information did you give or secure?

f. What facts did you or interviewee clarify?

g. What difficulties were considered?

In the exploratory, or fact-finding, interview one would stop at this point. If, however, a diagnosis has been made and if means of treatment have been worked out, the following questions are relevant.

h. What plan or possible solution did you or interviewee present?

i. What objections did you or interviewee encounter?

j. What compromise did you and interviewee work out?

k. What was the ultimate plan?

l. What reassurances or promises did you give or receive?

7. Summarize in not more than three sentences the results of interview.

QUESTIONS AND REFERENCES

Questions

1. Where can one find definitions of various forms of the interview?

2. What information can be secured by play interviews with young children?

3. How can the interview be used in diagnosis?

4. How are interpersonal situations explored in the interview?

5. How can the interviewer listen with the "third ear"?

References

1. Horace B. English and Eva Champney English, *A Comprehensive Dictionary of Psychological and Psychoanalytical Terms* (New York: Longmans, Green and Company, 1958).

2. Anni Weiss Frankl, "Play Interviews with Nursery School Children," in Robert I. Watson, ed. *Readings in the Clinical Method in Psychology* (New York: Harper & Row, 1949), pp. 385–394.

3. Robert I. Watson, *The Clinical Method in Psychology* (New York: Harper & Row, 1951).

4. Harry Stack Sullivan, *The Psychiatric Interview* (New York: W. W. Norton and Company, 1954).

5. Theodor Reik, *Listening with the Third Ear* (New York: Grove Press, 1948).

Questions	References
6. What are some interview techniques?	**6.** Ruth Strang, *Diagnostic Teaching of Reading* (New York: McGraw-Hill Book Company, 1964), Chap. 12.
7. How can the interview be used in counseling?	**7.** Lee J. Cronbach, *Essentials of Psychological Testing*, 2nd ed. (New York: Harper & Row, 1960), pp. 293–299.
8. How is family history related to present behavior?	**8.** E. Kuno Beller, *Clinical Process* (New York: The Free Press, 1962), Chap. IV.

Chapter 7

Making Use of Objective Measures

In this chapter we shall discuss the use of objective measures as tools in determining the child's reading needs and the causal factors related to his achievement in reading. It is assumed that the readers are acquainted with the administration, scoring, and interpretation of educational tests, and we shall not duplicate here the content of courses in mental testing, educational measurements, psychology of vision, audiology, personality testing, and projective techniques. We shall discuss what the teacher and reading therapist can expect to learn about the disabled reader from objective data resulting from various disciplines.

DEFINITION OF OBJECTIVE MEASURES

Objective measures are relatively free from personal and emotional bias. Accuracy of administration and scoring is dependent on the examiner, and the effectiveness of interpretation is directly related to his judgment. Objective measures result from the use of instruments such as the refractometer, audiometer, thermometer, Stanford-Binet, Wechsler scales, and standardized tests in many areas of investigation such as reading, spelling, and mathematics. Educational and psychological tests are standardized measures of a sample of behavior implying uniformity of procedure in administering and scoring. In order to maintain standard conditions, the examiner must adhere to the time limits, oral instructions, and all other details of the testing procedures set forth in the manual of directions. Raw scores may be interpreted in terms of standard scores, percentiles, grade equivalents, and achievement ages.

FACTORS TO BE CONSIDERED IN SELECTION AND USE OF TESTS

The value of any test is limited, for generally it is designed to accomplish a specific purpose. Some directives to be considered in selection are

- Determine *what* should be measured and *why*.
- What tests are available to accomplish this purpose?
- How good are these instruments?

Here it is necessary to consider reliability, validity, and ease of administration and scoring. Furthermore, one should discover whether or not scores are interpreted in terms of percentiles, grade scores, or achievement ages. Equivalent forms should be available, and cost should not be prohibitive. Test manuals should be complete but not too complicated. All tests should be used with caution and only by individuals who know how to administer, score, and interpret them. Adequate background and training is essential for their selection and effective use.

After tests have been administered and scored, the examiner should:

- Determine how data should be organized and reported.
- Set forth those inferences that actually are warranted by the data which have been secured. Keep in mind that test scores mean nothing aside from the conditions under which they were obtained and that they must be interpreted in terms of all known facts concerning the examinee.

The Index of Tests found in the appendix of *Diagnosis and Treatment of the Disabled Reader* is a list of representative tests from which the teacher and clinician can select those tools essential to their needs.

AREAS EXPLORED BY OBJECTIVE MEASURES

Objective tests are of value in investigating and analyzing individual capacities, abilities, and performances. Some measures discussed in this chapter that will be of concern to teachers and clinicians are

- Measures of mental maturity.
- Measures of visual functions.
- Measures of audition.
- Survey tests in reading.
- Measures designed for analysis of reading errors.
- Personality measures.
- Projective techniques.

Measurements in these areas are of little value unless they are obtained from well-selected tests administered, scored, and interpreted by individuals with adequate background, training, and experience, which generally results from internship under competent supervision.

TESTS OF MENTAL MATURITY

Mental maturity can be measured by individual or group tests of intelligence. Clinicians working with disabled readers employ individual rather than group tests, because group measures of intelligence generally require reading on the part of the examinee. Consequently, the discussion of tests of mental maturity will be limited to information concerning the Stanford-Binet and the Wechsler scales. The Illinois Test of Psycholinguistic Abilities will be briefly described.

Stanford-Binet Scale

The Stanford-Binet provides a mental age which can furnish a point of reference for comparing reading performance with mental maturity. A child, for example, may have a mental age of twelve years and a score on a reading test equivalent to an achievement age of ten years. This discrepancy of two years suggests that the child is not reading at his expected level.

Items passed and items failed on the Stanford-Binet may be relevant factors in a diagnosis of his reading disability. Such data can furnish a hypothesis which, after further study, can be accepted or rejected. The Stanford-Binet test items require (1) information and past learning, (2) verbal ability, (3) memory, (4) perception, and (5) reasoning ability. Levels of attainment range from two years to twenty-two years and eleven months.

In the interpretation of performance on the Stanford-Binet, the teacher should understand that:

- The test measures the individual's present level of intellectual functioning.
- It is heavily weighted toward verbal abilities.
- It makes use of mental content common to an urban culture.
- It is not a reliable measure of all abilities making up general intelligence.
- Scores are influenced by emotional and personality factors.

The reading clinician is concerned with more than the mental age and the IQ. Valuable clues can be utilized by studying the pattern of test performance in detail. The diagnostician is interested in *how* the child works even more than he is with the child's level of attainment. How the examinee fails or passes an item can be truly significant as a causal factor underlying his reading maladjustment. Scatter, or the range from the examinee's earliest failure to his highest success, is probably of little significance. The fact remains, however, that the child may have failed items one would expect him to pass and passed items one would expect him to fail. Whether this is due to lack of interest, lack of challenge, or to neurotic behavior is only a matter of conjecture.

The Wechsler Scales

The Wechsler scales, like the Stanford-Binet, provide an estimate of the individual's general level of development but, unlike the Stanford-Binet, they furnish a pattern of his mental functioning. Subtests evaluate Information, Comprehension, Digit Span, Similarities, Arithmetic, Vocabulary, Picture Completion, Block Design, Object Assembly, and Digit Symbol. Profiles based on these subtests can be drawn. Two types of interpretations may be made. The *signs* approach involves studying the profile for peaks and valleys known to be common in certain types of maladjustment. For example, several studies indicate that reading disability cases have significantly low scores on tests of Information, Arithmetic, and Coding. The *functional* approach involves interpretation in terms of the mental functions each test requires and an analysis of specific responses to test items. Often, observations of ability to comprehend directions, to concentrate, to criticize, and to correct one's responses are made during the administration of the Wechsler. The psychologist's observations are frequently of greater value to the reading clinician than the IQs obtained. In all instances the clinician is looking for clues or hypotheses which, if verified, can explain the cause of the disability in reading.

The Illinois Test of Psycholinguistic Abilities

The Illinois Test of Psycholinguistic Abilities is an individually administered diagnostic test designed to tap significant psycholinguistic abilities and disabilities in children between the ages of two and ten. The instrument consists of twelve tests which measure performance in ten separate and distinct areas. Three dimensions are investigated: (1) channels of communication (auditory-vocal and visual-motor); (2) psycholinguistic processes (the receptive process, the organizing process, and the expressive process); and (3) levels of organization (the automatic level and representational level). The subtests yield a composite psycholinguistic age which correlates highly with the Stanford-Binet mental age and an estimated Stanford-Binet mental age and IQ. Scale scores on each of the twelve subtests are profiled to determine discrepancies in growth so that an appropriate program of remediation may be prescribed.

MEASURES OF VISUAL FUNCTIONS

The clinician and classroom teacher should be acquainted with the more basic visual functions thought to be related to reading ability. Some of these are visual acuity, fusion at near and far points, lateral and vertical balance, stereopsis level, accommodation, convergence, and binocular vision. Such abnormalities as astigmatism, hyperopia, myopia, aniseikonia, and suppression should be understood. These terms are defined in the glossary, and the reader should be thoroughly acquainted with their use. Some visual difficulties may be indicated if the child:

• Rubs his eyes.
• Has watering or inflamed eyes.
• Holds his paper or book in a peculiar manner.
• Keeps a hand over one eye while reading.
• Reports letters blurred or running together.
• Frequently loses his place in reading.

Measures of visual functions should be made by the ophthalmologist, optometrist, or optician. Certain survey tests, however, can be made by the psychologist to identify those individuals who, if their history warrants, should be referred to the eye specialist for study. The question asked of the optician should be, "Is there a visual disability underlying the individual's inability to read effectively?" It is not the function of the psychologist or reading clinician to diagnose visual defects. Furthermore, visual training should be provided only under the guidance and supervision of the eye specialist.

Hyperopia, lack of binocular vision, eye muscle imbalance, and slow fusion have been found to be associated with reading disabilities. In the study of the child these factors can be investigated by such instruments as the Telebinocular, the Sight-Screener, and the Ortho-Rater.[1] Informal inventories involving visual discrimination and visual memory will be discussed in Chapter 8.

The Frostig Developmental Test of Visual Perception is designed to measure five perceptual skills. It requires the child to attempt carefully graded tasks in the following areas of visual perception: (1) eye-motor coordination, (2) figure-ground, (3) constancy of shape, (4) position in space, and (5) spatial relationships. In eye-hand coordination the child's task is to draw straight and curved lines between increasingly narrow boundaries or to draw a straight line to a target. In figure-ground perception the child is asked to discriminate between intersecting shapes and to find hidden figures. In the form-constancy subtest the task is to discriminate circles and squares in different shadings, sizes, and positions among other shapes on the page. In the fourth subtest the child is required to differentiate between figures in an identical position and those in a reversed or rotated position. In the subtest of spatial relationships, the task is to copy patterns by linking dots. The test can be used either as a screening device for nursery school, kindergarten, and first-grade children or as a clinical instrument for older children who suffer from learning difficulties.

The test materials consist of a thirty-five-page booklet, eleven demonstration cards, and three transparent scoring tissues. The time required for group administration is less than one hour. Individual administration takes about thirty to forty-five minutes. Scoring is

[1] The Telebinocular is manufactured by the Keystone View Company, the Sight-Screener by the American Optical Company, and the Ortho-Rater by Bausch and Lomb.

objective and requires approximately ten minutes. A perceptual age and scale scores for each subtest are computed, and a perceptual quotient is obtained from the sum of the subtest scale scores after correction for age variation. The five perceptual-age levels and the five scale scores indicate the child's development in each visual perceptual ability. The perceptual quotient is used as a prognostic indicator of the child's ability to profit from the customary learning situation provided in public schools.

MEASURES OF AUDITION

Hearing, like vision, is not a unitary factor. An individual may be superior in one aspect of hearing and deficient in another. *Auditory acuity* is one aspect of hearing in which reading clinicians are interested. Another term for auditory acuity is the *absolute threshold of hearing*, which refers to the faintest sound that the individual can hear. The pure tone audiometer is generally used for individual testing. Each ear is tested separately. Beginning with a sound too faint for the examinee to hear, the examiner gradually increases the tone until the examinee indicates that he hears it. Then the sound is decreased until he can no longer hear it. In this way the individual's threshold is determined for each frequency level, ranging, for example, on the Maico Audiometer, from 128 to 11,584. The subject's hearing loss in decibels can be read directly from the audiometer and from these readings the examiner prepares an audiogram, a graph showing the examinee's hearing loss at different frequencies. The zero point represents the intensity of sound which the "normal" ear can just barely hear. The examinee's hearing loss represents the number of decibels by which sound intensity must be increased above zero in order to be audible to him.

Hearing impairment is a matter of *degree* and *pattern* of loss. To determine whether hearing impairment is affecting a child's reading performance, the clinician needs to know the amount, if any, of hearing loss in the low, middle, and high frequencies. In general, a "flat" loss over the speech frequencies of 500, 1,000, and 2,000 results in little or no difficulty in discrimination, provided that speech is made loud enough to be heard. A rapidly increasing loss through the speech frequencies, with greater losses for the high frequencies, interferes with auditory discrimination because many consonants are distinguishable only through their high-frequency characteristics. For example, if the loss at frequencies 1,000 and 2,000 is markedly greater than at frequency 500, the examinee may confuse such consonants as p, k, s, t, f, sh, ch, and the voiceless th.

The reading clinician should keep in mind that some children with no measurable hearing loss have difficulty in auditory discrimination and in auditory blending. Some are unable to distinguish slight differences in sounds as in *bed* and *bid* or *grew* and *crew*. Auditory difficulties may be indicated if the child:

- Does not respond when called on.
- Favors the better ear by turning the head to one side.
- Listens with a tense facial expression.
- Confuses words which sound nearly alike.
- Ignores directions and appears inattentive.
- Has a history of earaches, running ears, or excessive wax.

There are other methods of testing hearing besides the use of the pure tone audiometer such as the crude watch-tick and whispered-voice tests, group audiometers, and speech audiometers. The use of audiometers requires considerable training and experience on the part of the examiner. Consequently, the reading clinician should cooperate with the experienced audiologist in studying the child who is suspected of having a hearing loss. Several authorities in the field of reading have expressed the opinion that auditory discrimination and auditory memory are in many instances more significant in the study of the disabled reader than measures of auditory acuity. Deficiencies in auditory discrimination may be detected by presenting to the child twenty alternate word-pairs from the Wepman Auditory Discrimination Test and by asking him to judge whether they sound the same or different. Informal measures of auditory discrimination and auditory memory will be discussed in Chapter 8.

SURVEY TESTS IN READING

Standardized tests of reading ability are generally of the survey type. They provide a general estimate of the reading level and the range of reading achievement within a class. Group scores are more reliable and valid than a single score of one individual. Survey tests as now constructed measure only a small part of reading ability. Most tests furnish measures of vocabulary and a vague and indefinite something called comprehension. Some survey tests indicate that they measure "rate of comprehension." Such measures are of little value for predictive purposes because the rate of reading will vary with the nature of material and purpose for which the selection was read. Individual scores on a survey test in reading merely indicate the presence or absence of certain reading skills. The test does not suggest causal factors underlying the child's success or failure. Scores can show, however, his comparative relationship to the performance of his fellows as determined by the test, and his relationship to existing standards.

No one knows what so-called tests of reading actually measure. Strang[2] has suggested that reading ability along with intelligence, educational opportunity, industry, and family background are being evaluated. Survey tests with all their shortcomings can be of value because by their use the teacher can estimate fairly well the achievement level of the individual and better still the performance level of the group as determined by that instrument of measurement. This information can help the teacher to adjust reading materials to both the reading and interest levels of her students. The reading clinician will make use of survey tests chiefly to measure achievement in reading both before and after treatment. The survey test has little value in diagnosis. Several survey tests in reading are listed in the Index of Tests in the appendix of *Diagnosis and Treatment of the Disabled Reader.*

MEASURES DESIGNED FOR ANALYSIS OF READING ERRORS

A detailed and intensive diagnosis of specific reading errors is essential for children with severe reading disabilities. Fortunately, there are standardized tests which can be used to determine the child's specific reading handicaps. These instruments combined with careful observation of the child provide valuable information in achieving a more comprehensive and valid understanding of the child's reading performance. The most commonly used techniques are (1) the Gates-McKillop Reading Diagnostic Tests, (2) the Monroe Diagnostic

[2] Ruth Strang, *Diagnostic Teaching of Reading* (New York: McGraw-Hill Book Company, 1964), pp. 132–133.

Examination, (3) the Spache Diagnostic Reading Scales, and (4) the Durrell Analysis of Reading Difficulty, and (5) the Stanford Diagnostic Reading Tests.

The Gates-McKillop Reading Diagnostic Tests

The Gates-McKillop program for analysis of reading difficulties is one of the most complete programs of diagnosis available. It requires thorough clinical training and considerable time for administration. Two equivalent forms are available. Each form consists of eight parts: (1) oral reading, (2) flash presentation of words, (3) untimed presentation of words, (4) flash presentation of phrases, (5) knowledge of word parts, (6) recognition of the visual form of sounds, (7) auditory blending, and (8) supplementary tests of spelling, oral vocabulary, syllabication, and auditory discrimination.

The oral reading test, composed of seven paragraphs of increasing difficulty, provides the examiner with an opportunity to analyze specific types of errors such as omissions of words, additions of words, repetitions, mispronunciations, full reversals, reversals of parts, and wrong beginnings, middles, and endings of words. The child's errors are recorded for each paragraph. Raw scores are converted into grade scores which range from 1.6 to 7.5. During the administration of this test the child's method of word attack, ability to phrase, habits of enunciation, and tendency toward tenseness in a reading situation can be observed.

The flash presentation of words consists of forty words which progress from short, easy words to larger, more difficult ones. The number of correct responses is converted to a grade score for comparison with mental grade and average reading grade. The purpose of this test is to determine how well a child can recognize words differing in difficulty when these words are exposed for one-half second. The untimed presentation of words is used to determine the child's ability to attack isolated words. Comparison of his performance on this test with his ability to read silently and orally provides information on how well he employs context clues in reading.

Four tests of knowledge of word parts are provided. They proceed from words to individual letters. The tests also involve recognizing and blending common word parts, giving letter sounds, and naming capital and lower-case letters.

Four tests are provided which require the child to recognize sounds and to associate them with their visual forms. Careful observation of the child's performance on these tests can help the examiner to answer such questions as: Which parts of words cause the student the most difficulty? Does he fail to distinguish between similar-appearing letters and letter groups? How much do general word configuration and structure help the pupil? Is he able to distinguish between two and three syllable words? When are word or letter reversals made?

The test of auditory blending requires the student to combine or blend sounds given orally. The supplementary tests provide the examiner with an opportunity to observe the pupil's methods of analyzing words in spelling. Does he attack words letter by letter or does he use groupings of letters? What letter combinations does he know? Does he make phonetic substitutions? The supplementary tests also measure his oral vocabulary, his skills in auditory discrimination, and his ability to combine syllables into words.

The skillful examiner can derive from the Gates-McKillop Reading Diagnostic Tests inferences concerning the pupil's specific reading handicaps. Each inference, however, should be considered a hypothesis to be checked in terms of the child's history, his responses on an informal reading inventory, and his reading performance in the classroom.

Monroe Diagnostic Reading Examination

The Marion Monroe technique of analyzing reading errors is one of the most carefully developed methods for dealing with the more difficult reading problems. The procedure provides an opportunity to determine a child's reading index and to analyze his reading errors.

Test materials include (1) the Gray's Oral Reading Paragraphs, (2) the Iota Word Test, (3) the Word-Discrimination Test, (4) a silent reading test selected by the clinician, (5) an arithmetic computation test, and (6) the Stanford-Binet scale. Gray's Oral Reading Paragraphs consists of twelve paragraphs of increasing difficulty. Grade scores on this test range from early first grade to grade eight. The Iota Word Test measures ability to read words in isolation. This test is composed of fifty-three words printed on three cards. Grade scores range from 1 to 5.5. The Word-Discrimination Test is made up of forty-seven words. Each is presented in a group of six confusion words printed on a series of six cards. The key word is spoken by the examiner and the child then points to the word he thinks he has heard. Grade scores range from 1 to 5.5.

The reading index is obtained by dividing the child's reading grade by his expectancy grade. In determining the reading grade, the average of the grade scores on the Gray's Oral Reading Paragraphs, a silent reading test, the Iota Word Test, and the Word-Discrimination Test is obtained. The expectancy grade is determined by finding the grade equivalent scores for the child's chronological age, mental age, and grade score on an arithmetic computation test. The average of these scores is the child's expectancy grade. For example, the grade equivalent scores for Tom's chronological age and mental age are 5.0 and 5.6, respectively. His arithmetic grade is 5.3. The average of these scores is 5.3. His grade equivalent scores on the Gray's Oral Reading Paragraphs, a silent reading test, the Iota Word Test, and the Word-Discrimination Test are 2.2, 2.4, 3.0, and 3.2, respectively. The average reading grade on the four measures is 2.7. The reading index, found by dividing the reading grade of 2.7 by the expectancy grade of 5.3 is 0.51. A reading index of 0.80 or below is significant and indicative of reading maladjustment.

Every error made on the Gray's Oral Reading Paragraphs, the Iota Word Test, and the Word-Discrimination Test is analyzed and classified into the following error types.

Faulty Vowels. This error is identified by each mispronunciation in which one or more vowel sounds of the test words are altered.

Faulty Consonants. A consonant error constitutes a mispronunciation in which one or more consonant sounds of the test word are changed.

Reversals. A reversal is a turning about of the orientation of letters, the sequence of letters, or the sequence of words.

Addition of Sounds. A sound addition is a mispronunciation in which one or more sounds are inserted.

Omission of Sounds. A sound omission is a mispronunciation in which one or more sounds of the test word are omitted.

Substitution of Words. A substitution of words is a replacement of a word by another word having no consonant or vowel sounds

similar to the test word and not related to the test word by
reversed letters or mistaken vowel or consonant sounds.

Repetition of Words. A repetition of words is the repeating of the
test words or their mispronunciations.

Addition of Words. An addition of words is the insertion of a word
or words into the text.

Omission of Words. An omission of words is the leaving out of a
word or words from the text.

Refusals and Words Aided. A refused or aided word is identified by
the child's statement, "I don't know that word," or by his delayed
response.

Tables are provided for converting number of errors for each type
into Z-scores. If the Z-score for any error type reaches or exceeds +1,
this suggests the need of corrective instruction. The Monroe method
is especially useful for diagnosing the specific reading needs of the
severely retarded reader.

The Spache Diagnostic Reading Scales

The Spache Diagnostic Reading Scales can be used to measure the
proficiency of readers in the elementary school and of disabled readers
at all levels. The tests consist of three word recognition lists, twenty-
two reading passages of graduated difficulty, and six supplementary
phonics tests.

The first word list ranges in difficulty from grades 1.3 to 2.3, the
second from grades 2.3 to 5.5, and the third from grades 3.8 to 6.5.
The purposes of the word recognition lists are (1) to estimate instructional level of reading, (2) to reveal the pupil's methods of word
attack and analysis, and (3) to evaluate the student's sight vocabulary.

The reading passages range from grades 1.6 to 8.5, and each
selection is accompanied by questions. The passages are similar to
reading material that is found in reading assignments and include
narrative, expository, and descriptive selections taken from such
sources as the natural and physical sciences, social studies, and
children's literature. The questions relating to each reading passage
sample the student's ability to interpret the feelings and actions of
characters, draw conclusions and inferences, recognize stated facts,

and recall specific terms. The reading of the passages permits the examiner to determine the child's instructional level, independent level, and his potential reading level.

The six supplementary phonics tests involve consonant sounds, vowel sounds, consonant blends, common syllables, blending, and letter sounds. Scores on these tests are interpreted by reference to a table of standards for phonics skills.

The Spache Diagnostic Reading Scales can be a useful tool in determining a child's oral and silent reading skills and his ability to understand material read to him. The reading clinician or classroom teacher using this material must keep in mind, however, that the terms *independent level* and *instructional level* do not have the same meanings as those set forth by other writers.

Durrell Analysis of Reading Difficulty

The primary purpose of the Durrell Analysis of Reading Difficulty is to discover weaknesses and faulty habits in reading. It consists of a series of tests and situations in which the examiner may observe in detail various aspects of reading, and it covers a range in reading ability from the nonreader to sixth-grade ability.

Materials for this test consist of a manual of directions, a booklet of reading paragraphs, a tachistoscope, various series of words on cards, and an individual record blank. The first test measures oral reading. Eight paragraphs are provided. A detailed record is made of all errors, and behavior symptomatic of reading difficulties is noted on the checklist provided in the record blank. A series of questions is asked at the end of each paragraph. Grade norms based on the time required for reading are provided.

The second test measures silent reading. A different set of graded paragraphs is used. Following the reading of each paragraph, the child is asked to tell everything he can remember in the story. Grade norms based on time and memory scores are provided. Another checklist accompanies this test.

A listening comprehension test is included. Graded paragraphs are read aloud by the examiner and a set of questions is asked. A word recognition and word analysis test comprises the next test. Lists of words printed on strips of cardboard are provided for presentation in the tachistoscope. Each word on the appropriate list is exposed for one-half second. The child's response is recorded. When he fails to respond to a word in the flash test, the word is exposed for a longer time so that he can try to work out the pronunciation of the word by analyzing it. Grade norms and a checklist are provided.

The next series of tests involves naming letters, identifying letters named, matching letters, and writing letters. The test Visual Memory of Words—Primary is for use with children whose reading grade is three or below. The Intermediate form of this test is for children with reading grades four to six. The next section, Hearing Sounds in Words, tests ability to identify beginning sounds, ending sounds, and both beginning and ending sounds in words. If a child fails this test, he should be given the test on Learning to Hear Sounds in Words in order to determine the severity of his difficulty in perceiving sounds in words. The Sounds of Letters test is given to children with less than second-grade reading ability to discover which letter sounds and blends are not known.

The Learning Rate test is given to severely retarded readers to discover the child's ability to remember words taught. Additional tests of Phonic Spelling of Words, a Spelling Test, and a Handwriting Test are provided.

The Stanford Diagnostic Reading Tests

The Stanford Diagnostic Reading Tests are group measures designed to identify needed areas of instruction in reading. The tests have been prepared in two levels with two forms at each level. Level I is intended for use from the latter part of grade two to the middle of grade four. Level II is intended for use from the latter part of grade four to the middle of grade eight. Level I consists of seven tests: (1) reading comprehension, (2) vocabulary, (3) auditory discrimination, (4) syllabication, (5) beginning and ending sounds, (6) blending, and (7) sound discrimination. Level II consists of six tests: (1) reading comprehension, (2) vocabulary, (3) syllabication, (4) sound discrimination, (5) blending, and (6) rate of reading.

The test of reading comprehension (Levels I and II) is used to establish the general reading level of the pupil in terms of his ability to understand the printed word as a form of communication. The paragraphs contain a wide variety of subject matter content, including social studies, health, and science. The questions require understanding of stated content, perception of important details, or ability to draw inferences. At Level II an attempt is made to assess both literal and inferential comprehension.

The test of vocabulary (Levels I and II) does not require reading ability. The items, taken from a variety of subject matter areas, are read to the child for the purpose of evaluating the child's auditory vocabulary.

In the test of auditory discrimination (Level I) the child is required to determine whether the two words read by the examiner contain the same sound in the beginning, middle, or ending of both words.

The test of syllabication (Levels I and II) requires the child to find the first syllable in words. Only the most frequently used syllabication rules are tested.

The test of beginning and ending sounds found in Level I evaluates the child's knowledge of the initial and ending sounds of words which begin or end with some of the more common sounds. The test involves visual recognition of certain letter combinations.

The test of blending (Levels I and II) requires the child to divide words and to know how each element sounds.

The test of sound discrimination (Levels I and II) assesses the individual's ability to determine sounds within words and his knowledge of the common and variant spellings of phonemes.

The test of rate of reading (Level II) determines the speed with which the pupil can read a story with understanding. The test is considered an index of the efficiency with which the individual utilizes his other reading skills.

The Stanford Diagnostic Reading Test is an effective device for identifying the individual's strengths and weaknesses in reading.

PERSONALITY MEASURES

In general, personality factors are related to reading and would involve investigation of the following loci of information.

- Physical records.
- Personal history.
- Social records.
- School history.

- Cultural background.
- Objective test data.
- Observational data.

A search for facts in one of these areas is not sufficient. Attention must be directed to the whole person and consequently a global approach must be utilized. If the examiner is to make use, for example, of objective test data, he must interpret his findings in terms of all known facts from all available sources. His test data to be of real value must fit into the general pattern of facts secured from other areas. If there are misfits or other inconsistencies, all sources should be re-examined.

In a study of the disabled reader, many personality factors are important. Some areas to be probed are the following:

Is the child emotionally mature?
Is he emotionally stable?
Is he apt to sustain effort?
Of what is he afraid?
How does he secure recognition?
Is he generally happy?
Is he well adjusted at home?
Is he well adjusted socially?
Does the child feel responsible for his success in reading?
What has he been successful in doing?
What are his interests?
What has been the effect of the home upon the child?
What is his ideal self?
What is his self-concept?
In what areas does he experience emotional conflicts?
What are his goals?
Are there physical clues as to the cause of his reading disability?
How has the personality of the child been affected by his environment?
Does he show creativity?
Is concentration a problem?

These questions are merely typical of the areas to be explored in the study of personality factors which can affect reading performance. Various personality tests and inventories, if wisely selected, can be helpful. Several means of evaluating factors related to personality are shown in Appendixes A and B.

In many instances it is necessary to investigate the attitudes of parents concerning family life and children. Studies[3] show that inferior readers come from homes where parents have failed to place a high value on the importance of reading, have failed to develop adequate language skills, and have failed to create an intellectual climate and to foster background conducive to effective reading and study. The following Inventory of Attitudes Concerning Family Life and Children consists of eighteen questions which have been carefully designed to identify three important attitudes related to reading. Three of the eighteen items are "rapport" items and are numbered 1, 8, and 15. The three scales are

I. *Triviality of Reading.* Each item in this scale reflects an attitude which suggests that parents consider reading to be relatively unimportant and of limited value. (Items 2, 5, 9, 12, and 16.)

II. *Hindering Development of Language Skills.* Each item making up this scale reflects an attitude which discourages children from asking questions, expressing ideas, reflecting their points of view, or listening to what others have to say. (Items 3, 6, 10, 13, and 17.)

III. *Restriction of Childhood Experiences.* Each item making up this scale reflects an attitude which favors holding children back from participating in activities which provide information, ideas, and experiential background. (Items 4, 7, 11, 14, and 18.)

A value of four points is given for a response which indicates strong agreement, three points for mild agreement, two points for mild disagreement, and one point for strong disagreement. A scale score is obtained by finding the sum of the item weights. A high score reflects an attitude in the direction of the title of the scale. For example, a high score on Scale I, Triviality of Reading, suggests that the person completing the inventory places little value on reading. The internal consistency of Scales I, II, and III are .89, .90, and .89, respectively.

[3] Dorothy J. McGinnis, *A Comparative Study of the Attitudes of Parents of Superior and Inferior Readers Toward Certain Child Rearing Practices, the Value of Reading, and the Development of Language Skills and Experiential Background Related to Reading.* Unpublished doctoral dissertation, Michigan State University, 1963.

Inventory of Attitudes Concerning Family Life and Children
Read each of the statements below and then rate them as follows:

A	a	d	D
strongly agree	mildly agree	mildly disagree	strongly disagree

Indicate your opinion by drawing a circle around the A if you strongly agree, around the a if you mildly agree, around the d if you mildly disagree, and around the D if you strongly disagree.

There are no right or wrong answers, so answer according to your own opinion. It is very important to the study that all questions be answered. Many of the statements will seem alike but all are necessary to show slight differences of opinion.

	Agree		Disagree	
1. As much as is reasonable, a parent should try to treat a child as an equal.	A	a	d	D
2. Being able to read well isn't as important as a lot of people think it is.	A	a	d	D
3. Most children ask too many questions.	A	a	d	D
4. Young children should not be encouraged to play with older boys and girls because they may have experiences that are not good for them.	A	a	d	D
5. Effective reading is not as important as effective speaking.	A	a	d	D
6. Most children ask questions merely for the purpose of having something to say.	A	a	d	D
7. Children under the age of five gain little worthwhile knowledge from trips.	A	a	d	D
8. Parents must earn the respect of their children by the way they act.	A	a	d	D
9. Time set aside to read is not essential to success in homemaking.	A	a	d	D
10. There is a lot of sense to the old adage, "Children should be seen and not heard."	A	a	d	D

	Agree		Disagree	
11. Some children are too curious for their own good.	A	a	d	D
12. Learning how to make friends is more important than learning how to read.	A	a	d	D
13. Children will monopolize the conversation if they are permitted to do so.	A	a	d	D
14. Children today have too much freedom to go places and do things.	A	a	d	D
15. Parents should adjust to children some rather than always expecting the children to adjust to the parents.	A	a	d	D
16. A man can read poorly and yet be successful in business.	A	a	d	D
17. Since many children have to be encouraged to eat at mealtime, the wise mother will discourage her children from talking while eating.	A	a	d	D
18. Most children play too much.	A	a	d	D

----

1. Age (check the correct category):
    Below 20 _____
    20–29   _____
    30–39   _____
    40–49   _____
    above 50 _____

2. Education (check highest level attended):
        Grade School Through High School
    Yourself   1 2 3 4 5 6 7 8 9 10 11 12

            College
            1 2 3 4

        Graduate School
        1 2 3 4

3. Occupation _____

4. How many children do you have? _____

5. Do you have a child who is an excellent reader?   Yes   No

6. Do you have a child who is a poor reader?   Yes   No

PROJECTIVE TECHNIQUES

Projective tests suggest to the examiner more about the whole child than many measures of personality. What an individual, especially an adult, says about himself is generally full of distortion and half-truths and characterized by many omitted details. It is difficult, indeed, to tell the whole truth and nothing but the truth. Projective methods make the task less difficult because we can assign our own unacceptable wishes and desires to another person or thing. We project ourselves and are not aware of what we are telling.

Every act and spoken word is a projection of the inner self, and to the perceptive observer these can have significant meanings. For example, three men on different occasions spent approximately thirty minutes in the office of a psychologist on the campus of a midwestern university. Each man found at hand a large mass of molding clay. During Mr. A's stay in the office, he formed a nearly perfect cube, 2 in. by 2 in. in size. While Mr. B was engaged later in an animated conversation, he molded an exotic woman with well-designed masses of feminine pulchritude. During Mr. C's visit, he formed with care the figure of a Beagle hound. Each of these men unconsciously expressed effectively certain aspects of his inner self. Obviously, they were not aware of the inferences that could be drawn from their performance. Little boys and girls when they talk about their friends and members of their family reveal much concerning themselves.

Some projective tests employed by psychologists and psychiatrists may be listed as follows:

- The Rorschach.
- The Children's Apperception Test.
- Bender Visual Motor Gestalt Test.
- The Blacky Pictures.
- Draw-a-Person.

The following questions related to reading may be answered in part by data from projective techniques.

How strong is the individual's dominant wish, or urge, to achieve?
Are emotional conflicts breaking up this drive to success?
Is there a gap between the individual's capacity and his functioning ability?

What personality vectors threaten his ability to function more adequately?

Is the individual depressed and worried about his relations with his friends and associates?

The use of projective tests should be the responsibility of psychologists and psychiatrists. Instruments such as the Rorschach and Thematic Apperception Test necessitate long and detailed training under careful supervision. Reading clinicians should cooperate with specialists in the study of the disabled reader.

SUMMARY

This chapter points out the value of some objective measures that can be applied in the study of the disabled reader. These instruments are tools, and their selection and use are dependent on the background, training, experience, and mental content of the examiner. Test scores should be interpreted in terms of all other known facts concerning the examinee. Frequently, how the individual reacts is more important than his scores.

GUIDED ACTIVITY 7

Aim

To review the use of objective measures.

Materials

1. Chapter 7 of *Diagnosis and Treatment of the Disabled Reader*.
2. Index of Tests, Appendix A of this book.
3. Chapter 3 of *Diagnosis and Treatment of the Disabled Reader*.
4. One of the described tests designed for analysis of reading errors.

Procedure

1. Read carefully the study of John's problem which is reported in Chapter 3. Show why you would accept or reject the use of a group intelligence test in this study.
2. State briefly your reaction to the use made of the Wechsler Intelligence Scale for Children.

3. Why was the Healy Pictorial used in John's case?

4. Show why you were satisfied or dissatisfied with the inferences made concerning certain measures of personality.

5. Show why you were satisfied or dissatisfied with the audiometric examination.

6. Show why, in your opinion, the visual examination was or was not relevant in John's case.

7. Explain the relevance of an arithmetic test in dealing with John's problem.

8. List facts in John's history which were substantiated by the audiometric examination.

9. Select from the Index of Tests found in Appendix A of this book two survey tests in reading which might be administered to any fifth-grade class.

10. Show, in general, the advantages and disadvantages of survey tests of reading.

11. Discuss the contributions of objective measures to diagnosis at the third and fourth levels.

12. List the various tests with which you believe you should become thoroughly acquainted.

13. Select a test which can be used to identify reading errors and administer it to an individual with a reading disability. Summarize your findings.

QUESTIONS AND REFERENCES

Questions	References
1. What objective measures can be used in predicting reading failure?	**1.** Katrina de Hirsch, Jeannette Jefferson Jansky, and William S. Langford, *Predicting Reading Failure* (New York: Harper & Row, 1966), Chap. 2.
2. What tests are of value in reading diagnosis?	**2.** Wayne Otto and Richard A. McMenemy, *Corrective and Remedial Teaching: Principles and Practices* (Boston: Houghton Mifflin Company, 1966), Chap. 5.
3. How valuable are group and individual tests?	**3.** Ruth Strang, *Diagnostic Teaching of Reading* (New York:

Questions	References
	McGraw-Hill Book Company, 1964), Chaps. 7 and 10.
4. Where can one find a representative list of reading and study skill tests?	**4.** Guy L. Bond and Miles A. Tinker, *Reading Difficulties, Their Diagnosis and Correction,* 2nd ed. (New York: Appleton-Century-Crofts, 1967), pp. 532–537.
5. What are some minimal requirements in statistics for teachers?	**5.** Henry E. Garrett, *Testing for Teachers* (New York: American Book Company, 1959), Chap. 2 and Appendix A.
6. What are some basic concepts of psychological testing?	**6.** Lee J. Cronbach, *Essentials of Psychological Testing,* 2nd ed. (New York: Harper & Row, 1960), pp. 3–153.
7. What are some principal characteristics of psychological tests?	**7.** Anne Anastasi, *Psychological Testing,* 3rd ed. (New York: The Macmillan Company, 1968), Chap. 2.
8. How can psychological tests be used?	**8.** *Ibid.,* Chap. 3.
9. Where can reading specialists find a comprehensive bibliography of all reading tests known to be in print as of May 1, 1968?	**9.** Oscar K. Buros, *Reading Tests and Reviews* (Highland Park, N.J.: The Gryphon Press, 1968).

Chapter 8

Making Use of
Informal Inventories

The classroom teacher and reading clinician need on-the-spot and practical means of studying the individual with a reading disability. Informal inventories can provide the teacher with an opportunity to observe the child so as to determine not only his reading deficiencies but why they may have developed. This chapter suggests that many areas other than reading can be investigated by observation of the child as he performs various kinds of informal inventories. The use of observations rather than testing procedures will be emphasized. Objectivity, validity, and reliability of the inventories themselves are not of primary concern.

WHAT ARE INFORMAL INVENTORIES?

An informal inventory is a tentative and unconventional means of identifying certain abilities and skills and of suggesting clues as to why they exist. They can be employed in determining interests, persistence, attitudes, and concentration. They can furnish information concerning the individual's breadth and depth of mental content and his ability to express his ideas orally. They can provide clues to various aspects of vision and hearing. In the field of reading, informal inventories can be used to appraise specific reading skills such as word recognition, location of data, identification and interpretation of main ideas with supporting detail, and the ability to answer *why* and *how* questions. They can be designed to investigate the student's ability to read for a purpose, to draw inferences, to locate and define key words, to follow directions, and to read in various content fields. They provide, furthermore, an opportunity for the examiner to observe the child's reaction to both silent and oral reading.

THE INFORMAL READING INVENTORY

The informal reading inventory is used to investigate a child's reading performance as he deals with materials of increasing difficulty. The initial purpose is to determine the level at which the child can function independently, the level at which he can profit from instruction, the point where he becomes frustrated with the material, and his level of understanding what is read to him. Another equally important purpose is the determination of the child's specific strengths and weaknesses.

Informal reading inventories may be constructed by the teacher. Materials representing a variety of levels should be selected. Two selections for each level from preprimer to the highest level to be measured should be chosen. One of these is to be used for oral reading at sight and the other for silent reading. The length of the material selected should be carefully considered so that the inventory can be administered without tiring the child. Some reading clinicians have utilized the Gray Oral Reading Paragraphs and have designed five questions for each paragraph. In general, four of these questions require recall of factual information such as *who, what, where,* and *when.* One of the five questions is inferential in nature and requires *why* and *how* responses. Each paragraph is printed on one side of a 5- by 8-in. card. On the reverse side are the questions. The following is an example of paragraph 5 from the Gray Oral Reading Paragraphs.

One of the most interesting birds which ever lived in my bird-room was a blue-jay named Jackie. He was full of business from morning till night, scarcely ever still. He had been stolen from a nest long before he could fly, and he had been reared in a house long before he had been given to me as a pet.

Front of Card

5

1. What was the bird's name?
2. Where did he live?
3. How did Jackie act?
4. What happened to him before he was able to fly?
5. Why do you think Jackie was a good pet?

Back of Card

Some teachers construct reading inventories from the pages of discarded basal readers or from children's magazines. Others employ commercially prepared informal reading inventories which can be obtained from publishing companies.

In administering the informal reading inventory, the first objective is to establish rapport and to explain to the child the procedure which will be followed. The examiner, during this time, has an excellent opportunity to observe the child's vocabulary, sentence structure, ability to concentrate, attitude toward himself, and his interests and attitudes toward reading. As soon as the examiner believes that he has the child's full cooperation, he should prepare the child for the first paragraph by establishing a purpose for reading. Then the child is asked to read the paragraph aloud. A record is kept of the child's reading errors. As soon as the paragraph has been read, the prepared questions and any supplementary questions which are needed are asked. When the child's performance on the first selection is ended, readiness for reading the second selection is established. The second selection is at the same level as the first, only this time the paragraph is read silently by the child. Questions on the silent reading should be asked. This same procedure is followed at each level until the frustration level has been established. When this is done, the examiner determines the capacity level by reading paragraphs to the child and by asking questions. Usually the examiner begins at the next level following the one at which frustration was reached and continues at successively higher levels until the child fails to maintain a level of 75 per cent accuracy in comprehension.

The *independent* reading level is the highest level at which the individual can read with full understanding and freedom from mechanical difficulties. The material should be read with 99 per cent accuracy in word recognition and a comprehension score of at least 90 per cent.

The *instructional* level is the highest reading level at which systematic instruction can be initiated. The material should be read with 95 per cent accuracy in word recognition and a comprehension score of 75 per cent.

The *frustration* level is the level at which the child is thwarted and baffled by the vocabulary, sentence structure, and complexity of ideas. Comprehension is usually 50 per cent or less and word recognition is 90 per cent or less. At this level tension and anxiety may be observed.

The *capacity* level is the highest level at which the student can comprehend what is read to him. This is the level for which he has adequate experiential background and mental content. It can serve as a point of reference.

In addition to establishing these four levels the administration of the informal reading inventory provides an excellent opportunity to observe the child. The following questions are suggestive of some of the factors to be detected with the aid of this valuable clinical device.

What is the child's attitude toward silent reading? Is it negative, hostile?

Does he make use of contextual clues?

Does he have control of detail? Can he respond to who, where, what, and when questions?

Were responses accurate?

Does his behavior suggest pleasure or displeasure?

Did the child read rapidly or slowly?

Did the child answer questions with complete sentences?

Did he answer why and how questions effectively?

Could he quickly find supporting data?

Was there depth in his responses or were they superficial?

Was he willing to venture a response?

Did he show initiative and creativity?

Did he go on a talking binge?

Were tics (involuntary movements) observed?

Was his voice high, low, or gasping?

Was attention poor, average, or excellent?

What extraneous movements were observed?

If oral reading was required, what errors were observed?

PURPOSES OF OTHER INFORMAL READING INVENTORIES

Informal reading inventories may be used for many different purposes. The following skills, arranged from the simple to the more complex, may aid the clinician and teacher in setting forth the objectives of other informal reading inventories they may devise.

- Looking at picture books and telling stories suggested by the pictures.
- Telling in response to questions what happened next in a familiar story.
- Recognizing words and their meanings.
- Identifying new words through (1) picture clues, (2) context clues, (3) phonetic analysis, (4) structural analysis.
- Interpreting short sentences and phrases.
- Reading silently to answer questions asked by the teacher.
- Asking questions and then reading to find the answers.
- Following printed or written directions in order to color, draw, make a toy, or play a game.
- Scanning printed materials to locate specific words, phrases, or facts.
- Skimming a selection to find the main thought or central idea.
- Looking for details and facts which support a main idea.
- Reading to others for their satisfaction.
- Appreciating humor and dramatic situations in books and magazines.
- Drawing a conclusion adequately based on facts.
- Remembering what is read.
- Making use of the dictionary.
- Determining central ideas or basic principles in various content areas.
- Selecting important points with their supporting details.
- Summarizing a paragraph, section, chapter, or entire text.
- Associating what is read with one's own experiences and background.
- Making a wise use of the card catalogue and *Readers' Guide to Periodical Literature.*
- Visualizing materials described in detail.
- Discovering problems through reading.

- Understanding essential conditions for a problem to be solved.
- Analyzing a situation into its several factors and understanding how they are related.
- Determining the validity of statements.
- Determining the relative importance of different facts and principles.
- Interpreting critically a point of view.
- Comparing inferences based on similar facts.
- Marshaling evidence to prove a point.
- Verifying conclusions.
- Making the most of the different parts of a book.
- Interpreting tables, charts, and graphs.
- Using rapidly and effectively train, bus, and plane schedules.
- Interpreting weather reports and maps.

INFORMAL APPRAISALS OF FACTORS AFFECTING
READING PERFORMANCE

Informal inventories can be utilized in areas other than reading. The child's motor coordination and ability to follow directions can be appraised as he reacts to such placing and turning instruments as the Minnesota Rate of Manipulation form board. His associative skills may be estimated as he responds to the visual-visual and the visual-auditory association cards prepared by Gates.[1] Dominance, certain visual and auditory skills, as well as reading interests and attitudes can be studied with teacher-made inventories. The individual's experiential background, personality characteristics, and motor skills may be observed as he draws a house, car, and person. Form boards, picture completion devices, and other materials of interest to the individual can be employed. Observation is the key to the effective use of these informal inventories, for the clinician is looking not for *scores* but for *clues* which may explain the child's difficulty.

Visual Discrimination

Visual discrimination means the ability to differentiate between two or more forms such as objects, written letters, or written words.

[1] Arthur I. Gates, *The Improvement of Reading*, 3rd ed. (New York: The Macmillan Company, 1947), pp. 651–652.

A child's vision may be excellent and still he may be unable to differentiate between similar objects, pictures, letters, or words presented in visual form. The ability to make fine visual discriminations is essential to effective reading. Many words look very much alike. Inability to differentiate between words obviously will affect the individual's ability to acquire an adequate reading vocabulary. Individuals who are deficient in visual discrimination can be detected by the use of observations and teacher-made informal inventories. Several types of informal measures of visual discrimination are described.

Letter Discrimination.   This inventory consists of lists of capital and lower-case letters, as the following illustrates. The child is asked to look at the first letter and to find another letter on the same line that is just like it. He is instructed to draw a circle around the letter he has selected.

Capital Letters

B	B	D	E	L
M	M	W	H	N
O	G	C	D	O
E	F	E	S	G
G	C	D	G	R
K	K	M	P	R
L	E	V	L	N
C	C	V	O	D
W	Z	U	V	W
N	N	E	M	A
A	B	A	P	L
D	D	P	C	O
Z	N	Y	Z	V
F	P	F	N	Z
P	O	F	D	P
U	V	W	U	N
Q	O	Q	C	Y
S	M	N	S	W
R	P	M	D	R
V	X	Z	U	V

Lower-Case Letters

d	q	p	b	d
f	f	k	t	l
b	e	b	p	d
m	n	m	w	u
r	t	f	r	d
n	a	u	m	n
a	a	b	c	o
o	p	c	e	o
p	p	q	d	b
b	p	q	b	d
c	d	c	e	o
s	z	s	m	u
h	n	l	u	h
t	f	t	l	n
i	g	i	i	y
k	l	z	k	w
q	p	d	b	q
w	v	w	m	n
g	y	g	q	d

Word Discrimination. Ability to discriminate between words can be determined by having the child select the word unlike the other words in a line.

mother	mother	brother	mother	mother
house	blouse	house	house	house
doll	doll	doll	doll	ball
saw	saw	saw	was	saw
jump	jump	bump	jump	jump

Number Discrimination. The child can be asked to underline the number exactly like the sample number on the left.

9	6	9	1	3
2	2	7	3	1
34	43	34	24	31
72	12	21	27	72

Visual Memory

Visual memory can be investigated by presenting to the child a picture rich in detail. Ask the child to look at the picture carefully. Then remove the picture and ask the child to recall as much of the picture as he can.

Visual memory can also be appraised by displaying for ten seconds a geometric design. Remove the card on which the design is drawn and ask the child to reproduce it.

Auditory Discrimination

Auditory discrimination means the ability to differentiate between sounds. Thompson[2] reports that there is a high correlation between auditory discrimination and success in reading. It is possible to have excellent hearing and yet be unable to distinguish between similar sounds.

The teacher can devise her own informal inventories for investigating auditory discrimination by selecting twenty pairs of words. In some of the pairs the two words will be the same. In others they will be different. While the child is sitting with his back to the examiner, two words of a pair will be pronounced by the examiner. The child is expected to indicate whether the two words spoken are the same or different.

Another example of an informal inventory that can be developed by the teacher or clinician to measure ability to perceive similarities and differences in sounds involves pronouncing two words, such as *can* and *king*, and having the child indicate whether or not they begin with the same sound. Another involves pronouncing two words and asking whether or not they end in the same sound. Variations of these two approaches can be developed by the teacher.

One type of inventory that has been found useful by many clinicians involves having the child encircle the beginning letters of words pronounced by the examiner. For example, the child is given a mimeograph sheet similar to the following illustration but containing twenty lines.

[2] Bertha Boya Thompson, "A Longitudinal Study of Auditory Discrimination," *Journal of Educational Research,* **56** (March, 1963), 376–378.

1.   e   s   r   t

2.   r   c   e   o

The child is instructed to listen carefully to a word which will be pronounced by the examiner. He is to listen to see if he can find the letter with which the word begins. A marker is placed below line 1. The examiner pronounces the word *receive*. The child draws a circle around the first letter in *receive*. Then the marker is moved to line 2 and the examiner says *calendar*. The child draws a circle around the first letter in *calendar*. This procedure is followed for the rest of the test. A similar inventory for listening to the final sounds in words can be developed by the teacher or clinician.

Auditory Memory

Auditory memory can be investigated by having the child repeat digits, nonsense syllables, words, and sentences. Some examples are provided.

Repetition of Digits.   The examiner can say to the child, "I am going to say some numbers. When I am through, say them after me. Be sure to listen carefully." The numbers should be said at the rate of one digit per second. Start with a three-digit series and increase each succeeding series by one number, for example, 5-9-4, 3-1-5-6, 9-6-3-7-8.

Repetition of Nonsense Syllables.   The examiner asks the child to repeat what she says. She pronounces a two-syllable nonsense word such as "la-glu;" next a three-syllable nonsense word, and then a four-syllable nonsense word.

Repetition of Words.   The child is again asked to repeat what the examiner says. She then pronounces a series of three words such as "run, boy, play." Next she says four words such as "toy, girl, ball, fun." Each succeeding series of words is increased by one word.

Repetition of Sentences.   The child is asked to repeat several sentences such as, "The boy likes to play baseball," and "John has a dog, and Mary has a kitten." Sentences in the series should increase in complexity of ideas.

Dominance

The dominant hand can be determined by observing which hand is used to throw a ball, to pick up objects from the floor, and to erase the chalkboard. Another method of determining handedness is to ask the child to make crosses with the right hand for three thirty-second periods, then to make crosses with the left hand for three thirty-second periods. The examiner counts the number of crosses made with each hand for each of the three periods. The median score for each hand is selected. Usually, a marked difference in the number of crosses made with each hand will be observed, with more crosses being made by the dominant hand.

The dominant eye can be determined by asking the child to look through a hole, ¼ in. in diameter, in the center of a sheet of cardboard, 8½ by 11 in. He is asked to hold the sheet in both hands at a distance of about 12 in. from his face, to keep both eyes open, and to look at a pencil held by the examiner about 8 in. from the sheet. As he looks at the pencil, he is to pull the paper closer to his face. The examiner observes which eye is being used to look through the peephole.

Another informal measure is to stand facing the child at a distance of 15 to 20 feet. The child is told to keep both eyes open as he extends his dominant arm and points his forefinger at a pencil held by the examiner. The sighting eye, the one in line with the forefinger, is the dominant eye.

Motor Skills

Gross motor coordination can be investigated by observing the child's ability to balance himself, to hop, and to throw a ball. Fine motor skill can be appraised by having the child fill in a pegboard, write his name, copy geometric designs, draw pictures, and by the informal use of instruments such as the Minnesota Rate of Manipulation Test and the Witmer Cylinder. While the child is performing these tasks, the examiner should observe carefully. The following questions may serve as a useful guide for this purpose.

Did the child use both hands?
Did he work quickly?
Were movements awkward?
Did he appear hyperactive?
Was he easily distracted?
Did he use force in trying to accomplish his purpose?
What were his remarks?
How did facial expressions change?
How did posture change?
Did the child sustain effort?
Did his hands tremble?
Which is the dominant hand?
Did he reverse forms or figures?
Did he turn paper or board to right or left?
Did he work from a near or far point?
Were child's hands dry or moist?

Background of Experiences

Through informal conversations with the child and observations of him in the classroom and on the playground, the teacher can form some conclusions concerning the child's mental content. Some clinicians have found that questions in the area of current events, travel, farm life, city life, religion, geography, and history provide clues to the child's background of experiences and knowledge. The following questions are samples of those which the teacher or clinician can ask to investigate the child's background of experiences.

Have you been to a farm?
Have you been to a circus?
Have you visited a zoo?
Have you been to a museum?
Have you been to an art center?
Have you taken a trip by airplane? by train? by bus? by car?
If so, where did you go?
What did you do during your last summer vacation?
Do you have a hobby?
If so, what is it?
Who is President of the United States?
Why do we celebrate Christmas?

Do you look at the newspaper funnies?
Does anyone read to you at home?
Is there a story that you like better than any other?
If so, what is it?
What toys or games do you have at home?
Does your father or mother play with you?
Do you go to church or Sunday School?
Do you help your father?
If so, how do you help him?
Do you go to the store with your mother and father?
Do you watch television?
If so, what are your favorite programs?
Have you been to a greenhouse?
Have you been to a dairy?
Have you been to a fire station?
Have you been to a department store?
Have you been to the beach?
Have you been to an airport?
Do you have a pet?
What do you do to take care of your pet?
Do you have a card for the public library?

Learning Ability

The teacher can obtain a crude measure of the child's learning rate
by providing him with practice in learning four or more words shown
in written form. The teacher can present each word on a card, name
the word, and ask the child to repeat the word. Next she can have
him match the cards with words written on the board. More practice
can be provided by having the child point to the words on the board
as the teacher pronounces them. After an interval of an hour or more,
the teacher can present the words again and ask the child to read
them. This will provide an approximation of the child's ability to
remember words presented in written form.

Associative Skills

In learning to read, children make use of visual, auditory, kinesthetic, and tactual imagery. These parts are associated in the process

of establishing meaning. Gates[3] has suggested the use of informal measures of associative learning. The materials for measuring visual-visual association consist of a set of ten cards, each with a simple geometric figure and picture. The child is told that he will be shown a number of pictures, below each of which is a figure. He is to remember the figure so that when it is shown alone he can tell which picture went with it. The figures are exposed one at a time for five seconds each. After the series has been presented, the cards are shuffled and each figure is shown to the child. He is to tell which picture goes with it. At no time does the examiner give the name of the object. If the child responds correctly, the card is turned so that he may see the correct response. Figure 8-1 is a sample of one of the visual-visual cards.

To measure visual-auditory association the child is shown ten cards, each containing a simple visual figure. Each figure is presented while the examiner pronounces the word printed on the back of the card. The exposure time is five seconds for each card. The word is pronounced twice during the exposure. The cards are then shuffled and presented one at a time. If the child's response is correct, the examiner says, "Yes, that is (giving the correct word);" if wrong, "No, that is ————." A sample of one of the visual-auditory cards is shown in Figure 8-2.

Many clinicians give the two inventories in the following order:

   I. First Trial
      A. Present the visual-visual cards.
      B. Test, using the visual-visual cards.
      C. Present the visual-auditory cards.
      D. Test, using the visual-auditory cards.
  II. Second Trial
      A. Present the visual-visual cards.
      B. Test, using the visual-visual cards.
      C. Present the visual-auditory cards.
      D. Test, using the visual-auditory cards.
 III. Third Trial
      A. Present the visual-visual cards.

---

[3] Arthur I. Gates, *The Improvement of Reading*, 3rd ed. (New York: The Macmillan Company, 1947), pp. 651–652.

Figure 8-1   A visual-visual card.

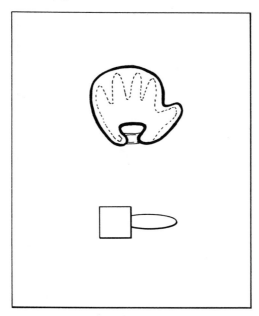

(a) Front of Card

(b) Back of Card

Figure 8-2 A visual-auditory card.

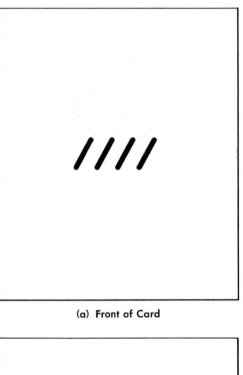

(a) Front of Card

(b) Back of Card

B. Test, using the visual-visual cards.

C. Present the visual-auditory cards.

D. Test, using the visual-auditory cards.

Reading Interests and Attitudes

Observations made during any reading period usually provide clues to the child's reading attitudes and interests. The student's remarks about reading and his behavior when asked to read can be revealing. One informal inventory of reading interests involves providing a child with a list of real or fictitious titles of books along with a short description of each story and asking him to select the ones he would really like to read. Another approach is to ask the student to talk about books he has read or would like to read. A graphic method of showing interest is through the use of *My Reading Design*.[4] This leaflet provides space for the student to list and number the books he has read. In the proper segment of a pie-shaped graph, he writes the number of each book. Each segment represents a type of book such as adventure, biography, fairy tale, animal, and nature stories.

Another approach that can be useful in revealing a child's interests and attitudes toward reading is the use of questions, similar to the following, which can be developed by the clinician or teacher.

When you have time to spend just as you please, what do you like to do?

What do you usually do on Saturday? On Sunday? After school?

What do you like to play best?

To what clubs or organizations do you belong?

Do you take special lessons outside of school? What kind are they? Do you like them?

Is there any toy, tool, or special equipment you would like to have? If so, what is it?

How often do you go to the movies?

What kind of movies do you like best?

What are your favorite television programs?

[4] *My Reading Design* by G. O. Simpson is published by Reading Circle, Inc., North Manchester, Indiana.

What do you like best in school?

If you could have three wishes which might come true, what would be your first wish? Your second wish? Your third wish?

Do you like to read?

Do you like to have someone read to you?

What have you been doing the last few weeks just for fun?

What music do you enjoy?

What books do you enjoy?

Do you like to travel?

What do you like best about your teacher?

What can the school do to help you?

These illustrative questions, which should not be used as items in a checklist, are sampling devices to appraise the child's interests and attitudes.

Personality

The informal use of the child's drawings and his comments about them can provide clues concerning certain facets of his personality. The clinician can ask the student to draw a house, a car, and a person. As the child draws, the clinician can make inferences about the degree of self-confidence shown, the amount of direction required by the child, the extent of originality and creativity, the need for encouragement and praise, the degree of perseverance, and the amount of cooperation. Upon completion of his drawing, the examinee can be asked to tell about the objects drawn. Questions can be asked, and fruitful areas can be investigated in detail. For example, the child can be encouraged to talk about the house he has drawn. Some exploratory questions are the following:

Who lives here?

Does the mother work?

Does the family like its neighborhood?

Do the folks like to read?

Do the parents think learning to read is important?

Are the people who live here happy?

Do they have enough money?

Are there many books and magazines of interest to children in this
   house?
Who does the scolding here?
Does the father play with his children?
Has this family had any trouble?
Does the mother read to her boys and girls?

Similar questions about the car and person can also reveal personality factors affecting reading maladjustment. After drawings have
been completed, the clinician can develop from his knowledge of the
situation hypotheses which can be explored by carefully designed
questions. The child's responses to these stimuli can be interpreted by
the perceptive teacher as she would interpret any relevant statement
or observed action. Here again it is essential to use one's intuitive
powers.

Another technique is the use of incomplete sentences which the
child is instructed to finish. Sentences designed to accomplish specific
purposes can be prepared, such as:

I worry over ———————.
I feel hurt when ———————.
I make believe that ———————.
I feel sorry when ———————.
I am afraid that ———————.
When I read, I ———————.
I feel proud when ———————.
I feel ashamed when ———————.
I like to ———————.
I hate to ———————.
I brag about my ———————.
Reading is ———————.
I become disgusted with ———————.
I am happy when ———————.
I like (boys, girls) who ———————.
I get angry when ———————.
I love ———————.
Most books are ———————.
Some teachers are ———————.
Some folks are ———————.

The stimuli in incomplete sentences are given in such a form as to arouse an emotional set and yet allow for all that may be implied in free response.

OBSERVATIONS: THE BASIS OF DIAGNOSIS AND TREATMENT

Observations can become the basis of hunches regarding the child and the causal factors underlying his achievement in reading. For example, Bill says he hates school and plans to drop out as soon as he is old enough. He is in the sixth grade and his teacher explains that in her opinion he is a bright boy who is reading only as well as a child six months in the third grade (3.6). Bill's father works in a dairy, and his mother is employed in a laundry. Both parents spend little time in reading activities. There are no other children. The school history shows that Bill is well liked by his associates and by other teachers who know him. He is eleven years and four months old.

In the reading clinic an informal reading inventory was administered to Bill. His independent, instructional, frustration, and capacity levels were 2, 3, 4, and 6, respectively. It was observed that he spent from two to three minutes in reading each paragraph. Factual questions were answered with less difficulty than questions involving why and how. To the observer, it appeared that Bill was reluctant to touch the informal reading cards. He frequently asked, "How much more time will this take?" As each card was handed to him, he scowled and said, "This reading is getting harder and harder, and I don't like it. My father says reading is not as important as some people think it is." As the paragraphs became more difficult, perspiration became apparent on his forehead. Again he asked, "Isn't it time for us to stop?" As the examiner attempted to determine the capacity level, it was observed that his responses to the questions on card five were made quickly, accurately, and with interest. Bill's responses to the questions on card six were accurate, and it was apparent that he was more interested in what was read to him, for he wanted to discuss the activity of making maple syrup. In discussing this operation, Bill said, "If I had been there, I would have helped myself to the syrup just as soon as it was cool enough to eat." Bill's interpretation of the Healy Pictorial I was completed in less than three minutes, and all the situations were correctly identified, interpreted, and evaluated. His reactions to several incomplete sentences are recorded as follows:

Stimulus	Response
I like to read	comics, not school books.
When I have to read,	my hands tremble.
My teacher says	I am not a good reader.
I feel bad when	I make a mistake.
I worry about	being dumb.
I am proud of	my dad.
I get angry when	the kids make fun of my reading.

In discussing his drawing of a house, Bill said, "The boy who lives here is a poor reader and a lousy speller. His mother and father did not go to school very long. They are good people, and they have a nice home and a new car. This boy is going to leave school as soon as he can, and his father is going to help him get a good job. This boy is brighter than the school principal thinks he is, and one of these days he will have a good job and earn a lot of money."

Observations made during Bill's performance on these informal inventories led to the following inferences.

- Bill is a boy of average intelligence or better.
- He has no difficulty in identifying and interpreting words. His reading of factual materials is quite satisfactory.
- He does not respond well to why and how questions. In fact, it appears that reading for Bill is not a thinking process.
- He has a strong negative feeling toward reading.
- He rationalizes his limited ability in the language arts, especially reading and spelling, by saying that his father is a poor reader and yet a successful man.
- Bill needs to learn how to read for the purpose of identifying, interpreting, and evaluating concepts.

A tentative diagnosis based on these inferences may be briefly stated as follows: Bill is a boy of average intelligence who has failed to make a satisfactory adjustment in the language arts, especially reading and spelling, chiefly because of an inadequate home environment which has failed to make known to him the importance of reading in a highly competitive society. Furthermore, the home has failed to provide an experiential background which would prepare and stimulate Bill to activities of an academic nature.

SUMMARY

Informal inventories can provide an opportunity for the teacher and reading clinician to observe the child so as to determine not only his reading disabilities but why they may have developed. Those who use these tools are seeking clues and hunches and not numerical scores. Informal inventories are not tests, and consequently those who employ them are not concerned with such characteristics of tests as validity and reliability. Careful observation and the wise interpretation of facts are the keys to the effective use of informal inventories.

Caution. A clinical study of a minor should not be attempted without the consent of the parent or guardian.

GUIDED ACTIVITY 8

Aim

To make effective use of informal inventories.

Materials

1. *Informal Reading Inventories* by Marjorie S. Johnson and Roy A. Kress (International Reading Association, Newark, Delaware), 1965.

Procedure

1. Prepare an informal reading inventory following the suggestions provided in this chapter and in the booklet, *Informal Reading Inventories*, by Johnson and Kress.
2. Administer your informal reading inventory to several children to be sure your questions are well designed and clearly stated.
3. When you are satisfied that you have improved your instrument to the point where you have a useful informal reading inventory, administer it to a fifth-grade child who is a fairly good reader.
4. Determine his independent, instructional, frustration, and capacity levels.
5. List clearly your observations.
6. Summarize briefly his reading needs.
7. Select a child who is having difficulty in reading. Administer your informal reading inventory to him.

8. Determine his independent, instructional, frustration, and capacity levels.

9. Summarize your observations and list the kind of errors made by the child.

10. Investigate his experiential background, learning ability, dominance, and personality characteristics using the procedures suggested in this chapter.

11. Draw inferences concerning his reading needs and the effect of the factors investigated on his reading achievement.

12. List the advantages and the disadvantages of informal inventories to a teacher in your position.

QUESTIONS AND REFERENCES

Questions

1. How can teachers make use of informal reading inventories?

2. What are the visual visual and visual auditory association cards?

3. How useful are informal reading inventories?

4. Where can one find a reading inventory for college students and adults?

5. What are the techniques for developing and using informal reading inventories?

6. Where can one find a questionnaire which can be used to de-

References

1. Homer L. J. Carter and Dorothy J. McGinnis, *Teaching Individuals to Read* (Boston: D. C. Heath and Company, 1962), pp. 123–127.

2. Arthur I. Gates, *The Improvement of Reading*, 3rd ed. (New York: The Macmillan Company, 1947), pp. 651–652.

3. Joseph P. Kender, "How Useful Are Informal Reading Tests?" *Journal of Reading*, 11 (February 1968), 337–342.

4. Homer L. J. Carter and Dorothy J. McGinnis, *Reading, A Key to Academic Success* (Dubuque, Iowa: William C. Brown Company, 1967), Appendix A.

5. Marjorie S. Johnson and Roy A. Kress, *Informal Reading Inventories* (Newark, Delaware: International Reading Association, 1965).

6. Paul Witty and David Kopel, *Reading and the Educative Proc-*

Questions	References
termine handedness and laterality?	*ess* (Boston: Ginn and Company, 1939), pp. 313–315.
7. Where can suggestions be found concerning the use of observations made in the classroom?	**7.** Ruth Strang, *Diagnostic Teaching of Reading* (New York: McGraw-Hill Book Company, 1964), Chap. 3.
8. Where can one find descriptions of several informal inventories for use in determining reading readiness?	**8.** Donald D. Durrell, *Improving Reading Instruction* (Yonkers-on-Hudson, N.Y.: World Book Company, 1956), Chap. 4.

Chapter 9

Diagnosis

In the study of the disabled reader at all levels, diagnosis is of the essence. In this chapter the importance of diagnosis will be discussed, and the essential acts of diagnosis and their sequence will be presented. In a factor-Gestalt approach, facts will be evaluated as to whether they are relevant, material, and consequential. Diagnosis is thought of as an ongoing process in which experiential background is essential to the diagnostician.

THE IMPORTANCE OF DIAGNOSIS

In classroom or clinic, diagnosis is essential to the implementation of instruction and the facilitation of treatment. With proper diagnosis instruction can be effectively designed and treatment provided to remedy specific disabilities. Without diagnosis at levels one, two, and three, teachers are merely babysitters who keep children contented, busy, and happy. Teachers must stimulate, inform, and guide. In order to accomplish these goals, a knowledge of the child's needs, interests, and attitudes is imperative. Those who stimulate and guide must know the child in his environment and must aid him in the accomplishment of his purpose. They must do more than "just teach" and follow blindly a basic text, a happy routine, or a ritualistic approach.

Treatment is dependent on diagnosis. In order to prescribe, the diagnostician must know and understand the disability he intends to remedy. No qualified physician would attempt to treat a high

153

temperature and abdominal pains until he had made a thorough diagnosis. If palliative measures are applied, they too are dependent on diagnosis. Routine safeguards are considered, and the patient's welfare is never needlessly placed in jeopardy. In a similar manner, the well-trained reading clinician will insist upon a diagnosis before he attempts to provide treatment. If he makes use of palliative measures, he will be reasonably sure that they will not do more damage than good.

The chief cornerstone of corrective work in the classroom and of all activities in the clinic is valid and reliable diagnosis. Instruction and treatment without preliminary diagnosis are nothing but guesswork and drugstore therapy. Unproved methods, even if successful, do not permit one to evaluate their effectiveness in the absence of a diagnostic consideration of the variables being manipulated.

DIAGNOSIS AT FOUR LEVELS

The alert teacher can identify the child in her class who is failing to make satisfactory academic progress because of a reading disability. This *identification* is diagnosis at the first level. Furthermore, the capable teacher can become aware of the child in her fifth-grade class who is reading at the second-grade level (2.0) and who is severely penalized both academically and socially as a result of a marked reading defect. This is an example of the second level of diagnosis, which involves measurement and *classification*. By means of test data, school history, observations, and informal reading inventories, the classroom teacher can diagnose at the third level, *identification of reading needs,* those skills which the child needs to acquire if he is to make the progress expected of him in reading.

These levels of diagnosis can be accomplished by the teacher on her own without the aid of the reading clinician. In her daily association with her students she can *observe, diagnose, adjust instruction,* and *evaluate* success of treatment. By means of anecdotal records she can summarize relevant information concerning each child and consequently gain an understanding of her class as a whole. With this appraisal of the reading needs of her students the teacher can utilize flexible grouping and, later if she wishes, she can individualize her instruction. In the classroom, diagnosis at levels one, two, and three should be made before the teacher begins her consideration of aims to be accomplished, materials to be employed, and procedures to be utilized. To be effective, instruction must be based on the reading interests and needs of the students as they attempt to accomplish their goals.

Diagnosis at the fourth and highest level involves the determination of causal factors which may be found by a team of specialists in such disciplines as physiology, psychology, sociology, and education. At this level a clinical study is made of the child in his environment. Diagnosis based on data from many sources is established, and treatment in the form of instruction or psychotherapy is outlined. The child is then referred back to his homeroom teacher or to a reading therapist. Diagnosis at level four, although distinctive in many aspects, really involves identification, classification, and the determination of individual needs. There is, of course, much overlapping of function. Diagnosis at any level is an on-going process which continues until maladjustment is at an end. The individual changes, and consequently his remediation, that is, his diagnosis and treatment, must change. Diagnosis is not complete until the disability and need no longer exist.

DIAGNOSIS OF SPECIFIC READING NEEDS

An analysis of the reading strengths and weaknesses of the disabled reader is essential in diagnosis and treatment. The clinician must locate the student's faulty reading techniques and specific reading needs. Only then can an effective program of remediation be planned. The following questions have been developed to serve as a guide in determining the child's fundamental reading disabilities.

FAULTY VOCABULARY

Is the child's sight vocabulary insufficient?
Does the child have difficulty using context and other meaning clues?
Is the child deficient in phonetic and structural analysis?
Does the child have difficulty in auditory discrimination or visual discrimination?
What types of errors appear most frequently?
Is there a pattern of vowel or consonant errors?
Is the child unfamiliar with the sounds of letters?
Can he identify the letters of the alphabet?

Do errors occur in the beginning, middle, or ending of words?

Does the child repeatedly reverse letters? If so, which ones?

Does the child show evidence of being overanalytical by breaking words into too many parts or spelling out words letter by letter?

DEFICIENCIES IN IDENTIFICATION, INTERPRETATION, AND EVALUATION

Does the child have an inadequate meaning vocabulary?

Does the child read word by word instead of by thought units?

Does the child encounter greater difficulty as he attempts to read larger units of material?

Does he have difficulty in following written directions?

Does he fail to identify the central idea in a paragraph?

Does he fail to recall details and facts he has read?

Does he have difficulty in finding answers to specific questions?

Does he have difficulty in finding facts which support a main idea?

Is he unable to summarize a paragraph, section, or chapter?

Is he unable to interpret critically what he reads?

Does he experience difficulty in finding words, phrases, or facts in printed materials?

Is he unable to associate what he reads with his own experiences and background?

Does he have trouble remembering what he has read?

Is he unable to read well to others for their satisfaction?

Does he fail to appreciate humor and dramatic situations in books and papers?

Does he draw valid inferences from material he has read?

DEFICIENCIES IN READING-STUDY SKILLS

Is he unable to make effective use of the dictionary?

Does he fail to understand the essential conditions for a problem to be solved?

Is he unable to use aids in locating materials to be read?

Is he inadequate in his ability to organize what he has read?

Does he have difficulty reading charts, maps, graphs, and tables?

Does he have a limited knowledge of specialized, technical vocabularies?

 unable to adapt reading techniques to the special demands of
  ent fields?

Is he unable to adapt his rate of reading to his purposes and the difficulty of the materials?

SOME PRINCIPLES OF DIAGNOSIS

The principles of diagnosis in the field of reading are identical with the fundamental laws of diagnosis in other clinical fields. Behind every behavior pattern there are material and consequential causes. The process of diagnosis becomes effective when it is carried out on a background of scientific investigation and according to principles generally accepted by students of human behavior. Some of these principles are as follows.

Causal factors are important to the degree to which they affect reading performance. Not every relevant factor is material or consequential, because in one case it may exert primary causal influence whereas in another instance it may be immaterial and even inconsequential. It is necessary not only to identify a factor but to determine its contribution to the effect.

The individual should always be studied as a whole, relating disorders of parts to the pattern of the whole personality. The dysfunction of parts of the individual's behavior must be interpreted and evaluated in terms of his total personality pattern. Isolated performance is meaningless and can only be understood as it becomes figure upon ground.

Simple interpretations of the individual's behavior should have preference over the more complex. The individual's disability in reading should be explained in terms of the fewest possible causal factors. If one is sufficient, the others are superficial and of little consequence. In general, causation is multiple. In individual cases, however, a *single* factor can set off a chain reaction of several factors which are contributory and even material to the disability.

It is always necessary to recognize the possibility of several diagnoses, which must be differentiated. In a complex reading problem it is necessary to identify the symptoms to be considered. The clinician must then evaluate the observed facts so as to establish cause-effect relationships, and must reject improbable hypotheses so as to reach a diagnosis which explains the disability in the simplest manner possible.

Diagnosis must be scientifically oriented if it is to become the basis of instruction and the cornerstone of clinical study. The diagnostician, whether teacher or clinician, must know research in the field of reading and be able to judge its worth. He must have the attitudes of the scientist and be able to sense cause-effect relationships. He should be able to determine whether observed facts are relevant, material, and consequential. He should be cautious, conservative, and uninfluenced by subjective feelings. He must be aware of his own biases and be ready to compensate for his own idiosyncrasies. He must be mature in experience and judgment and at all times a doubter.

MENTAL CONTENT AND EXPERIENTIAL BACKGROUND OF THE DIAGNOSTICIAN

The reading teacher, and especially the reading clinician, must be able to apply information from the life sciences effectively. He must have both theoretical and practical training with reading performance at all levels and with children in various economic and social climates. He cannot become a specialist in all areas, but he can gather facts from several fields and integrate his findings. His educational background should make him both scientific in his diagnosis and creative in his treatment. The training obtained from curricula leading to the M.A. and Ph.D. degrees is but the beginning of professional study. He should have experience in the classroom, in a reading clinic, child-guidance center, and hospital for mentally retarded and emotionally disturbed children. He should "hear, read, mark, learn, and inwardly digest" contemporary research. He should progress from being a "mental tester" to a competent reading clinician.

The team approach to the study of the disabled reader assumes that a greater breadth and depth of mental content and experiential background will be utilized than can be brought to bear on the problem by a clinician working alone. This advantage of the team approach, however, can be threatened if team agreement on a diagnosis is adversely affected by a dominant member who is not necessarily the most competent clinical worker.

The remediation of any abnormality of human behavior, and especially one as complicated as a disability in reading, requires a multi-disciplinary approach. In dealing with the seriously disabled reader, neither the educator nor the psychologist should attempt to muddle through alone. In some instances the individual should be referred, with the concurrence of the family physician, to a neurologist, otologist, ophthalmologist or endocrinologist. In the study of the disabled reader each specialist should be willing to cooperate with representatives of other disciplines in the diagnosis of the individual's disability.

ACTS OF DIAGNOSIS

As in all problem-solving activities, diagnosis depends on the identification of the immediate problem and of all relevant variables. Furthermore, some of these factors are only *relevant;* some are essential to a solution and are *material;* others may be *consequential* and lead directly to the effect. The greatest difficulty in diagnosis consists in discovering the true nature of the problem. In achieving this objective, the clinician must be aware of possible etiological factors. He attempts to

- *Identify* the problem and possible causal factors.
- *Assume* and *reject* hypothesis after hypothesis until one can finally be *accepted.*
- *Discover* possible determinant and *explain* consequential relationship.
- *Predict* with treatment ultimate effect and *verify.*

These acts in many instances may vary in order and sequence. They, however, are an integral part of every complete diagnosis.

APPLICATION IN FIELD OF MECHANICS

A mechanic in a local garage was having trouble with a new car. The motor would start, run for a few minutes, backfire, and stop. His problem was to determine the cause of this faulty performance, which was quite unusual for a car just off the assembly line.

The mechanic *identified* the problem and was aware of several possible causes such as: a plugged gas line, water in the gasoline, defective ignition. He *assumed* that the cause of the problem was a plugged gas line. After disconnecting the gas line at the carburetor, gasoline flowed freely and this hypothesis was *rejected.* His second hypothesis, that water was in the gasoline, was also rejected. His third hypothesis, that defective ignition was a causal factor, was carefully investigated as he considered wiring and spark plugs. When the mechanic examined the commutator, he exclaimed, "This can be the cause of the difficulty." He had made a *discovery* and he *explained* its significance. He pointed out that the cap of the distributor had a crack in the top and that when the temperature of the motor increased, this crack became wider because of expansion of the cap. This widened gap caused the faulty ignition. The broken cap was the determinant which led directly to the effect. This factor was both material and consequential. The mechanic immediately *predicted* that if a new distributor cap was installed, the motor would operate effectively. Later he *verified* this prediction, and the diagnosis was complete.

It is obvious from the illustration that the skilled mechanic with his experiential background and training was able to apply the following acts of diagnosis: identification, assumption, rejection, acceptance, discovery, explanation, prediction, and verification. The mechanic was able to determine what factors were relevant, material, and consequential. Even though he may not have had experience in a physics laboratory, his thinking was objective, systematic, and goal oriented. He was a good diagnostician. Let us see now how the reading clinician can handle the problem of a disabled reader.

DIAGNOSIS OF READING DISABILITY

The clinical study of Stephen is briefly summarized in the form of statements organized under several headings.

THE PROBLEM

Stephen is a shy and courteous lad who is having trouble not only in reading but in all his academic subjects. At the time of referral, Stephen was thirteen years and six months old and weighed 142 pounds. His grade placement was that of a pupil two months in the sixth grade. His teacher reported that Stephen was beginning to lose confidence in himself because of a marked reading disability, which was adversely affecting his achievement in the classroom. In an interview she explained that in her opinion Stephen could do better in reading if he would put forth the necessary effort.

HOME ENVIRONMENT

Stephen and his parents live in a beautiful home in the suburban area of a Midwestern city. Both parents are teachers in the public schools, and both are actively engaged in the academic affairs of their schools and the social activities of their neighborhood. Stephen is their only child, and he has been left in the care of a paternal grandmother who lives in the home. Stephen's father is interested in sports, especially football, and reports that he cannot understand why his son lacks an aggressive and active interest in outdoor activities. In fact, the father is at times so critical of Stephen that both the mother and grandmother come to the boy's defense. This reaction, the mother reports, is the cause of emotional tension and frustration in the home. Both parents report that they have little time to do any reading except that which is required of them in preparation for their classes.

Stephen, they add, is reading only as well as a second-grade child. They say his training in phonics has been neglected and that he is unwilling to try to read. There are many interesting books for a growing boy of fourteen years in the home; however, the grandmother points out that there is little stimulation provided by the adult members of the family that would contribute to Stephen's interest in books. He has no responsibilities in the home.

DEVELOPMENTAL HISTORY

The parents report that Stephen's birth was normal. He sat up at nine months, walked at thirteen months, and talked at fourteen months. The only illnesses were whooping cough, mumps, and measles. The child was well nourished, and there was a history of endogenous obesity. Development of sex organs had not been normal. The physician reported fat deposits over the hips and pubes, but no pubic hair. The penis was infantile and the testes, at the age of thirteen years, had not descended into the scrotum. There was a long history of enuresis, which was disturbing to the parents and frustrating to Stephen.

SCHOOL HISTORY

When Stephen was five years of age, he entered kindergarten. At the end of the school year he was promoted to the first grade even though his teacher stated that he was not mature enough for reading. She reported that throughout the year Stephen would seldom come to school without his grandmother bringing him to the entrance of the building. He cried easily and demonstrated little responsibility in putting on his rubbers and raincoat. The children tolerated him and assisted him with his projects. In the first grade there was a history of reversals and orientation difficulties. During his stay in the elementary grades his teachers reported that he was happy, careless, and unwilling to do anything that was difficult. He was retained twice, once in the first grade and again in the fourth grade. This did not trouble Stephen, according to his teacher.

ANTHROPOMETRIC MEASURES

Stephen's standing height was scored at the 65th percentile, his sitting height at the 60th percentile, and his weight at the 92nd percentile. His right grip, left grip, and lung capacity were placed at the 30, 40, and 90 percentiles, respectively. These physical measurements indicate that Stephen is a boy of high average height who is significantly overweight.

A comparison of the first three measures with the last three measures suggests that Stephen did not put forth his best efforts in acts involving the expression of volition.

SOME EDUCATIONAL AND PSYCHOLOGICAL MEASURES

Measures of achievement in reading, spelling, and arithmetic interpreted in terms of grade scores are 3.6, 3.8, and 4.9, respectively. Data resulting from an informal reading inventory suggest a capacity level of a sixth-grade child and the frustration level of a fourth grader. Instructional and independent-reading levels were at third-grade and second-grade levels, respectively. Rapport was not difficult to establish, and Stephen showed a higher degree of spontaneity than the examiner had expected. He made effective use of contextual clues and responded well to questions concerning the materials read at the independent and instructional levels.

When asked to read orally, Stephen made frequent substitutions of words. A tendency toward reversals was apparent from his performance on the Morrison-McCall Spelling Scale. A dislike for spelling was inferred by observers. Stephen's errors on the arithmetic test were, in the opinion of the examiner, due to carelessness.

The clinician reported that Stephen's IQs as determined by the Wechsler Intelligence Scale for Children were 114, 115, and 116 on the verbal, performance, and full scales, respectively. Stephen's highest scores were on subtests involving vocabulary, similarities, and comprehension. In the opinion of the examiner, rapport was well established but Stephen did not put forth effort commensurate with his assumed ability. His present level of intellectual functioning is within the high average range.

MEDICAL REPORT

The physician's report gave the general impression of pluriglandular insufficiency. A lowered basal metabolism, a characteristic of the Frohlich syndrome, was reported. X-rays showed that the metacarpals and phalanges were normal and that the sella turcica was of the closed type. Secondary sex characteristics were not present. There was marked overweight with fat distributed more about hips and thighs than other parts of the body. The infantile penis and partially undescended testes completed the picture of a glandular problem. Vision and hearing were normal.

ACTS OF DIAGNOSIS APPLIED AT LEVEL FOUR

The *problem* briefly stated is, "Why is Stephen reading so far below his expected level?"

The staff of the clinic after studying the known facts have made several *assumptions* which must be *accepted* or *rejected.* It must determine what is only relevant, what is material, and what is consequential. The hypotheses are the following:

1. The home climate has contributed little to develop an interest in and readiness for the work of the classroom.
2. Stephen's unwillingness to put forth and sustain effort is a primary factor.
3. A glandular dysfunction may be significant.
4. Perceptual factors may have been causal in nature.
5. Marked feelings of inadequacy may have caused Stephen's disability.
6. A mental set against reading is a cause of limited attainment.

Each of these hypotheses represents a constellation of factors which must be evaluated to determine whether the configuration is relevant, material, or consequential. As the result of this evaluation, it was the consensus that hypotheses 1, 4, 5, and 6 were only relevant and that hypothesis 2 was a likely explanation of Stephen's maladjustment in reading. In a further study of the available data, it was *discovered* that a glandular dysfunction known as the Frohlich syndrome, hypothesis 3, could cause emotional immaturity, which in turn would be manifested by unwillingness to put forth and sustain effort. As a result of this *discovery* and *explanation*, it is assumed that dyspituitarism is both a material and consequential factor leading directly to the effect. It is hypothesized, then, that the other factors are only relevant but not essential to the diagnosis. They may be contributory, but not causal. It was predicted that if this physical condition could be remedied, mitigated, or set aside, Stephen would make improvement in reading. Because this actually happened, after an interim of ten months, theoretically the acts of diagnosis were complete, for *prediction* actually led to *verification*.

The diagnosis could then be stated as follows: Stephen is a youth of average intelligence who has made unsatisfactory progress in reading because of a glandular dysfunction and emotional immaturity. His unwillingness to put forth and sustain effort and his dislike for reading are manifestations of this immaturity. The home climate and his feeling of inadequacy are contributing factors.

DIAGNOSIS: AN ONGOING PROCESS

Diagnosis at any level is an ongoing process never completed until the accepted hypothesis has been proved beyond reasonable doubt. Time is a requisite for evaluation of diagnosis, and frequently mistrust can cloud the issue. Diagnostic formulations are based on the judgments of the clinical team and are frequently unprovable because causal factors and dynamics of human behavior are not always susceptible to analysis. The proof of clinical procedures in any case is adversely affected by a lack of control over a large number of variables.

TREATMENT

In providing treatment for Stephen, the following procedures and acts were carried out.

- Glandular therapy was prescribed for treatment of maldevelopment of testes and delayed puberty.
- Interesting reading materials at second- and third-grade levels were made available for Stephen. He was encouraged to select only those of special concern to him. It was suggested that the therapist and the classroom teacher encourage Stephen to read to answer why and how questions. It was reported that he enjoyed this activity and learned to construct his own queries.
- In conferences with the parents it was pointed out that the home could stimulate Stephen's desire to read and could provide an environment accepting of him as a growing adult with interests and goals of his own.
- Stephen, as a member of a family, was encouraged to assume responsibilities about the home. His interest in and care of the family car was encouraged and he was given fundamental information preparatory to learning to drive.
- Stephen's growing achievement in the classroom and his acceptance of responsibility for lawn and garden were reinforced by praise and commendation. He was in the process of becoming a man.

Approximately ten months after the initiation of corrective measures, Stephen was reported to have lost 12 pounds. His reading level was that of an individual two months in the sixth grade (6.2). This was a significant gain of two years and six months. Marked changes in sex development occurred. It was reported that his attitude toward reading and the work of the classroom was drastically changed. He became more aggressive and developed both an interest in and an aptitude for football. Subsequent reports received nearly a year later indicated that Stephen was reading as well as a boy six months in the seventh grade and that he was making a satisfactory academic adjustment. Sex development was normal.

In reviewing the case of Stephen the following questions become apparent:

- What was the effect of Stephen's acceptance by his parents?
- What was accomplished by the adjustment of reading materials?
- What was gained by Stephen's change in self-concept?
- What was achieved by the fact that special attention was focused on Stephen by the reading therapist whom he liked very much?
- Would Stephen have made significant gains in reading without glandular therapy?

These questions, because of a lack of control over several variables, cannot be answered. The fact does remain, however, that Stephen made marked and significant gains in reading and furthermore his academic adjustment improved so that he was able to complete both junior and senior high school.

SUMMARY

Diagnosis is essential in the study of the disabled reader. It involves a search for current causal factors and a study of the child's reading strengths and weaknesses. It plays an important role in the planning of classroom instruction and clinical treatment. In this chapter the acts of diagnosis have been set forth and illustrated. Some principles governing diagnosis have been explained in a factor-Gestalt approach, and the importance of determining which facts are relevant, material, and consequential has been emphasized. The contribution of the mental content and experiential background of the teacher and clinician making the diagnosis has been stressed.

GUIDED ACTIVITY 9

Aim

To understand the acts of diagnosis.

Materials

1. Chapter 9 of *Diagnosis and Treatment of the Disabled Reader.*
2. Chapter 3, *Ibid.*

Procedure

1. In Chapter 9 the writers have illustrated the diagnosis of a mechanical difficulty and of a reading disability. Show how causal factors differ in each problem.
2. In these illustrations of diagnosis, show how *adjustment* of mechanical parts and *treatment* of Stephen are similar in nature.
3. Show how prediction in one case can be verified *without doubt.*
4. Show how diagnosis is dependent upon the experiential background and training of the diagnostician.
5. List several factors in Stephen's case which you believe to be relevant but not material and consequential.

6. In the mechanical problem described in Chapter 9, why was the consequential factor so easily verified?

7. In dealing with a reading disability, when is diagnosis at the third level quite sufficient?

8. Reread the clinical study of John in Chapter 3. Explain why diagnosis at level three was or was not sufficient.

9. In making a diagnosis what one attitude on the part of the diagnostician is most important? Explain your inference.

10. In diagnosis can a factor be material but not consequential? Illustrate your point of view.

11. Show how a classroom teacher can improve her ability to determine the causal factors affecting the reading performance of her students.

12. Select a child with a reading disability and, after securing permission from the school and from his parents, determine to the extent of your ability the causal factors affecting his performance. Make use of his school history, your observations in the classroom, informal inventories, and information resulting from interviews. Report briefly your diagnosis.

13. Observe, if possible, a clinical team at work with a disabled reader. Report your observations and inferences.

QUESTIONS AND REFERENCES

Questions

References

1. What are some general principles of diagnosis?

1. Guy L. Bond and Miles A. Tinker, *Reading Difficulties, Their Diagnosis and Correction,* 2nd ed. (New York: Appleton-Century-Crofts, 1967), Chap. 7. Marion Monroe, "General Principles of Diagnosis of Reading Disabilities," in Delwyn G. Schubert and Theodore L. Torgerson, eds. *Readings in Reading* (New York: Thomas Y. Crowell, 1968), pp. 359–362.

2. What factors should be considered in an analysis of reading difficulties?

2. Guy L. Bond and Miles A. Tinker, *Reading Difficulties, Their Diagnosis and Correction,* 2nd ed. (New York: Appleton-Century-Crofts, 1967), Chap. 8.

3. What are some specific approaches to diagnosis?

3. *Ibid.,* Chap. 9.

Questions	References
4. What is the relation between clinical sensitivity and hypothesis making?	**4.** Richard W. Wallen, *Clinical Psychology* (New York: McGraw-Hill Book Company, 1956), Chap. 3.
5. What constitutes educational diagnosis?	**5.** Robert M. Wilson, *Diagnostic and Remedial Reading* (Columbus, Ohio: Charles E. Merrill Books, 1967), Chap. 4.
6. How is the technique of the reading survey related to diagnosis?	**6.** Mary C. Austin, Clifford L. Bush, and Mildred H. Heubner, *Reading Evaluation* (New York: The Ronald Press Company, 1961), Chap. 4.
7. How can the teacher investigate classroom learning environments?	**7.** Robert Fox, Margaret Barron Luszke, and Richard Schmuck, *Diagnosing Classroom Learning Environments.* (Chicago: Science Research Associates, Inc., 1966).
8. Why should the cause of reading maladjustment be determined before applying therapy?	**8.** Delwyn G. Schubert, "Know the Cause Before Applying the Cure," in Delwyn G. Schubert and Theodore L. Torgerson, eds. *Readings in Reading* (New York: Thomas Y. Crowell Company, 1968), pp. 333–335.
9. What specific principles are essential to classroom diagnosis?	**9.** William D. Sheldon, "Specific Principles Essential to Classroom Diagnosis," in Delwyn G. Schubert and Theodore L. Torgerson, eds., *Readings in Reading* (New York: Thomas Y. Crowell Company, 1968), pp. 351–359.
10. What clinical procedures should be followed in diagnosing seriously retarded readers?	**10.** Helen M. Robinson, "Clinical Procedures in Diagnosing Seriously Retarded Readers," in Delwyn G. Schubert and Theodore L. Torgerson, eds. *Readings in Reading* (New York: Thomas Y. Crowell Company, 1968), pp. 363–369.

Chapter 10

Treatment

In this chapter treatment will be defined and discussed in relation to the remediation of reading disabilities. Seven principles of treatment will be set forth and some suggestions for planning a program of remediation outlined. Special emphasis will be given to a discussion of personality factors in remediation and several commonly asked questions involving treatment answered. This chapter is designed to give an overall view of factors to be considered in the treatment of the disabled reader.

DEFINITION

Treatment is the systematic act, method, and manner of providing care in order to accomplish a specific purpose. It is an endeavor to help a person attain better health or better adjustment by means of medical care, psychotherapeutic aid, counseling, and instruction. It is designed to remedy, cure, or mitigate a disability in order to aid the individual in the realization of his goal. Treatment of the disabled reader may consist of both instruction and therapy. It may be general, specific, palliative, or preventive. In all instances, however, it must be a direct response to a diagnostic study of the individual or to an immediate anticipation of his needs. Treatment is the natural outcome of diagnosis at one or more of the four levels. It is directed to a well-defined purpose.

Instruction as Treatment

If instruction is to be effective, it must be based on the interests and reading needs of the child. This involves diagnosis at the third level. Instruction may be both developmental and corrective, for seldom does any individual learn completely at the first presentation. Furthermore, developmental and corrective procedures have much in common, because all instructional activities have, in part, a corrective nature. In all instances, effective teaching is designed to accomplish a specific purpose.

Remediation, on the other hand, is carried on by the clinician, reading therapist, and teacher as they attempt to determine why the child has a disability in reading and how they can best remedy this situation. For example, Bill, an intelligent eight-year-old boy, was a nonreader. During the course of diagnosis, it was discovered that Bill had difficulties in fusion, which resulted in double vision. He was referred to an ophthalmologist for treatment, and no aid in reading was provided until the visual difficulty had been corrected. When the cause of this boy's reading problem was removed, instruction in reading was given, and he made significant improvement in a surprisingly short time. In remediation it is assumed that the therapist has an adequate background in several disciplines. Remediation at the fourth level consists of both diagnosis and treatment.

General Versus Specific Treatment

General treatment occurs daily in response to diagnosis at the first, second, and third levels. It is on-the-spot action taken to alleviate the student's immediate difficulty and does not lead to marked changes in classroom instruction of the child. General treatment provided by the teacher is a part of regular instruction and can be preventive. It may be group oriented and only indirectly applied to the individual. A teacher, for example, has five children in her sixth-grade class who have trouble in reading for detail. Two of them are reading at third-grade level, two at fourth-grade level, and one at sixth-grade level. She has instructed these children as a group and has utilized materials at three levels. General treatment in many instances can be most effective.

Specific treatment is individualized. The child may be taken from the classroom by the therapist for special remediation which is too difficult to apply in the usual group situation. Children subjected to clinical studies require multidisciplinary approaches which necessitate cooperation between the reading therapist and other specialists. These boys and girls will generally spend a specified amount of time each day in a reading laboratory. Joel, for example, is a seventh-grade boy who has difficulty in reading textbook material. His IQs as determined by the Wechsler Intelligence Scale for Children are 120, 108, and 115. His capacity level on an informal reading inventory is that of an eighth-grade student. His independent, instructional, and frustration levels are 3, 4, and 5, respectively. Joel reports that he is "dull and stupid and cannot live up to the expectations of my father." Joel needs to be shown how to read for main ideas, how to read for a purpose, and how to make ideas his own. Specific treatment is necessary to accomplish these goals. More important still, Joel requires therapy to develop his self-concept. He needs to identify himself with the young man who is providing remediation until he can gain more self-confidence. Specific treatment is designed to effect a cure of a particular disability. In the field of medicine, quinine is a specific in the treatment of malaria, and a visual, auditory, kinesthetic, and tactual technique is regarded by some reading clinicians as a specific in the treatment of reversal tendencies.

Palliative Treatment

Palliative treatment in reading is designed to relieve symptoms or undesired effects without removing the cause. Its purpose is to alleviate inability to identify, interpret, and evaluate ideas expressed by written symbols. It is not a cure but merely a means of making the student more effective in his academic and social environment. The use of a liner to keep one's place, for example, can provide temporary palliative benefits. In the treatment of the disabled reader, as in the practice of medicine, few measures are specific and many are palliative. The selection of suitable materials, the grouping of children, and the giving of praise and commendation are palliative in that they do not effect an immediate cure for problems in reading.

Preventive Treatment

The case load in reading clinics is evidence enough of the need for prevention of reading disabilities. Many children who are left on their own fail to develop needed skills which can lead to independent reading. Many of these children develop acute emotional disturbances, and others drop out of school, only to become more seriously maladjusted.

Prevention of reading disabilities occurs through early identification of those children who are apt to become disabled readers, such as, for example, the immature child, the disadvantaged child, the emotionally unstable child, and the physically handicapped child. Whenever necessary, referrals to a reading therapist or clinic should be made as early as possible. In the classroom teachers can prevent reading disabilities by aiding the child in developing a readiness for reading. The choice of teaching and learning methods which meet the needs of the child also constitutes preventive treatment. Prevention is a function of both the home and school.

SOME PRINCIPLES OF TREATMENT

Remediation involves diagnosis and treatment. Furthermore, treatment consists of both instruction and therapy. It can be applied by the classroom teacher, the reading therapist, and the clinician. Some principles underlying its application are briefly summarized.

Attention to the Individual

The retarded reader needs to be accepted as a person and at his level of development. He needs to be understood, respected, and liked by his teachers and his associates. Rapport is of the utmost importance. It is essential that the reading therapist have a thorough knowledge of the child, his abilities, interests, and attitudes as well as the skills he possesses and does not possess. In both diagnosis and treatment attention must be focused on the individual. Physical, psychological, environmental, and educational factors must be given careful consideration. The child's developmental, social, and school histories provide a moving picture of him over the greater part of his life rather than a snapshot of him at the time of his observation and study in the clinic. Treatment must be based on his needs and disabilities and on full consideration of his interests and his goals. Treatment must be designed to fit the individual, and not necessarily the members of his group.

Emphasis on Interpretation

Interpretation of the child's performance should be emphasized, rather than evaluation of his achievement. Diagnosis and treatment are reciprocals, with diagnosis always coming first. Both are acts of remediation. Frequently, persons lacking clinical training or having preconceived ideas evaluate the child's achievement rather than interpret his performance. They make value judgments without determining why the individual did what he did.

Some teachers, for example, may discover that a student is unable to read effectively for detail. Instead of trying to determine why this disability exists, they may prescribe drill in reading for detail and display annoyance when the child fails to respond adequately. There can be no effective treatment until needs or causal factors have been identified. Interpretation of all known data must precede treatment at any level.

Adequate Materials

Instructional materials should be selected which are appropriate to the needs, reading level, interest, and goals of the student. Valid treatment necessitates providing the child with interesting material which he can actually read. The needs, abilities, and interests of retarded readers differ greatly. Consequently, no one book is adequate for all. The therapist should evaluate materials in terms of the appropriateness for the student and should select only those that will further the reading growth of the child. Under no circumstances should materials be utilized only because they are available at the time. They should always be used to accomplish a specific purpose.

At the beginning of therapy, materials should be sufficiently simple that the student experiences immediate success. As progress is made, it is essential that the therapist maintain a balance of easy materials to insure success and more difficult ones to provide stimulation and growth. All materials that students associate with failure in reading should be avoided. If adequate materials are not available, the therapist and child can construct and design them by developing experience charts, which can be made immediately into small books having a special interest to the young author. Some teachers have helped the child in this manner to build up a vocabulary of 250 to 300 words before formal texts were utilized.

In all instances, the reading and interest levels of materials must fit the child. Publishers and manufacturers have produced many mechanical devices and well-designed materials which can prove of great value to the therapist and classroom teacher. A few have been listed in Appendix C. Many of these, although constructed to accomplish a specific purpose, can be used successfully in a variety of ways. The creative therapist will make many clever adaptations.

Specific Objectives

Instructional procedures should be selected and modified to accomplish specific objectives. There is no one way to teach reading, for some children learn one way and some another. In fact, what is beneficial to some may be detrimental to others. Trial and error procedures may be employed to determine a satisfactory approach. Some children learn by a visual-visual approach, some by a visual-auditory, some by a visual-kinesthetic, and some by a visual-tactual. Others may make satisfactory progress by various combinations of these approaches. In providing treatment utilizing instruction, the therapist should consider the importance of specific *aims*, well-selected *materials*, and carefully planned *procedures*. Treatment involves more than "just teaching."

Emphasis in instruction should be placed on the skills and abilities the student does not have but that are essential for his immediate success in reading. Sometimes teachers drill on all reading skills, whether or not the student possesses and uses them. Because time is of the essence to the retarded reader, skills which have already been learned should not be emphasized unless they can serve as the basis for the development of needed skills. All stress should be placed on mastering abilities that will help the student to move forward quickly. At the same time, instruction must be balanced. It must be directed toward helping the student overcome specific weaknesses, while keeping the total reading program in balance.

Skills should be developed sequentially and not haphazardly. For example, the student must learn to identify concepts before he can interpret them. He must learn to interpret before he evaluates. Each instructional period should be well planned. Because the attention span of retarded readers is usually short, the teacher should plan several activities for each instructional period. These activities should be in harmony with the requirements of the student. Remedial instruction should be well organized and systematically developed for each retarded reader.

Much meaningful practice is essential if the newly learned reading skills are to be developed and maintained. Practice must minimize isolated drill and emphasize the use of these skills and abilities in a goal-oriented activity. Furthermore, it is not sufficient that the student learn about reading or be proficient in stating principles. He must be able to use reading skills automatically when he reads. All remedial instruction should be meaningful to the student, and he should know his weaknesses, the goals of instruction, and the methods by which these goals are to be achieved. In addition, he should know the purpose of each lesson and how mastery of the abilities acquired will help him to become a better reader. Students soon become bored with practice and drill for which they do not see a real purpose.

Stimulation, Information, and Guidance

The therapist should guide the student step by step, demonstrating the human interest of the parent for his child and at the same time the objective attitude of the laboratory technician. The most important principle of successful remedial teaching is motivation. The main task is to arouse within the child the drive necessary to improve his reading. Frequently, the retarded reader's previous failure has convinced him that the task is hopeless. These feelings about reading and about himself must be changed, and he must be helped to realize that improvement is possible and desirable. This can be accomplished by securing his cooperation in the diagnosis of his problem, the planning of his activities, and the evaluation of his progress. Active effort can be stimulated by using interesting materials and dramatizing progress.

Treatment involves guidance from difficulty to success. It furnishes praise and commendation whenever deserved. It accentuates the positive. It builds the child's self-concept and causes the child to feel that the therapist knows all about him and accepts him. On the other hand, treatment must be based upon hard, cold facts that have been obtained objectively and interpreted without emotional bias.

Avoidance of Frustration

Frustration and emotional set against reading should be avoided. The individual is seeking *satisfaction, security,* and *recognition,* and when these goals are threatened, frustration and emotional reactions occur. The child who is required to read materials far too difficult for him or who is expected to read again and again stories of little interest to him will learn to hate not only reading but other activities of an academic nature as well. Reading can and should provide pleasure and satisfaction. Success must be an integral part of therapy, and the retarded reader must experience success early and continuously.

Continuity of Learning

The wholeness and continuity of the instructional process in reading should be emphasized. Reading is an act of the whole organism and not merely an accumulation of specific skills. Treatment should make clear to the student that reading is a way of life and an aspect of living that begins in the home and continues throughout the life span of the normal, healthy person. Learning to read is a continuous process, and one is never too old to improve if the drive is strong and effort is sustained. No individual can learn today all that will be required of him in the years to come. As the result of research, new information and new points of view are bringing about change with which one must adjust. Continued reading and study, will aid one in maintaining effective social and economic adjustment.

PLANNING A PROGRAM FOR TREATMENT

In planning a program for scheduled treatment, the following acts should be given consideration.

Review and Restatement of Problem

Review all information provided by parents and teachers, including, if possible, clinical history and school data blanks. This reappraisal may bring the problem into sharper focus, making advisable its restatement. Hunches as to means of dealing with the child may be suggested by a review of histories and of all known data.

Careful Consideration of the Diagnosis

Review the diagnosis and the recommendations made by the reading clinician and his team of specialists. If a clinical study has not been made, the teacher or therapist can plan to meet the child's reading needs as shown by the history, observations, informal inventories, and available test data. The therapist and teacher should understand that a diagnosis can change and that it is seldom static. When new conditions are discovered and additional disabilities identified, they should be discussed immediately with the reading clinician or person in charge of the case. Treatment should be modified when necessary and aims, materials, and procedures adjusted creatively.

Planning the Schedule of Appointments

A schedule of appointments should be planned which is satisfactory to the child, his parents, and the school personnel. Time and place of meeting should be thoroughly understood. In general, thirty-minute work periods are satisfactory, and under no consideration should tutoring periods be scheduled during a time when the child's peers are scheduled for swimming, a bus trip, or an interesting film.

Planning of Treatment

Before corrective work with the child is attempted, the therapist must have a clear and concise plan of the treatment that is to be applied. She must understand exactly what is to be accomplished over the long-range period of remediation. The activities of each daily period should be planned so as to contribute to the realization of this major objective. Each day's work must become a step toward the ultimate goal. The therapist must not lose sight in her planning of the diagnosis and the treatment recommended to facilitate effective reading.

Rapport should be established at the first meeting and maintained throughout all periods of instruction and treatment. The work of each period should be wisely planned in regard to aims, materials, and procedures, yet the therapist should be ready to modify all three if the situation and needs of the child require it. The emphasis should be on aims and methods, rather than on materials which happen to be available at the time. Activities should be interesting and challenging. The child should have an opportunity to talk freely and ask questions. The therapist can observe him during his work and prepare anecdotal records reporting new and unusual forms of his behavior. Some therapists administer informal reading inventories at least twice during the semester. Emphasis is placed upon how the child responds to these inventories, rather than on levels of attainment. It is suggested that teachers and therapists confer frequently with the reading consultant or clinician who is supervising the remedial program. Just talking the problem over with a good leader helps.

Writing Adequate Reports

Parents and teachers who have referred the child for treatment are entitled to a brief, yet comprehensive report of what has been attempted and what has been accomplished. The following topics are suggestive of data to be included.

Identifying information.
Objectives of instruction.
Material utilized.
Procedures followed.
Evaluation of progress.
Recommendations.

At least one interview should be held with the child's parents. The therapist should plan in advance what she wants to accomplish and how to establish rapport. Face-to-face conferences are more effective than written communications.

SOME PERSONALITY FACTORS IN REMEDIATION

The child or adult with good mental health has been able to obtain satisfaction, security, and recognition in a manner both satisfying to himself and satisfactory to society. In general, happy, healthy parent-child relationships will contribute much toward developing a well-adjusted youth who can become a good reader. Some prophylactic suggestions are presented.

Self-acceptance

Retarded readers frequently feel inferior and insecure because of their inability to read and respond as well academically as their peers. Pressures are applied in the home by parents, on the playground by associates, and in the classroom by teachers. Frustration can, and frequently does, become so intense that unsocial acts are committed, or, on the other hand, the frustration is inhibited and concealed to the detriment of the child. In both instances, feelings of inadequacy are expanded.

Children can learn to perceive themselves as they are and put forth real effort to improve their performance. They can say, "I am as I am, and I am going to do something about it." To accomplish this objective, they will need aid from both the home and the school. Teachers and reading therapists can reduce frustration by selecting materials at the child's interest and reading levels and by relating reading activities to the child's goals. Oral reading can be eliminated until the student can, after practice, contribute both to his satisfaction and to the pleasure of his listeners. The therapist who does no more than listen sympathetically to the student as he haltingly tells of his fears and worries is encouraging a release of anxiety and tension and is contributing to catharsis. Teachers and therapists can discover what the child can do well and then assure him of success.

Parents can aid the child to accept himself by knowing all about him and by loving him just as he is. They can understand that he is seeking *satisfaction, security,* and *recognition,* and that they must aid and not retard him in the realization of these goals. Parents should learn to accept their children as they are, to aid them in achieving all they can, and not to insist on more.

Desire to Improve Competencies

The disabled reader must really want to develop and improve his reading skills. He should hunger for success. For some students to learn to read effectively, it is necessary for them to put forth and sustain effort. Taking responsibility for learning to read and study is a concomitant of purposeful living in both the home and the school and is associated with both mental and emotional maturity. It is interesting to ask, "Why did Lincoln walk 22 miles to secure a book? Why was his desire to improve his competence so strong? It is reported that he felt reading was essential to the realization of those goals which he was most anxious to achieve."

Knowing What Can Be Changed and Accepting What Cannot

As the individual becomes more emotionally mature, he discovers that he can do some things unusually well, that many of his achievements are only average, and that there are some things he cannot do with any degree of success. In the process of growing up, he realizes that he cannot have all that he may desire, and consequently he decides what he can change successfully and what he must accept without frustration and resentment. This attitude must be acquired through conditioning and education, and its inculcation is the responsibility of both parents and teachers.

Some individuals will never become good readers, nor will they become excellent students. Many such individuals have found success in other attainments and joy in what they have achieved. The teacher should recognize these underachievers in the classroom and meet their needs rather than demand that the child fit the school and all its requirements. The therapist in order to understand the child and his environment should be well oriented in the world in which the child and his parents live. Home visitations should be an integral part of the therapist's responsibilities, for a conference with parents in the home will aid in the identification of factors in the child's environment which should be understood and evaluated.

Learning to Become Involved

The activities of successful individuals possessing good mental health are generally goal oriented. These people are busily engaged in constructive work, social activities, and group participation. They are going somewhere and doing something of interest to themselves.

Alert and active children in the classroom soon discover that if they are to do what they want to accomplish, it will be necessary for them to learn to read and study effectively. If the disabled reader has a goal to achieve and is willing to become involved in its attainment, remediation becomes less difficult to achieve. Cooperation between therapist and the classroom teacher will aid in securing a common understanding of the student's goals, interests, and reading needs. This information is especially needed in the treatment of the culturally disadvantaged.

Re-evaluation of Distressing Problems

Distressing situations are not always as serious as they appear to be. On many occasions a re-evaluation of the difficulty shows that it is not as troublesome as originally assumed. The disabled reader is sensitive and easily frustrated by statements made by his teacher which he has probably misinterpreted. He is dismayed by reading errors which are insignificant in reference to the total situation, and consequently he feels rejected. Obviously, the student needs someone with whom he can discuss his worries and secure a new look at his problem. The therapist should guard against making a faulty judgment of a student and should listen sympathetically to his fears and worries. Frequently, this is more beneficial than technical help.

ILLUSTRATION OF READING PROBLEM AND SUGGESTED TREATMENT

Remediation of a reading disability consists of both diagnosis and treatment. Attention is focused upon the individual, and the therapist is concerned with the child's disability, why it developed, and means of correction. Let us examine such a problem.

PROBLEM AND RELATED FACTORS

Charles, who is in the sixth grade, is a boy of high average intelligence whose achievement in reading is far below the expected level. His parents report that they do "everything" for their son and that his mother assumes responsibility for his homework. He has difficulty in identifying and interpreting unfamiliar words. Furthermore, he has trouble in locating words in the dictionary. He has no adequate method of word attack. Charles resorts to projection as he ascribes his difficulty to his former teachers. His frustration frequently manifests itself by daydreaming and by a defiant and quarrelsome attitude. His interests are chiefly sports and music.

DIAGNOSIS

Charles is a boy of average intelligence who is not making satisfactory progress in reading chiefly because of his unwillingness to assume the responsibility of acquiring certain specific reading skills. Overindulgent parents provide the consequential factor in Charles' difficulty.

TREATMENT

It is recommended that both the home and the school reinforce by praise and commendation any attempt on Charles' part to assume responsibility.

His interests in sports and music should be utilized in stimulating an interest in reading.

Charles should be shown how to make use of contextual clues as he reads. The meaning of words determined in this manner should be verified by the use of a dictionary.

It is suggested that Mildred, whom Charles likes and admires, be assigned the responsibility of showing him how to make effective use of the dictionary and other reference materials.

The use of structural analysis should be demonstrated to Charles and to the other members of the class who are not making effective use of this method of word attack.

It is recommended that Charles' parents refrain from discussing his teachers in his hearing. Furthermore, it is suggested that they aid him in developing more responsibility for his success in the classroom and for the management of his affairs in the home.

ROLE OF LIBRARY IN TREATMENT

The use that is made of the library by teachers and students can be a measure of the effectiveness of the reading program. Books should be used for personal reading and independent study and not only for purposes of display. The classroom teacher and reading therapist should be acquainted with the shelves filled with literature for children, reference materials, and supplementary books for young students. The teacher can supplement her collections of materials on various topics which she plans on presenting to her classes by cooperation with the librarian and her staff. The reading corner can become well known to children as a place where they can go to read for enjoyment. It can be one of the most attractive places in the building, and one of the most frequently used. The reading program must develop readers who read.

ADMINISTRATOR'S ROLE IN TREATMENT

Administrators are responsible for the success of the reading program. They are acquainted with its objectives and with the entire hierarchy of reading consultants, reading clinicians, reading therapists, and classroom teachers of reading. They are familiar with the role of the school nurse, the visiting teacher, and the librarian and their contributions to the success of the reading program. They are not only acquainted with the program but also with the cost of personnel, room space, and materials.

They are also concerned with the responsibilities of effective public relations. They want to prevent parents and school personnel from developing the idea that reading specialists work only with mentally retarded and maladjusted children who are failures and dropouts. They must promote the idea that many intelligent individuals at all age levels have difficulty in reading effectively. Parents must understand that reading is more successfully taught today than at any period in the history of modern education. They must understand that reading at the present time is taught universally to all the children of all the people and not only to the elite and that learning to read for all is a lifelong process. Bringing this message to parents and the general public is one of the many responsibilities of all administrators in the field of public education.

Administrators in the school system can develop an awareness of reading maladjustment at all levels and direct an attack on the problem. Creative leadership, cognizant of what can be achieved, is required for the establishment of reading programs and corrective measures from the kindergarten through the high school. An understanding of objectives and a unification of effort are essential to an effective program.

The administrator can clarify the contributions made by the reading specialists and stress the need for cooperation between teachers and all the various specialized professional workers. Some administrators have found that an annual staff meeting with ample opportunity for discussion is appreciated by the participants.

The school administrator is responsible for the selection of well-prepared personnel. The reading specialists should not be recruited from the ranks of unsuccessful teachers from various fields. The training, personality, and experience of each candidate should be given careful consideration. Graduate study in education, psychology, and sociology should be required. A desire to help the student with a reading problem is mandatory.

SOME PROBLEMS INVOLVING TREATMENT

Directors of reading clinics, reading clinicians, and therapists along with school administrators are confronted with problems which are difficult to resolve. Some of these are briefly discussed.

Shall disabled readers be referred to summer school? In answering this question, the child, his parents, and his teachers should be considered. Much will depend on the nature of the reading program. Does it provide remediation or is it merely a review of previous instruction in reading? The student's health is frequently a factor, and consequently the family physician should be consulted. Vacation plans and the welfare of the family can be deciding factors.

Where can the reading laboratory and instructional facilities be housed? No reading program should be put into operation until adequate housing has been found. Dark basements, the teachers' lounge, and attics are being used by reading clinicians, reading therapists, and reading consultants. Clinical studies are being made in noisy, poorly heated, and inadequately ventilated quarters. In many localities remedial reading, because of this neglect and lack of consideration, is in disrepute. Some school systems are building an annex to an older structure and are supplying the rooms with new furniture, new equipment, and new books. In planning for these additions the clinician, therapist, and reading consultant along with all teachers and librarians concerned with the project should be consulted.

How large a load can the reading specialist be expected to carry? The reading clinician working with his team will need to spend approximately six hours with each child referred for study. Furthermore, interviews must be held with parents and the child's classroom teacher. The reading therapist working six hours per day should spend four hours each day with not more than twelve children per hour. The remaining two hours of the day must be spent in preparation, interviews, and conferences. It is not unusual, however, to find reading specialists attempting to perform diagnostic and remedial activities with 120 or more children in a working day of six hours. This over-loading limits the effectiveness of the program.

How can tutoring be supervised? Qualified teachers are required for tutoring. The reading clinician is generally responsible for the direction and supervision of these individuals. Tutors must be acquainted with the reading needs of those with whom they work. They will need remedial materials and suggestions on how they can be utilized. Contacts with the homeroom teacher and parents must be maintained. All such activities are the responsibility of the reading clinician. The reading consultant, when available, can supervise instruction and make valuable suggestions on the selection and use of materials. Cooperation is essential.

How can therapist and parents facilitate changes in the home? Reading problems can have their origin within the home environment. Parents, when acquainted with the difficulties of their children, are generally willing to cooperate with the teacher and therapist in helping their boys and girls remedy their disabilities in reading. To be of assistance, the therapist must be acquainted with conditions within the home and neighborhood. Some school administrators make it possible for therapists to spend from six to eight weeks of the year in home visitations and conferences with parents. These teachers become aware of the child's needs, interests, and goals. They understand his background and how it has affected him. They are sensitive to the problems of the home and in many instances are able to mitigate, if not remedy, detrimental circumstances. Many therapists find that it is as essential to work with parents as with their children. Some achieve this objective by means of seminars for parents in which mothers and fathers have an opportunity to discuss freely their children and their problems.

How can teachers and reading specialists cooperate? Classroom teachers need the aid which can be provided by reading clinicians, consultants, and therapists. On the other hand, the reading clinician and therapist are largely dependent on the teacher for information concerning the child and his performance in the classroom. Each has much to gain from the other. Aims, materials, and procedures prescribed by the clinician and utilized by the therapist should be understood and employed by the homeroom teacher as time and occasion may permit. A unification of effort is essential. As the teacher carries out the recommended treatment, she will be able to evaluate its effectiveness and the student's reaction to the various materials being employed. She may be able to suggest in a biweekly report modifications that may prove beneficial.

An evaluation of aims, materials, and procedures should be freely discussed by teacher, clinician, and therapist. Well-organized staff meetings with agenda set forth in advance can prove helpful. Teachers can provide, on request, anecdotal records of children under consideration. Reading specialists participating in the conference can outline principles resulting from research in the field which are relevant and material to the problem being investigated. Discussion should be encouraged and ample time should be provided at each meeting. No one individual should be permitted to dominate the proceedings.

Should daily records be kept of remedial instruction? Each day the therapist should prepare for the therapy session by planning and recording the aims she hopes to achieve, the materials she has selected, and the procedures she plans to follow. As soon as the therapy period has ended, she should record pertinent observations of the child's reactions, relevant inferences, and an evaluation of the effectiveness of her instruction. Any modification or deviation from the original plan should be noted. Her records should be brief.

How long should a child receive specialized instruction from a reading therapist? In general, specialized instruction by a reading therapist should continue so long as the student is making progress and until he is able to profit from instruction provided in the regular classroom. The seriousness of the child's reading problem and the expectation of success should be determining factors. The therapist's interest in a particular child should not allow her to carry on prolonged instruction which is needed much more by another student. The reactions and desires of the child receiving treatment should always be given consideration.

Have specialized procedures been devised for teaching the disabled reader? Several specialized procedures have been devised for teaching disabled readers. Some of the best known methods are those developed by Fernald, Monroe, Kephart, Frostig, Kirk, Delacato, and Gillingham.

One of the best-known methods of teaching remedial reading is the Fernald Kinesthetic Method.[1] In this approach the teacher writes the

---

[1] Grace Fernald, *Remedial Techniques in Basic School Subjects* (New York: McGraw-Hill Book Company, 1943).

word to be learned in large letters as the child watches her. The child then traces the word with his finger as he says each syllable, and later he tries to write it from memory. He compares his writing of the word with the original, and if an error has been made, he tries to learn the word again by applying the same method. The words chosen for study are those that the child wants to learn and are useful to him in describing his experiences. Consequently, words learned are frequently used in experience stories which the child writes with the help of the teacher. When the child has learned a sizable number of words, he is no longer required to trace but is instructed to write each word that he learns on a card and to file it in his word box. As soon as the child demonstrates ability to learn words without tracing them, new words are presented to him in print.

Monroe's method[2] is primarily phonetic and is designed to correct specific reading errors. Materials are selected at the level of the child's reading achievement, and the child's understanding of the materials read is checked by questions.

Kephart's methods[3] are based on the theory that slow-learning children need extended practice in perceptual-motor development. He recommends specific training activities in sensory-motor learning, ocular control, and form perception.

The Frostig Program for the Development of Visual Perception[4] provides training in five specific areas: (1) perception of position in space, (2) perception of spatial relationships, (3) perceptual constancy, (4) visual-motor coordination, and (5) figure-ground perception. The authors of this program recommend that perceptual training be provided as early as possible, preferably while the child is in kindergarten or first grade. Nevertheless, the materials can also be used in remedial programs for children at any grade level whose visual-perceptual development has been impaired.

The program consists of 359 exercises in the form of individual worksheets. Thirty-six worksheets are used to develop the child's ability to recognize the form and directionality of figures and char-

[2] Marion Monroe, *Children Who Cannot Read* (Chicago: University of Chicago Press, 1932).

[3] Newell C. Kephart, *The Slow Learner in the Classroom* (Columbus, Ohio: Charles E. Merrill Books, Inc., 1960).

[4] Marianne Frostig and David Horne, *The Frostig Program for the Development of Visual Perception* (Chicago: Follett Publishing Company, 1964).

acters. Another set, consisting of eighty-five worksheets, is designed to develop ability to perceive positional relationships between various objects, for example, the order of letters in a word or the arrangement of material on a page. Perceptual constancy is developed by means of seventy worksheets which provide practice in perceiving and identifying forms regardless of differences in size, color, position, background, or angle of viewing. The skill of visual-motor coordination is developed through practice in such specific areas as tracing, drawing from point to point, completing patterns, and duplicating patterns and figures. Visual and kinesthetic methods are employed. The purpose of the seventy-eight worksheets involving figure-ground perception is to develop the child's facility in reading without running words together. The total program provides step-by-step training from the simplest activities of discriminating body position through complex problems involving perception, identification, and creative thinking.

Samuel Kirk[5] recommends a reading program which stresses phonics. In this approach much drill is provided, accompanied by repeated associations of objects with sounds. The child says a new sound, writes it, and uses it in words with other sounds he has learned.

Delacato's approach[6] to reading maladjustment is based on the concept that children who have problems with reading have been either traumatized or deprived environmentally, resulting in a lack of complete neurological organization. He maintains that the diagnosis of a reading problem must include an evaluation of the state of neurological organization and that treatment must involve the development of the nervous system if the reading problem is to be eliminated.

Another specialized method developed by Gillingham[7] is based on the work of Orton. In this approach no words are taught by sight. Instead, the first principle is to teach the sounds of the letters and then to build these letter sounds into words. The Gillingham technique is based on the close association of visual, auditory, and kinesthetic elements. Each new phonogram is taught by associations between "visual, auditory and kinesthetic records on the brain." The core of

[5] Samuel A. Kirk, *Teaching Reading to Slow-Learning Children* (Boston: Houghton Mifflin Co., 1940).

[6] Carl H. Delacato, *The Treatment and Prevention of Reading Problems* (Springfield, Ill.: Charles C Thomas, 1963).

[7] Anna Gillingham and Bessie W. Stillman, *Remedial Training for Children with Specific Disability in Reading, Spelling, and Penmanship* (Cambridge, Mass.: Educators Publishing Service, Inc., 1965).

this alphabetic approach is to establish the concept of words as built out of phonetic units.

All the procedures just described have reportedly been used successfully. Nevertheless, the therapist should remember that in general the methods which are most effective with disabled readers are the same as those recommended for other boys and girls. The reader should be reminded that no one approach to remediation can be equally effective for all children.

Is remedial reading instruction effective? Remediation is not always effective. Failure may be due to the therapist, the student, or the classroom teacher. A faulty diagnosis may have been made, and inadequate treatment may have been applied. The student may not have been willing to put forth and sustain effort, and the classroom teacher may not have provided sufficient guidance after the student was dismissed from therapy. Treatment may have been discontinued too soon. Balow[8] reports that long-term rather than short-term treatment produces unusually satisfactory results for the severely retarded reader. He states that "severe reading disability is probably best considered a relatively chronic illness needing long-term treatment rather than the short course typically organized in current programs." In any remedial program it is essential that the clinician, therapist, and classroom teacher cooperate in helping the child adjust to the regular classroom work. Follow-up programs and evaluation studies should be a regular part of the reading therapist's responsibilities.

How can coordination of various specialists be accomplished? In some school systems there are, in addition to specialists in reading, other professional workers, such as the school psychologist, the nurse, the visiting teacher, and the speech therapist. In many instances, the disabled reader is brought in contact with several specialists, each of whom works independently and remains unaware of what has been achieved by others. There is in many cases not only a duplication of effort but a confusion of treatment. The child is troubled and parents are at a loss to determine what is taking place.

Coordination of effort and a pooling of information is necessary for successful treatment. This can be accomplished by a team approach to the whole problem of maladjustment and by a central index in which

---

[8] Bruce Balow, "The Long-Term Effect of Remedial Reading Instruction," *The Reading Teacher,* **18** (April, 1965), 581–586.

all clinical and educational data related to the disabled reader are filed and kept securely by a mature and competent secretary.

Members of the clinical team can work under the guidance of a consulting psychologist or they may wish to select from their number a temporary chairman who serves for one year. Such a plan can bring about a unity of effort without confusion and misunderstanding.

How can reading specialists be secured? Reading consultants, clinicians, and therapists are not easily secured as staff members. If one is found, his salary may exceed by far the funds available. Consequently, some school systems select from their staffs keen, alert young men and women who are excellent teachers interested in reading and desirous of doing graduate work in the field. These teachers are encouraged to prepare themselves for specialized careers in reading and at the same time remain on the staff.

SUMMARY

Treatment is designed to remedy, cure, or mitigate a disability. In remediation of the disabled reader, it should consist simultaneously of both instruction and therapy, and it must be a direct response to a diagnostic study of the individual. It may be general, specific, palliative, or preventive. In this chapter several principles involving treatment and the planning of a program for the disabled reader have been outlined. In providing for remediation in reading, some personality factors have been discussed. Several critical problems confronting school administrators have been brought to the attention of the reader. Remediation of reading disabilities is but a part of a whole school program devoted to the development of readers who read and enjoy books.

GUIDED ACTIVITY 10

Aim

To review factors involved in treatment.

Materials

1. Chapter 3 of the text, *Diagnosis and Treatment of the Disabled Reader.*
2. Chapter 9 of the same book.

Procedure

1. Reread Chapters 3 and 9 of this book, keeping in mind diagnosis and treatment at levels three and four.
2. Show where, in Chapter 3, instruction was employed as treatment.
3. Show where, in Chapter 3, treatment was general and where it was specific.
4. What palliative treatment was recommended in Chapter 3?
5. What examples of preventive treatment can you find in Chapter 9?
6. How would you differentiate treatment and remediation?
7. Show how diagnosis and treatment are reciprocals.
8. In Chapter 9 what examples of specific treatment do you find?
9. What are the dangers of permitting materials to determine techniques and methods?
10. Show how aims and objectives of treatment are determined.
11. In Chapter 9 how was remediation evaluated?

QUESTIONS AND REFERENCES

Questions

1. How can remedial instruction in reading be carried on in the classroom?

2. What criteria should be used for selecting materials and instruments for corrective reading?

3. What has been accomplished during five decades of remedial reading?

References

1. Miles A. Tinker and Constance M. McCullough, *Teaching Elementary Reading*, 3rd ed. (New York: Appleton-Century-Crofts, 1968), Chap. 26.

2. A. Sterl Artley, "Criteria for Selecting Materials and Instruments for Corrective Reading," in Leo M. Schell and Paul C. Burns, eds. *Remedial Reading, An Anthology of Sources* (Boston: Allyn and Bacon, 1968), pp. 348–354.

3. Albert J. Harris, "Five Decades of Remedial Reading," *Forging Ahead in Reading* (Newark, Del.: International Reading Association Conference Proceedings, 1968), pp. 25–34.

Questions

References

4. Where can one find some helpful suggestions on the organization and administration of a
remedial reading program?

4. Leo M. Schell and Paul C.
Burns, *Remedial Reading, An
Anthology of Sources* (Boston:
Allyn and Bacon, 1968), pp.
377–420.

5. What are some basic principles
of remedial instruction?

5. Guy L. Bond and Miles A.
Tinker, "Basic Principles of
Remedial Instruction," in Del-
wyn G. Schubert and Theodore
L. Torgerson, eds., *Readings in
Reading: Practice, Theory, Re-
search* (New York: Thomas Y.
Crowell Company, 1968), pp.
372–397.

6. What are the remedial implications of dyslexia?

6. N. Dale Bryant, "Characteristics
of Dyslexia and Their Remedial
Implications," in William K.
Durr, ed., *Reading Instruction,
Dimensions and Issues* (Boston:
Houghton Mifflin, 1967), pp.
344–349.

7. How can psychotherapy be
combined with remedial reading?

7. Charles C. Dahlberg, Florence
Roswell, and Jeanne Chall,
"Psychotherapeutic Principles as
Applied to Remedial Reading,"
in Oscar S. Causey, ed., *The
Reading Teacher's Reader*
(New York: The Ronald Press,
1958), pp. 280–285.

8. How can the teacher make use
of bibliotherapy?

8. Caroline Shrodes, "Bibliotherapy," in Oscar S. Causey, ed.,
The Reading Teacher's Reader
(New York: The Ronald Press,
1958), pp. 285–289.

9. How can instruction be employed as treatment of reading
disabilities?

9. Homer L. J. Carter and Dorothy
J. McGinnis, *Teaching Indi-
viduals to Read* (Boston: D.C.
Heath and Company, 1962),
Chaps. 3–8.

10. How can remediation be initiated?

10. Robert M. Wilson, *Diagnostic
and Remedial Reading* (Colum-

Questions	References
	bus, Ohio: Charles E. Merrill Books, 1967), Chap. 5.
11. How can perceptual difficulties be overcome?	11. Newell C. Kephart, *The Slow Learner in the Classroom* (Columbus, Ohio: Charles E. Merrill Books, 1960), Chaps. 7, 8, 9, and 10.

Chapter 11

Treatment of Children with Orientation Difficulties

Some disabled readers have difficulty in following lines of print. They often lose their place while reading, habitually omit words, and frequently show evidence of reversals and letter confusions. These symptoms appear to be related, in that faulty perception of word form and directional sense may be involved. This chapter considers some causal factors of defective form perception and an inadequate directional sense. A psychological basis for perception is outlined and related to remediation. Several techniques involving treatment are suggested.

PSYCHOLOGICAL BASIS FOR PERCEPTION

Perception, according to Gestalt psychology, is an act of the total organism which results from excitation of sensory receptors and interpretation in terms of the experiential background of the organism. Perception is a fusion of mental content which has sensory data as its core. It is sensation in a context of experiences that provides meaning. Some psychologists, however, doubt that perception refers to an act having scientific unity or coherence. These individuals avoid the use of the term entirely. In this chapter, perception is considered to be a psychological process whereby a sensation gains meaning through the organization and integration of experiential background historically called mental content.

Perceptions are unique and personal and consequently cannot be completely shared with others. A farmer, for example, sees an oak tree in his field and bemoans the fact that he has had to work around it for twenty years. An artist sees this tree and, admiring its beauty, plans to use it as a theme in a picture. A lumberman sees the tree and considers the number of feet of lumber it would provide. The woodman, seeing the tree, methodically calculates the cords of fireplace wood it would furnish. Two lovers, after an absence of several years, return to "their tree" and find again their initials. The stimulus *tree* was constant. The perception varied with each observer. In the field of reading, visual, auditory, kinesthetic, and tactual sensations are utilized in the process of instruction. Obviously, when given the same stimulus no two children will see, hear, and feel the same. Gestalt theory claims that sensations as such cannot be independent units. Instead they are part of a unified whole.

The perception of a tree by a young child differs from that of an older individual. Experiential background and mental content increase with maturity. In the growing organism, organization and integration develop from the simple to the more complex but always with a wholeness and relatedness of parts to parts and figure to ground. In the perception of a simple object such as ::, visual sensation is interpreted in terms of mental content. The observer may report that he sees four dots or he may say that he sees a square. His perception is dependent on his previous experience. In both instances, visual sensation is figure upon ground, and perception may be of four dots or squareness. There is a constancy of relationship between stimulus (::) and mental content and not between stimulus (::) and the end product, perception. The gestalt of an object depends on many things other than stimulation. The sum of the factors that make up the perceptual field are, when taken together, the total configuration.

Perception involves integration of previously understood "parts" into a new "whole." This integration is creative and is more than the summation of parts. Water, for example, has properties other than those of hydrogen and oxygen, its constituent parts. The ability to integrate parts into wholes is determined by the quantitative and qualitative aspects of mental content and the effectiveness of the total organism. Many children have difficulty in learning to identify the elements in a perceptual impression and to integrate them into a form. These children may be unable to differentiate between two figures such as a square and a triangle seen together unless they count the corners.

In order to copy a square the child must organize the figure on a ground and differentiate all the essential qualities of the figure. This ability is necessary in the identification of word forms. Many young or mentally immature children have difficulty in differentiating elements from the mass. They cannot attend to the details, and consequently these details are not recognized. Many other individuals become lost in details and fail to integrate parts into a usable form. They fail to react to the totality, or "whole," and respond only to disorganized minutiae or "parts." In the sentence, "Se eDi ckan dJa ne," it may be difficult for the reader to organize and integrate the parts into the whole, "See Dick and Jane." The process is more difficult for some than for others. Similar reactions are observed in dealing with students as they attempt to read paragraphs, chapters, and even longer thought units. Inadequate perception is involved.

PERCEPTION OF FORM AND DIRECTION

Children showing difficulties of form perception are frequently unable to react to words as a unified whole. Monroe[1] has shown that these children try to identify word patterns by tracing them with the finger and that their reading errors consist of omissions of sounds and words with consequential vowel and consonant errors. Faulty orientation of letters are frequently observed. Children may confuse, for example, *b, d; p, q; was, saw; no, on.* Orton[2] has labeled this *strephosymbolia,* or twisted symbols. Some individuals, even adults, have difficulty in the perception of the temporal sequence of sounds. For example, *economy* may be pronounced and spelled *ecomony.* Some children have difficulty in following a line of print from left to right. Others may skip whole lines and repeatedly lose their place. It is

[1] Marion Monroe, *Children Who Cannot Read* (Chicago: University of Chicago Press, 1932), p. 106.
[2] Samuel Orton, "Specific Reading Disability—Strephosymbolia," *Journal of the American Medical Association,* XC (1928), Part II, 1095–1099.

obvious, then, that faulty perception of word form and directional confusion can be causal factors affecting reading maladjustment.

Faulty perception may be due to inadequate experiential background, faulty teaching methods, and factors within the organism. All loci need investigation. Faulty perception is a phenomenon common to all individuals who are adjusting to new situations. It is possible that in a majority of instances experiential background and mental content are the critical factors. The student, for example, who pronounces and spells *economy* as *ecomony* probably has not taken a course in economics, which is labeled "Econ" by the students. Neither has he studied the origin of the word—*oikos* meaning "house" and *nomos* meaning "manager." Furthermore, he is not familiar with the Latin word, *economus,* meaning *steward.* In brief, his experiential background is inadequate for the correct pronunciation and spelling of the unfamiliar word *economy.*

Confusion of left-right directions is related to perceptual disorder in the recognition of words. To the very young child, there is no left and right, up and down. He has not yet learned to make the center of his body the point of reference for determining directions. Even with some adults a quick command to turn left will bring the opposite response. Under emotional stress the confusion still exists. The old experiential patterns have interfered under stress with the new and sudden demands of the situation. This, in some instances, causes difficulty in sensing the temporal sequence of speech sounds and difficulty in coordinating these sequences of sound with left to right direction in words. Many adults have this perceptual disorder.

Children who confuse *b* and *d, saw* and *was* have perceptual difficulties that can be explained as an inability to integrate parts into meaningful wholes. In the perception of both *b* and *d*, a coordination of visual and kinesthetic imagery is involved. Without doubt, the child is familiar with the drawing of a vertical line and of a circle. This imagery has been established and is a part of his past experience. His immediate difficulty is one of integration, that is, to understand when the circle is supposed to be at the bottom of the line on the left side (d) and when it should be at the bottom of the line on the right side (b). This inability to perceive and discriminate *b* and *d* and to write *b* and *d* can be due to inability to shift figure-ground relationships. This assumption may not be true in all instances.

One of the most reasonable explanations of perceptual difficulties is set forth by Kephart.[3] He shows that integration of simultaneous inputs and of past and present experiences are essential to perception. This concept emphasizes what takes place between stimulus and response, that is, the integration of the new with the old. In other words, the child fails to perceive the new because his experiential background has been quite inadequate.

Faulty teaching methods, such as a marked emphasis upon word endings, can cause perceptual errors. The use of initial sounds and especially consonants, as suggested by Dolch,[4] is recommended by experienced therapists. They reject, however, the practice of teaching word endings such as those found in *make, cake, bake.* Young children enjoy and recall rhymes, and it is easy for them to remember the endings and not the initial consonant sound. An overemphasis on word endings can encourage the child to look from the familiar to the unfamiliar in a word or, in this case, from right to left. This reaction, common with many children, can actually develop reversal errors.

The premature introduction of many new words can cause perceptual difficulties among children who are beginning to read. The tense and hurried examination of the beginnings and endings of unfamiliar words can interfere with directional movements from left to right. Consequently, the child may fail to integrate word parts and to experience success. Words may be reversed and meaning confused or lost entirely.

Phonetic analysis of words, if introduced before the child has attained a degree of readiness, may cause perceptual difficulties. An unfamiliar word, for example, may be identified and even correctly pronounced and yet be worthless to the child because he is unable to fit it into the context. Perception has not taken place. Furthermore, the child may have been taught, for example, "When a one-syllable word contains two vowels, one of which is the final *e*, the first vowel is usually long and the final *e* is silent, as in the words *fate* and *pine*." Consequently, he looks at the final *e* and then back to the vowel and establishes the fact that the vowel is long. This back-and-forth eye movement can lead to faulty habits of word perception.

There are conditions within the body which can adversely affect

[3] Newell C. Kephart, *The Slow Learner in the Classroom* (Columbus, Ohio: Charles E. Merrill Books, Inc., 1960), Chap. 4.

[4] Edward W. Dolch, *Teaching Primary Reading*, 2nd ed. (Champaign, Ill.: Garrard Press, 1950).

perception. Any sensory disturbance, lesions in the brain and nervous system, along with developmental lags, and any impairment of physical function can retard and affect the efficiency of the whole organism. There is evidence, for example, that perceptual difficulties are related to visual defects. This too is a reasonable assumption, for any unclear word form can cause faulty perception. Defects of fusion, astigmatism, hyperopia, and myopia are commonly found in the examinations of school children. It is suggested that in any diagnostic study of the disabled reader medical and physical factors be given preference at the time of investigation over psychological, sociological, and educational data relating to the individual.

REMEDIATION OF PERCEPTUAL DIFFICULTIES

Perceptual difficulties have been of special interest to many authorities in the field of reading. As a result, several specific techniques for remediation have been suggested.

Inability to Follow Lines of Print

Studies of eye movement during reading indicate faulty directional habits of individuals who show the following symptoms: repetition of words, omission of words, transposition of words, skipping lines of print, jerky oral reading. The child's inability to follow a line of print from left to right can be due chiefly to a lack of adequate experiential background. There may have been little in his previous experience to prepare him for this new and, for him, unusual situation. His concepts of up and down, left and right may have been inadequately developed. Inaccurate responses may have been reinforced and faulty habits may have been acquired. Relearning must take place and new habits must be established. When children begin to read, they should be taught proper directional orientation. They should be shown that words are to be observed from left to right and lines of print are to be read from left to right. These directional habits must become firmly established.

To the young child there is no right or left, up or down in objective space, nor are there clues to these directions until a point of reference has been established. Some children learn early to establish coordinates centered in the body and extended into space. Others fail to make this differentiation until they are much older. Children can be taught to identify their right hand and their left hand and to perceive that some objects are on their right side and that other objects are on their left side. This can be taught incidentally at home and at school by means of plays and games. Alert teachers can make use of many opportunities to stress left-to-right sequences in the classroom. An important task is to insure a transfer of this left-to-right orientation to the reading of written and printed materials.

In providing treatment for disabled readers who demonstrate directional confusion, it is suggested that the chalkboard training outlined by Kephart[5] be given careful consideration. He describes training activities which are designed to strengthen perceptual-motor development. These activities involve scribbling, finger painting, the dot game, the clock game, chalkboard orientation exercises, and the drawing and copying of geometrical figures.

Faulty perception of direction may be further modified by the following means.

- Oral reading of experience charts with sweeping movement of pointer from left to right. Integration of ideas is essential and will be manifest by fluency of reading.
- Choral reading so as to develop perception and expression of ideas from left to right. The chorus of voices accentuates the left-to-right flow of ideas.
- Encouragement of child to type sentences which he has composed. This activity is of interest to the child and develops left-to-right movement.
- Tachistoscopic exercises making use of words, phrases, and short sentences. The teacher can show the child where to focus his eyes on the screen or chalkboard. She can explain that he should look at the word, phrase, or sentence from left to right, trying to get an "eyeful" at each exposure.
- Reinforcement of desired response by praise and commendation.

Faulty Perception of Words

Reversals are common among individuals at all ages and especially among severely retarded readers. They are symptoms of an inadequate

[5] Newell C. Kephart, *The Slow Learner in the Classroom* (Columbus, Ohio: Charles E. Merrill Books, Inc., 1960), Chap. 7.

experiential background and of severe eye defects in some instances; in many situations they have been intensified by improper phonetic instruction and structural analysis techniques. Spache[6] boldly states that reversals do not cause poor reading, nor are they even related to it. He says, "They are a universal phenomenon present among learners of all ages who are attacking a new and strange group of symbols. Reversals are not related to handedness or eyedness or cerebral dominance, nor are they indicative of laterality or visual handicaps." According to Spache, they indicate only that the individual is unfamiliar with the particular symbols he is trying to learn. Obviously not all students concerned with remediation of disabled readers agree with this statement. There is, however, little evidence, recently produced, which can substantiate their conflicting points of view.

Reversal tendencies are symptoms which, in cases of severely retarded readers, should be investigated. Treatment, following diagnosis, should not be too difficult to apply. Some practical suggestions for teacher and therapist are explained.

A Visual, Auditory, Kinesthetic, and Tactual approach[7] to word study has been found to be helpful. The following sequence is recommended.

1. Look at the word from beginning to ending. The analysis of elements within words should be restricted to those prefixes, roots, inflectional endings, and suffixes which convey direct meaning.
2. Pronounce the word silently, being sure to associate each syllable with its corresponding sound and being certain that the proper sequence of syllables is maintained.
3. Spell the word silently, paying careful attention to each syllable.
4. Trace the word with index finger.
5. Write the word.
6. Compare the word written with the word selected for study.
7. Repeat this process until the word can be spelled and written correctly.

Words taught in this manner should be used in context. For example,

[6] George D. Spache, "Factors Which Produce Defective Reading," *Corrective Reading in Classroom and Clinic.* Supplementary Educational Monographs, No. 79 (1953), pp. 50–51.

[7] Homer L. J. Carter and Dorothy J. McGinnis, *Teaching Individuals to Read* (Boston: D. C. Heath and Company, 1962), p. 97.

the word *mother* may have been taught and a flashcard containing the word prepared. The teacher can ask, "Does your ———— make gingerbread?" At the proper time in asking the question, the word *mother* can be shown and the child would be expected to answer, "Yes, my *mother* makes gingerbread."

Monroe[8] has suggested a combined phonetic and sounding-tracing procedure which many therapists have found to be effective. Her approach to word study is illustrated as follows: The word *man* is written in large handwriting on a piece of paper. The child is asked to look at the word and is told that the word is *man*. He is then asked to say *man*. He is asked again to say *man* as slowly as he can. He is asked then to take his pencil and trace over the word while saying *man* slowly and deliberately. He is encouraged to trace rapidly and to speak slowly so that tracing and speaking end at the same time. The purpose of these acts is to establish firmly the sequence of sounds. Later the child is taught to glide the voice from one sound to the next in order to pronounce the word as an integrated whole.

As a variation of this tracing method a sound-dictation technique can be substituted. The child is asked to write words as the teacher dictates the sounds and then reread those dictated. Monroe[9] points out that the writing is as beneficial as the tracing and that some children like to write better than to trace. The words are presented to the child in the following sequence.

1. The teacher says to the child in preparation for the teaching of words, "These words are all short a words."
2. The word *man* is pronounced by the teacher.
3. It is then said slowly so that the child can hear the separate sounds.
4. The child then says the word slowly as he writes the letters of each sound. For example, *man*, m-ă-n.

Some additional suggestions for teacher and therapist are listed.

• Games with anagrams. This activity is of interest to young children, and it has been found effective. The child is given a box of letters and is encouraged to reproduce words, phrases, and short sentences which have been written on the chalkboard.

---

[8] Marion Monroe, *Children Who Cannot Read* (Chicago: The University of Chicago Press, 1932), pp. 120–121.
[9] *Ibid.*, p. 123.

- Encouragement of child to write or print words, phrases, and short sentences on chalkboard.
- Use of dictionary. It can be helpful in establishing a left-to-right habit pattern. The student can be taught to use the guide words at the top of columns and pages. Even young children who construct picture dictionaries have an opportunity to acquire alphabetizing skills.
- Alphabetizing. Words selected from context and learned by the child can be correctly filed in his word box according to the arrangement and sequence of letters in each word.
- Typing of words. This activity can develop proper orientation in word perception.
- Word beginnings. At all times stress should be placed upon word beginnings rather than word endings.
- Awareness of errors. Help the child to perceive the *kind* of errors he is making. For example, the stimulus word is *left* and the child's response is *felt*. The student should compare the two words. He should be taught to look at the beginning consonant and then at the remaining letters as he says the stimulus word aloud.
- Avoidance of undue stress. The teacher and reading therapist are cautioned against an overemphasis on the correction of reversal errors. This correction should not be made at the expense of the total instructional program.
- Avoidance of analytic techniques. An overemphasis on phonetic and structural analysis before the child is sufficiently mature may accentuate reversal tendencies.
- Visual examination. A possibility of visual abnormality should be investigated by an ophthalmologist.

Loss of Place and Omission of Words

Some children habitually lose their place while reading. They skip lines and words, and their reading errors consist of omission of words, omission of sounds, reversals, and repetitions. Their perception of what is on the printed page is impaired. Monroe[10] suggests that lack of

---

[10] Marion Monroe, *Children Who Cannot Read* (Chicago: The University of Chicago Press, 1932), pp. 107–108.

precision in the motor control of the eyes may be a causal factor. Some individuals who frequently lose their place are aware of having made an error while others are unconscious of what they have done. Lack of attention, which can be related to faulty perception, can be a significant factor. An early emphasis upon rate of reading should be avoided by the teacher. Treatment, following careful diagnosis, may be facilitated by these suggestions.

- Exclude the possibility of an ocular difficulty with an examination by an ophthalmologist.
- Permit children who habitually lose their place to use a liner. This crutch should be cast aside as soon as possible.
- Make the child aware that he frequently omits words and loses his place by the use of a tape recording of his reading performance. This can be accomplished by having the child listen to his recording as he silently reads the text.
- Encourage the child to *want* to improve his reading achievement. Knowledge of the success he is making can help.
- Emphasize flexibility of reading rate and not speed. Encourage a slower rate of reading until accuracy is obtained. Some children believe that the good reader reads rapidly, consequently, they hurry and make errors they would not make if they read with greater deliberation. It is the responsibility of the therapist to change, if possible, this attitude on the part of many individuals.
- Motivate the child so as to increase attention by asking questions and by having the child read carefully for specific answers. The sequence of ideas expressed in the text should be maintained.
- Demonstrate to the child the progress he is making by means of a graph. This can be shown by the increment of correct responses. Let the child know that he is succeeding.

SUMMARY

The treatment of children showing perceptual difficulties in reading has been discussed. A psychological basis for perception has been outlined and related to remediation. Techniques designed to remedy faulty perception of words, reversal errors, loss of place while reading, and omission of words have been suggested. It has been pointed out that perception results from the activities of the organism, and consequently sensory-motor factors should be given consideration in both diagnosis and treatment.

GUIDED ACTIVITY 11

Aim

To treat children with orientation difficulties.

Materials

1. Tape recorder.
2. Tagboard for making 4- by 15-in. word cards.
3. Felt pen.

Procedure

1. Select a child in the elementary grades who has shown a marked tendency to make reversals.
2. Choose three words which the child has recently reversed. Write each word on a 4- by 15-in. card.
3. Teach these three words, using the visual-auditory-kinesthetic-tactual approach described in this chapter. Observe the child's reactions carefully.
4. State briefly your interpretation of his difficulty and summarize the results of your work.
5. Select a child who loses his place while reading or who omits words.
6. Make a tape recording of the child as he reads material at his instructional level in reading.
7. Help the child to become aware of his tendency to omit words or lose his place while reading by playing the recording and permitting him to identify his reading errors.
8. Discuss these errors with the child and listen to his explanation of why he made them.
9. Apply, when working with the child, some of the suggestions made in this chapter.
10. Summarize briefly the results of your work with the child.

QUESTIONS AND REFERENCES

Questions

References

1. How is form perception related to learning?

2. How are form perception and directional sense related to reading?

3. How can orientation difficulties be treated?

4. How can the therapist make use of imagery in treating children having reversal tendencies?

5. How can words be taught?

6. How can orientation difficulties be treated in classroom and clinic?

7. What factors produce defective readers?

8. How can sensory-motor training be provided?

1. Newell C. Kephart, *The Slow Learner in the Classroom* (Columbus, Ohio: Charles E. Merrill Books, 1960), pp. 30–31, 62, and 76–87.

2. Arthur L. Benton, "Dyslexia in Relation to Form Perception and Directional Sense," in John Money, ed., *Reading Disability* (Baltimore: The Johns Hopkins Press, 1962), Chap. 6.

3. Guy L. Bond and Miles A. Tinker, *Reading Difficulties, Their Diagnosis and Correction,* 2nd ed. (New York: Appleton-Century-Crofts, 1967), Chap. 13.

4. Homer L. J. Carter and Dorothy J. McGinnis, *Teaching Individuals to Read* (Boston: D. C. Heath and Company, 1962), pp. 97–98.

5. *Ibid.*, Chap. 5.

6. Robert M. Wilson, *Diagnostic and Remedial Reading* (Columbus, Ohio: Charles E. Merrill Books, 1967), Chap. 6.

7. George D. Spache, "Factors Which Produce Defective Reading," *Corrective Reading in Classroom and Clinic.* Supplementary Educational Monographs, No. 79, The University of Chicago (1953), pp. 49–57.

8. Newell C. Kephart, *The Slow Learner in the Classroom* (Columbus, Ohio: Charles E. Merrill Books, 1960), Chap. 8.

Chapter 12

Treatment of Children with Vocabulary Disabilities

Adequate sight vocabularies and effective word-attack skills are essential to effective reading. The study of words, the symbols of thought, is mandatory if the individual is to read, live, and adjust in the modern world. This chapter is primarily concerned with the remediation of specific difficulties of word perception generally called word recognition. Techniques and materials for treatment will be suggested. Their application, which can be made in a variety of ways, is left to the discretion and creativity of the therapist.

INADEQUATE SIGHT VOCABULARIES

Words which the child can quickly identify, pronounce, and understand make up his sight vocabulary. These words are like funds in the bank which are immediately available upon call for instant use. Some individuals, however, have a limited source from which to draw as they attempt to read sentences, paragraphs, and even larger thought units. A child with an inadequate sight vocabulary may show many of the following characteristics.

- He needs to be told words.
- He is a word-by-word reader.

- He attempts to "sound out" words previously "read" correctly and those with which he is acquainted.
- He makes even more errors on small common words than on polysyllabic words.
- He may know a word in one situation but not in another.
- He may make the same percentage of word errors at his independent reading level as he does at his instructional level.
- He may be able to pronounce the word but may fail to associate it with the correct meaning.

Sight vocabulary can be easily measured by tachistoscopic devices, for it can generally be assumed that if the child makes a greater number of word errors when the device is used than he does when viewing the same words for longer periods of time, he may have an inadequate sight vocabulary.

Sight vocabularies do not just happen but instead are built up by word study which consists of learning to associate meaning with word symbols and of developing techniques with which to identify new words with ease and effectiveness. The study of words should be a selective process, for not all words in the language need to become a part of one's vocabulary. It appears reasonable to assume that *need* and the necessity for *use* should determine what words should be studied. In the reading of a story or textbook the unknown words are the ones that demand attention. Some reading therapists, with the aid of the student, identify the unfamiliar words in a selection and introduce them by discussing their meaning and using them in sentences. Then the material is read silently by the child in response to guiding questions asked by the therapist.

Treatment designed for increasing the sight vocabulary of a disabled reader may be applied in the following manner.

- Develop and enhance the child's experiential background for the meaning of words comes from the organism and not from the printed page. The child can be prepared for his experience of reading. Concepts can be developed and background can be established by discussion. *The Peabody Language Development Kits*[1] contain 180 lessons in language development; their use is suggested.

[1] Refer to Appendix C.

- Make use of experience charts to establish a sight vocabulary of 150 to 300 words. This can be done in groups of three to twelve children. The use of experience charts provides the child practice in auditory perception and in pronunciation as he learns the visual forms of words which are meaningful to him. Experience records can be used successfully with disabled readers at all age levels.
- Utilize interesting materials at a level of difficulty which is easy for the child to read with pleasure and satisfaction.
- Make use of or construct exercises which will encourage the child to view words *rapidly* rather than inspect them in a detailed manner. The use of a tachistoscope can be helpful.
- Make use of *The Merrill Linguistic Readers*[2] if the child misses small, similar words.
- Teach abstract words in context. For example, "The boy *then* went to the car." This sentence can be written on the chalkboard and the word *then* enclosed in a box or plainly designated by colored chalk.
- Utilize the Dolch Games[3] in developing mastery of sight words.
- Encourage the child to prepare and maintain a card file of words he has recently added to his vocabulary. Emphasize the importance of meaning, pronunciation, and use in a sentence. Overlearning can be helpful.
- Utilize novel and interesting materials which introduce new words gradually and repeat them at carefully spaced intervals. New basic readers are helpful in developing sight vocabularies.

INABILITY TO USE MEANING CLUES

Rightly used as a reasoning process, meaning clues can facilitate word recognition. The reader who makes use of the context is apt to recognize an unfamiliar word with ease, and consequently the selection of the appropriate meaning is facilitated. Meaning clues can be useful as determinants of the adequacy of definitions found in a dictionary and as a means of evaluating meaning derived from other word recognition techniques. Some anticipatory and contextual clues are illustrated.

[2] *Ibid.*
[3] *Ibid.*

- An unknown word may be defined in the context. *Example:* "The reading therapist used a *tachistoscope* to expose groups of words for short periods of time."
- The clue can consist of a known synonym for the unfamiliar word. *Example:* "He was an *inveterate* or habitual smoker."
- Mature readers may depend upon their experience and mental content to supply the meaning of a new word. *Example:* "During his devotions the priest reads the *collect* for the day."
- The meaning clue may consist of a comparison or contrast of the unknown word with a well-known word. *Example:* "The old woman, usually *taciturn,* became talkative."
- The clue may consist of an association of the unfamiliar word with a familiar expression which is a part of the reader's language pattern. *Example:* "Necessity is the mother of *invention.*"
- The clue to the unknown word may be a summary of the ideas which precede it. *Example:* "It was observed that John frequently called *saw, was; no, on;* and confused *d* and *b.* This reaction may be called *strephosymbolia.*"
- The clue may be a reflection of a situation or mood, for in some instances the general tone of a series of ideas suggests the meaning of an unfamiliar word. *Example:* "The teacher set forth her plan, and the children listened with anticipation. They nodded their heads and smiled in apparent agreement. It was obvious that they would *acquiesce.*"

Skill in using meaning clues along with word-recognition techniques is essential if an adequate identification, interpretation, and evaluation of the printed symbol is to be made. The student should understand, however, that the use of meaning clues is not always sufficient. In many instances he should resort to the dictionary to determine the best possible meaning.

Treatment of the individual's inability to use anticipatory and contextual clues can be facilitated by means of the following suggestions.

- Demonstrate to the student the importance of his experiential background and his mental content. Show him how to make use of his knowledge of a subject as an aid to word recognition.
- Develop a readiness for reading a story, acquiring information on a new topic, and studying a new text. Readiness is an essential factor in reading any subject at any level.

- Show the student the value of pictures, drawings, charts, graphs, and tables in making effective use of meaning and contextual clues.
- Select materials of such a level of difficulty that only 2 or 3 per cent of the words are unknown. Encourage the student to read for detail and a thorough understanding. Such activities will accentuate the importance of contextual clues in the search for meaning.
- Encourage the more mature student to scan various writing styles in several subject matter fields so as to identify anticipatory and contextual clues. These can be listed and discussed.
- Consult the teacher's manual of the basal series which the child is using for suggestions concerning use of contextual clues in that series of books.
- Utilize the ideas and the materials suggested in *Using the Context*, Specific Skills Series,[4] which can be employed at elementary and intermediate levels. Here the child must relate the whole to parts and the parts to the whole.

INABILITY TO ASSOCIATE MEANING WITH PRINTED SYMBOLS

Meaning is an essential element in word recognition. Some children and adults will pronounce a word correctly and yet be unable to interpret and evaluate its meaning. Generally this is due to a lack of experiential background which can give meaning to the symbol. A child, for example, may say or recite the word *temptation* without any real knowledge of its meaning or application. The term may even be a part of his listening vocabulary and yet be of little significance to him. Meaning is dependent upon the mental content of the reader.

In providing treatment for children who have difficulty in associating meaning with printed symbols the acts of perception should be at all times in a meaningful setting. The word form must become a part of the individual's experiential background. The following instructional procedure is designed to help the individual utilize his mental content as he learns to associate meaning with written symbols.

1. Project a picture upon the chalkboard. Use slide of interest to the child.
2. Discuss objects in the picture with him and relate these to his experiences.

[4] Refer to Appendix C.

3. Label the objects in the picture, such as *Lake Michigan, pine trees, log, water, Stephen, rocks,* and *sky.* With young children manuscript writing may be advisable.
4. Point to each word and have the child "read" it. Repeat this process until mastery is apparent.
5. Turn off the current and ask the child to identify words. If errors are made, restore the picture. This procedure reinforces the association of object, written symbol, and pronunciation. In other words, visual image of the word, visual image of the object, and auditory image of the spoken word are utilized in the learning process. Spatial relationships are also helpful to the child.
6. Have the child dictate a story suggested by the picture, making use of the words on the chalkboard.
7. In writing the story use short sentences and as few additional words as possible.
8. Aid the child in suggesting a title for the story.
9. Have the child read the story as a whole. Then ask questions and have the child read for answers. In testing for mastery, have the child *identify and read phrases.*

Drill on words in isolation should be completely rejected. The recognition of words should be, at all times, in a contextual setting so that not only identification takes place but interpretation as well. The "cloze procedure" described by Taylor[5] can be used for appraising the child's ability to associate meaning with word symbols. The therapist can select a composition at the child's instructional level which is also of interest to him. In reproducing this passage every eighth word can be omitted, with the exception of proper nouns and the beginning word of a sentence. The child should then be encouraged to read the incomplete sentences and add the missing words. In concluding this exercise it will be necessary for the reader to associate meaning with word symbols, to understand the ideas expressed, and to predict the thoughts of the writer. This closure technique can be utilized in elementary grades or high school and for a number of purposes.

Therapists and teachers at all levels should emphasize and develop competence in the use of the dictionary. The selection of a definition

[5] W. L. Taylor, "Cloze Procedure, a New Tool for Measuring Readability," *Journalism Quarterly,* **30** (Fall 1953), pp. 415–433.

requires an understanding of the context in order to avoid an inappropriate meaning. The following sequential acts may be helpful to the child in using his dictionary.

1. Find correct alphabetical section.
2. Scan page headings to find the first, second, third, and fourth letters of the word.
3. Look for the word in the column under the correct page heading.
4. Skim the various meanings of the word.
5. Observe the different parts of speech proper to this word and how they affect its meaning.
6. Select meaning of word which fits the context.

VOCABULARIES OF THE CULTURALLY DISADVANTAGED CHILD

Illiteracy and faulty English in the home prevent children from understanding and enjoying the language of books and especially some of those found in the classroom. Unfavorable attitudes toward books, stories, and poems are developed in many middle-class homes. Some of these parents do little reading and even less frequently do they discuss what they have read in a manner which would interest their children. Many of the more affluent homes fail to provide an educational and emotional climate which would encourage children to talk freely of their experiences and to express their opinions. Consequently, they do not have an opportunity to share experiences and add new words to their vocabulary. Children in some homes are neglected by their parents. The language skills of these boys and girls are acquired only incidentally as the result of their play with other children. They learn the dialect of the neighborhood and say, for example, *tahr* for *tire* and *fahr* for *fire*. They fail to appreciate the language of books.

Linguists believe that the child's initial reading experience should be in the language as close as possible to his speech. Whipple[6] too emphasizes the fact that culturally disadvantaged children should have reading materials prepared for them that are appropriate both in content and in difficulty. Thomas[7] found in his study of the oral

[6] Gertrude Whipple, "A Report of the Progress of the Writers Committee of the Great Cities School Improvement Project" (Detroit, Michigan; March, 1960).
[7] Dominic Thomas, *Oral Language Sentence Structure and Vocabulary of Kindergarten Children Living in Low Socioeconomic Urban Areas.* Unpublished doctoral dissertation, Wayne State University, 1961.

language of culturally disadvantaged children that the vocabulary of his subjects differed substantially from both first-grade readers and standard primary-grade word lists. Furthermore, many children, especially those coming from economically disadvantaged homes, have little opportunity to visit zoos, playgrounds, and the lake shores near where they live. The parents of these children have failed to provide experiential background which can contribute to readiness for reading.

The following are some suggestions for aiding these boys and girls.

- Mental content should be developed by visiting interesting places and events. The children, however, should be prepared for the visits, and topics growing out of the visitations should be freely discussed upon return to the classroom.
- Experience charts and experience records based upon the child's background can be prepared and used for vocabulary development.
- Newly taught words should be employed in a variety of contexts familiar to the child.
- Interesting materials should be selected and used only after adequate preparation has been made so as to stimulate and guide the child as he reads.
- Stories should be discussed in terms of the child's own experiences.
- Culturally disadvantaged children need help in developing word-attack skills, sentence structure, and basic understanding of correct word usage.
- Use of records and tape recorders can be helpful in showing the child how he has expressed himself both before and after receiving aid.

INABILITY TO INTEGRATE WORD PARTS

Words have parts that go together; like hydrogen and oxygen, they too can form an entity having new properties. Words have elements, such as syllables, prefixes, roots, and suffixes, and each element has its unique contribution to meaning. Words are composed of printed forms, each with appropriate sounds. In order to analyze words in terms of their sound elements, the child must possess the following knowledge and skills.

- He should know how to divide words into syllables and apply phonics effectively.

- He should learn how to perceive initial and final consonants.
- He should know how to make consonant blends.
- He should know short and long vowels.
- He should be able to recognize silent letters in words.

The child, in order to become an effective reader, must be aware of these parts and their significance; at the same time he must be able to *integrate* them into a whole having adequate meaning in the context. Both analysis and synthesis must contribute to the correct evaluation of the word in its setting. Smith[8] explains that there are at least four separate skills involved in the total phonic process—(1) visual discrimination, (2) auditory discrimination, (3) blending, and (4) contextual application. Most authorities advocate the practice of teaching children the phonics they need in connection with words that give them difficulty in their daily reading. In other words, phonics can become an integral part of a corrective program in working with the disabled reader. It is suggested that the teacher and therapist become acquainted with the suggestions made by Smith concerning the development of phonetic skills.

Phonics is a useful tool in the blending of sounds into meaningful wholes. Another member of the analytical and synthetic team is structural analysis, which is faster than phonetic analysis. In analyzing the structure of a word, the reader is concerned with prefixes, roots, suffixes, and inflectional endings. Many words in our language can be studied structurally if the student has the informational background to accomplish this end. Smith[9] sets forth some principles for teaching structural analysis as well as some cautions which the teacher should heed.

In providing treatment for inability to integrate word parts, the following suggestions are made by the writers.

- Demonstrate to the child how to locate the most useful elements in words such as root, prefix, suffix, or phonetic element.
- Suggest that the student try one element of the word and if it does not help, try another until a satisfactory interpretation has been worked out.
- Discourage letter-by-letter spelling or sounding of letters. Little

[8] Nila B. Smith, *Reading Instruction for Today's Children* (Englewood Cliffs, N.J.: Prentice-Hall, 1963), pp. 187–214.
[9] *Ibid.*, pp. 215–242.

meaning, for example, can be secured from the sentence *She has insomnia,* by spelling or sounding the letters in the unknown word.

- Consult manuals of basic readers used by the child for exercises designed to aid in developing knowledge of word parts and their integration.
- Make use of devices such as word wheels, word slips, and word tachistoscopes. These mechanisms are helpful with young children for they illustrate valuable principles of word recognition. Their effectiveness, however, is soon dissipated by meaningless drill.
- Encourage the child to use a variety of approaches to word attack and not specialize in any one.
- Make use of visual, auditory, kinesthetic, and tactual imagery in the study of words. The following procedure has been found to be effective.

    1. Look at the beginning and ending of the word. The analysis of elements within words should be restricted to those prefixes, roots, suffixes, and inflectional endings which convey direct meaning.
    2. Pronounce the word silently, being sure to associate each syllable with its corresponding sound and being certain that the proper sequence of syllables is maintained.
    3. Spell the word silently, paying careful attention to each syllable.
    4. Trace the word with the index finger.
    5. Write the word.
    6. Compare the word written with the word selected for study.
    7. Repeat this process until the word can be spelled and written correctly. Words taught by this procedure should always be used in context. For example, if the word *construction* has been taught, it can be written or printed on a card. It can then be shown to the child at its proper place in the sentence, "Did you see the ———— of the garage?" The child would then be encouraged to respond, "Yes, I did see the construction of the garage."

- Make use of *SRA Word Games Laboratory*[10] for development of skills in use of prefixes and suffixes.
- Make use of the tachistoscope or other rapid exposure technique in helping the child to integrate word elements. Project, for example, on the chalkboard the word *pro-duc-tion* and have the student

[10] Refer to Appendix C.

integrate the elements and respond by using the word in a sentence as *The production of silver was limited.*

INABILITY TO INTEGRATE WORDS INTO MEANINGFUL WHOLES

Frequently young children and adults who are learning a new language experience difficulty in blending words into completed sentences. Words are thought symbols and like stones, bricks, and mortar they must be placed and manipulated to complete a predetermined design. Words are "parts" which have little value in themselves. They must be used to develop an idea. The child or student may know what he wants to say and yet lack the knowledge and techniques for self-expression. What he does say may have meaning to him and yet lack the approval of the more sophisticated listener. Many children coming from culturally disadvantaged homes need not only to increase their vocabularies but to develop their ability to speak in sentences. These children can learn to integrate their thought symbols and yet retain their picturesque expressions.

In providing treatment for these boys and girls, the therapist and classroom teacher can apply the following suggestions.

- Help the child to have something to say. "Bring and tell" experiences can be utilized.
- Show the children how to speak in complete sentences. This can be done in groups more effectively than individually.
- Develop the concept that a sentence is a group of words containing a subject and its verb and expressing a completed thought. The meaning of such terms as *noun, pronoun, verb,* and so on should be developed in a way that will interest children and hold their attention. Avoid memorization of definitions.
- Encourage the child to dictate sentences which can be written on the chalkboard and later read orally.
- Provide the child with an opportunity to match meanings he has secured from words or sentences with pictures expressing the same ideas. The use of flashcards directing the child to act out printed directions can be helpful in aiding the child to integrate words into meaningful wholes.
- Make use of the tachistoscope in teaching the child to recognize thought units or phrases at a single fixation. Assist the child to

transfer this skill immediately to the identification of similar units in sentences, making certain the reader is able to tell what is accomplished by each in the sentence. The following thought units can be used in a sentence.

> The red-headed boy
> rode his bicycle
> to school
> during the storm.

Each thought unit accomplishes a definite purpose, for example,

> Who went to school?
> How did the red-headed boy get to school?
> When did he go?

- Help the child to make effective use of capital letters and punctuation in securing meaning. Call attention to the use of capital letters at the beginning of sentences, commas, periods, and question marks. Oral reading can show the effectiveness of such instruction.
- Use the tape recorder to show the child the progress he has made in his expression of ideas as a result of these suggestions.
- Read and apply the suggestions made in this chapter under the heading *A Goal-Oriented Process of Word Study*.

LIMITED VOCABULARIES IN THE CONTENT FIELDS

Children in the elementary grades and even older students acquire the habit of "skipping" unknown words as they read in the content areas. In doing this, the essential idea in the sentence may be missed, and consequently the central thought of the paragraph may be lost and a gap in the flow of meaning from paragraph to paragraph may occur. Rereading can only result in frustration unless the unknown word is identified, interpreted, and evaluated. These unfortunate experiences on the part of readers take place far more commonly than many teachers realize. Many individuals who "skip" words do so because of their inability to secure the meaning from context. Generally this inability to make use of contextual clues is chiefly due to limited knowledge of the subject they are reading. They lack a readiness for reading in that area.

Frequently students who skip unknown words report that they are in a hurry and do not want to take the time to consult the dictionary or to apply word-attack techniques even if they are familiar with them. "It takes too long," they explain. Emotional immaturity is a characteristic of some of these individuals. The reading therapist and teacher can prescribe treatment for the more mature students which can be beneficial. Some suggestions are set forth.

1. As the student reads or listens to his teachers, he should list the words unfamiliar to him.
2. He should look in his books for clues to the word's meaning in the context. He should refer to the glossary, if there is one, for usable meanings.
3. He should examine the prefix, root, and suffix for clues to its meaning.
4. If these approaches are insufficient, he should consult the dictionary and make sure that the meaning selected actually fits the context. The use of the dictionary is the most reliable way of determining word meaning.
5. The student can build up a reading and spelling vocabulary simultaneously by means of a Visual, Auditory, Kinesthetic, and Tactual approach which has been described in this chapter.
6. He should make use of the word in a complete sentence so that its full meaning is adequately expressed.
7. He should keep a card file of the words studied and review them frequently.
8. The student should understand that there is no short-cut to a good vocabulary.

HELPING THE OVERLY CAREFUL READER

Some individuals become unduly concerned with word parts. They attempt to analyze and take apart words that are well known to them. Some children have acquired the habit of analyzing familiar words to such an extent that when given unlimited time they make more errors than when required to identify words quickly at sight. Frequently these children are obsessed with the desire to attend to prefixes, roots, and suffixes. They seem entranced with phonetic elements and sound out word forms that they can pronounce at once. Such procedures are time-consuming and retard effective reading.

Some possible causes of this common word recognition disorder follow.

- Inability to integrate word parts immediately.
- Overemphasis on structural and phonetic analysis.
- Too much drill on word parts.
- Abnormal desire on the part of the child to be careful and exact.

In providing treatment for the overly careful reader, the following suggestions may prove helpful.

- Make use of the materials found in the SRA Reading Laboratory[11] designed to develop sight vocabulary, word-attack skills, and meaning.
- Encourage the child to read interesting materials at his independent reading level so that he will experience little difficulty with unfamiliar words. Stimulate rapid reading for the purpose of securing answers to specific questions.
- Encourage the child to make use of meaning clues and the information he already possesses.
- Suggest that the student "skip the word with discretion" and go on until he experiences a meaning difficulty. His attention to the word will then be justified.

GUIDING PRINCIPLES FOR THE THERAPIST

The reading therapist or teacher in her work with the disabled reader should employ many methods of teaching the individual to unlock the meaning of words in the process of reading. Some principles that can aid in developing word-recognition skills are listed.

- Words should be taught in situations where the child has a well-defined *need* for the word. Furthermore, it is essential that the materials being read be *meaningful* to the reader and at his *instructional* level.
- The teacher should make sure that the student has the necessary background for the study of the word so that he can understand and appreciate its meaning.
- Words should be taught as they will be used. Consequently, isolated

[11] Refer to Appendix C.

drill and mechanical approaches using single words should be avoided except in rare instances where the needs of the individual make them advisable.

- The child should be taught to inspect the unfamiliar word from left to right before he attempts to sound it, for in this manner he can identify the usable elements of the word and that part which needs to be studied phonically.
- The teacher should aid the child in developing ability to identify similarities and differences in the visual forms of words which he is to learn.
- The therapist should develop word-attack skills as the need arises and as they can be applied in the daily work of the individual.
- She should teach phonics gradually and incidentally and only as a device for recognizing and pronouncing unfamiliar words.
- Generally, structural analysis should precede phonetic analysis, for it does not take as long to perceive whole structural units in a word as it does to sound out letters and letter combinations.
- The child should be encouraged to develop a liturgical approach to word recognition which is helpful to him. The following sequential acts are suggested: (1) Try meaning clues found in context. (2) Beginning at the left and moving to the right, examine word parts such as prefixes, roots, and suffixes. (3) Pronounce the word, paying attention to syllables and vowel sounds. (4) Look up the word in the dictionary for appropriate meaning and pronunciation. (5) Use the word in a sentence.
- Disabled readers at all levels need to acquire the effective use of the dictionary as a means of securing meaning and as an aid to pronunciation. Information concerning construction and word forms can also be obtained.
- All treatment and instruction should be adjusted to the needs of the child as he attempts to accomplish his purpose.
- The teacher should maintain a balance, as suggested by Bond and Tinker,[12] between (1) word recognition and meaning vocabularies, (2) sight vocabularies and word recognition skills, (3) meaning clues and analytical aids, (4) phonetic analysis and structural analysis, and (5) word parts and left to right inspection.

[12] Guy L. Bond and Miles A. Tinker, *Reading Difficulties, Their Diagnosis and Correction*, 2nd ed. (New York: Appleton-Century-Crofts, 1967), pp. 305–307.

A GOAL-ORIENTED PROCESS OF WORD STUDY

Learning words can accompany a project of real interest to the individual. This is especially true of the reluctant learner and the culturally disadvantaged child. In the following sequence of activities, which begins with *stimulation* and ends with *achievement*, effective learning can take place with resulting feedback. The child, for example, who wants to write a book which he can show to his friends and read to his parents has acquired a readiness for an activity which

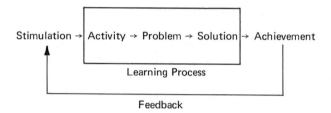

Figure 12-1. Goal-oriented process.

can be utilized in teaching words and their use in sentences. Short stories for the child's book can come from experience charts based upon a picture projected upon the chalkboard and from experience records resulting from an interesting trip, or they can be based upon the child's drawings. In all instances the story should be dictated by the young writer and should be his creation. During the writing of the composition difficulties will be experienced and problems will need to be solved. All of this is part of the learning process, and the child will need information and guidance. When the picture is projected on the chalkboard and the objects in the picture labeled, words will be seen in spatial relationships to each other and to the picture as a whole. These same words will be seen again in relation to each other in sentences and related to the completed story. Structural analysis and even phonics can be utilized in the process. The words taught and the necessary helping words become integrated into a meaningful and pleasing whole. This achievement on the part of the child is stimulating and results in "feedback" and even more information and more stimulation. The whole process is goal oriented and ever expanding.

In guiding the child to success the following suggestions will prove helpful in making his book. These directions are a part of the goal-oriented process and are not "just busywork."

- The teacher or therapist can type or assist the child in typing his story.
- The teacher or therapist can encourage the child to illustrate his characters, the setting, or the events in his story.
- In preparing the cover the child will need the following materials: (1) Stiff cardboard. Corrugated cardboard works quite well. (2) Cloth which is colorful, firm, but not too heavy. (3) Drymount. This will adhere to both sides when heat is applied. (4) An iron which should be used at rayon setting. (5) Masking tape. (6) A ruler.
- The following steps should be taken in preparing the cover.

    1. Cut cardboard ¼ in. larger than pages of book. Leave ¼ to ½ in. space between the front and back cover, depending upon number of pages in the book. This will allow the book to close and lie flat when completed. Hold covers in place with masking tape. See Figure 12-2.

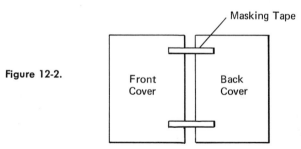

Figure 12-2.

    2. Cut cloth 1½ in. wider and longer than overall length and width of two covers, including the allowance between back and front covers. See Figure 12-3.

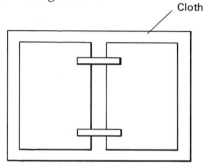

Figure 12-3.

3. Cut piece of drymount same size as cloth cover. Lay cloth aside. Place drymount over the top of cardboard covers. With tip of iron touch drymount at several places indicated by X in Figure 12-4. This will hold drymount in place.

4. Place cloth on top of the drymount and cardboard covers. Press with warm iron from inside edges of covers to outside edges, thus eliminating wrinkles. See Figure 12-5.

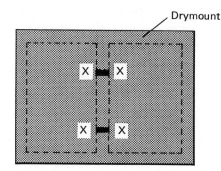

Figure 12-4.

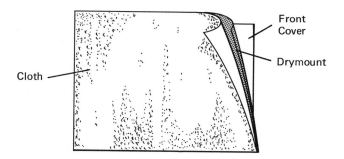

Figure 12-5.

5. Turn cover over. Cut the corners of cloth and drymount within ¾ in. of cardboard corners. Turn cloth over the cardboard and with warm iron press down corners, top, bottom, and sides. See Figures 12-6 and 12-7. The cover is now complete.

• In preparing pages for the book, the child will need white paper (the stronger, the better), drymount, heavy thread, and a darning needle.

Figure 12-6.

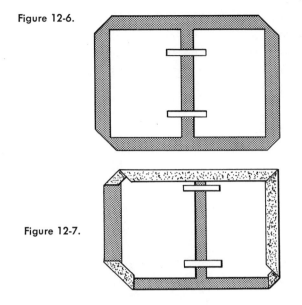

Figure 12-7.

1. The white sheets of paper need to be twice the desired size of each page of the book. The cover should be ¼ in. larger than the pages of the book on all open edges. Fold each sheet of paper exactly in half, making two pages. This is called a folio. Allow four extra pages. Two of these extra pages will be fastened to the front and back covers, and two pages will become the end papers. See Figure 12-8.

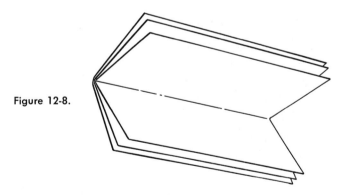

Figure 12-8.

2. With a large sharp pin or needle, punch holes through all thicknesses of the folios, along the fold. This makes sewing easier. Holes should be about ¼ in. apart. With threaded needle start

sewing from the outside. Pull thread through leaving about 3 in. of thread hanging loose on outside. Continue stitching through punched holes until you are back where you started. Finish by tying a knot using the thread left hanging and the thread in the needle. See Figure 12-9.

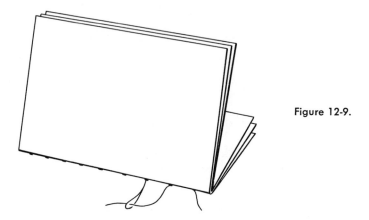

Figure 12-9.

3. Cut two pieces of drymount the same size as the first and last pages of the book. With the warm iron, tack the drymount to the first and last pages. See Figure 12-10.

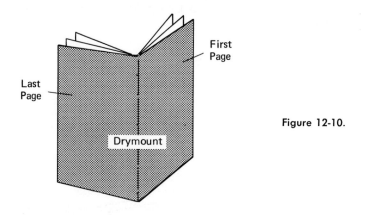

Figure 12-10.

4. Center the prepared pages of the book in the space left between the front and back covers. Holding the pages firmly with one hand, press, with warm iron, the first page onto the inside of the front cover. Do the same with the last page, being careful not to

let the pages get off center. Press the book between heavy weights for several hours. The finished book should lie flat.[13]

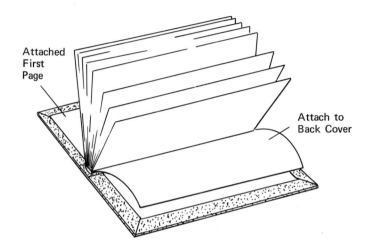

Attached
First
Page

Attach to
Back Cover

Figure 12-11.

SUMMARY

This chapter has discussed remediation of children with deficiencies of sight vocabularies and word-attack skills. Specific suggestions for treatment have been made, and some guiding principles for the therapist have been suggested. Furthermore, the writers have described a goal-oriented process of word study which can lead to an integration of ideas and to creativity on the part of the child.

GUIDED ACTIVITY 12

Aim

To aid children with vocabulary disabilities.

Materials

1. Chapters 12 and 15 of *Diagnosis and Treatment of the Disabled Reader.*

[13] Prepared by Leona D. Hefner of the Portage Public Schools, Portage, Michigan.

2. Tachistoscope.
3. Stiff cardboard.
4. Cloth.
5. Drymount.
6. Iron.
7. Masking tape.
8. Ruler.
9. Crayons or paints.
10. White paper.
11. Heavy thread.
12. Darning needle.

Procedure

1. Select a child reported to be of average intelligence who has a limited sight vocabulary and is unfamiliar with adequate word-attack procedures.
2. Take time to establish rapport.
3. Administer an informal reading inventory and observe carefully his approach to unfamiliar words.
4. Consider thoughtfully the following questions.
   - Does he show a lack of mental content?
   - Does he make effective use of the context and meaning clues?
   - Does he use structural analysis?
   - Can he integrate word parts?
   - Is he a word-by-word reader?
   - Does he "sound out" words?
   - Does he skip words?
   - Does he really want to improve his vocabulary?
   - Can he use the dictionary effectively?
5. Work your diagnosis of his vocabulary needs out carefully and state it in not more than three sentences.
6. Outline treatment in detail, making use, if necessary, of some of the materials and equipment mentioned in this chapter.
7. Apply treatment, maintaining at all times rapport with the child. Make the work interesting to him.
8. Report systematically and in detail your observations. Make use of anecdotal records. Do not spend more than thirty minutes with the child at one time.
9. Summarize briefly the results of your work. Skim Chapter 15 for suggestions.
10. Select a little girl whose reading ability has been retarded by a vocabu-

lary deficiency and apply the suggestions made in Chapter 12 under the heading *A Goal-Oriented Process of Word Study*. After her book has been completed, encourage her to show her parents what she has accomplished and how effectively she can read her story aloud to them.

QUESTIONS AND REFERENCES

Questions

1. How can word recognition difficulties be overcome?

2. What vocabularies?

3. How can the student learn to make the most of words?

4. How can the reading therapist work with handicapped children?

5. How can sight vocabulary and word-attack skills be developed?

6. How can experience charts be used in vocabulary development?

References

1. Guy L. Bond and Miles A. Tinker, *Reading Difficulties, Their Diagnosis and Correction*, 2nd ed. (New York: Appleton-Century-Crofts, 1967), Chap. 12.

2. Helen M. Robinson, "Vocabulary: Speaking, Listening, Reading, and Writing," in H. Alan Robinson, ed., *Reading and the Language Arts*, Supplementary Educational Monographs, No. 93 (Chicago: University of Chicago Press, 1963), Chap. XIV.

3. Homer L. J. Carter and Dorothy J. McGinnis, *Reading, A Key to Academic Success* (Dubuque, Iowa: Wm. C. Brown Company, Publisher, 1967), Chap. 5.

4. Dorris M. Lee and R. V. Allen, *Learning to Read Through Experience*, 2nd ed. (New York: Appleton-Century-Crofts, 1963).

5. Morton Botel, *How to Teach Reading* (Chicago: Follett Publishing Company, 1962), Chaps. III and V.

6. Virgil E. Herrick and Marcella Nerbovig, *Using Experience Charts with Children* (Columbus, Ohio: Charles E. Merrill Books, 1964).

Questions	References
7. How does a linguist approach the problem of reading?	**7.** Charles C. Fries, *Linguistics and Reading* (New York: Holt, Rinehart and Winston, 1963).
8. How can skills in word recognition be developed?	**8.** John J. DeBoer and Martha Dallmann, *The Teaching of Reading*, rev. ed. (New York: Holt, Rinehart and Winston, 1964), Chap. 6b.
9. What are some practical suggestions for teaching culturally disadvantaged students?	**9.** Arnold B. Cheyney, *Teaching Culturally Disadvantaged in the Elementary School* (Columbus, Ohio: Charles E. Merrill Books, 1967).
10. How can the reading needs of culturally disadvantaged children be met?	**10.** Gertrude Whipple and Millard H. Black, *Reading for Children Without—Our Disadvantaged Youth* (Newark, Del.: International Reading Association, 1966).
11. How can linguistics be employed effectively in reading?	**11.** William K. Durr, ed., *Reading Instruction* (Boston: Houghton Mifflin Company, 1967), Chap. 12.

Chapter 13

Treatment of Individuals Who Have Difficulty in Reading for Meaning

Meaning emerges as the reader identifies, interprets, and evaluates symbols and ideas. It develops and grows as new facts and experiences are introduced. The reader is concerned with words, phrases, sentences, paragraphs, and finally the chapter. These, however, are but parts of a growing whole, the reader's total awareness of the subject. Some individuals, of all ages, are unable to obtain meaning and carry on a thoughtful reading process which is goal oriented. This chapter will suggest procedures for remediation. There are many ways in which these techniques can be applied. Their selection and use will be determined by the needs of the student and the ingenuity and insight of the therapist.

DIAGNOSIS BEFORE TREATMENT

As previously pointed out, the teacher and therapist must determine *what* difficulties the student has in reading for meaning and *why* they have developed before effective treatment can be applied. The therapist is reminded of some causal factors which should be considered. They are the following:

- Visual defects.
- Inability to sustain attention.
- Lack of experiential background.
- Lack of knowledge of *how* to read effectively.
- Inability to maintain effort.
- Marked feelings of inadequacy.

Information resulting from interviews, the student's academic history, informal reading inventories, and tests may suggest *what* reading disabilities the individual possesses. When these needs have been determined, the student can be shown *how* to achieve the basic skills which are lacking. This is diagnosis at the third level. Later observations of the student as he works may reveal "hunches" concerning the causal factors affecting his reading achievement. In some instances, therapy as well as instruction must be provided.

WORDS, MEANING, AND CONCEPTS

Words are thought symbols or signs which have no significance of their own but instead derive their meaning from their context and the mental content of the reader. Meaning, which cannot be adequately defined, is determined by continuous experience and is in part the total significance of an object, process, and situation. It is interesting to ask, "From what source did meaning come, and how was it associated with words?" Concepts are generally developed incidentally in a goal-oriented pursuit and are modified by mental content resulting from one's experiential background. Some students at various age levels have difficulty with words. They omit them, skip them, misspell them, and otherwise treat them with disrespect. Consequently, ideas and concepts are confused or lost entirely. In Chapter 12 of this book remediation for these individuals has been suggested. Let us turn to the larger thought units and determine not only how to read for meaning but how to identify main ideas, how to read for a purpose, and how to make ideas one's own.

INADEQUATE SENTENCE MEANING

Sentence meaning is based upon word symbols and the manner of their integration, for a sentence is more than an accumulation of words.

It has a subject and a predicate. It has a verb whose meaning can be changed by other words, called adverbs. The sentence may contain a pronoun which takes the place of a noun. Phrases and adjectives may be used to modify the meaning of nouns and pronouns. Independent and dependent clauses may be introduced so that compound and complex sentences are utilized. Figures of speech and symbolic expressions may be employed. The usual order of a sentence may be changed to accomplish a specific purpose. Obviously, sentence reading for the immature reader can be difficult.

Individuals most apt to have difficulty in sentence reading are those classified as nonreaders and children who have lived in homes where they have seen and heard little to stimulate their interest in books and the expression of ideas. Experience has shown that some of these boys and girls have physical defects which can retard their growth in reading; some have difficulties in visual and auditory discrimination; and nearly all lack a readiness for language and reading experiences. Remediation of difficulties involved in sentence reading may be accomplished by first determining the source of the disability and then by providing treatment. Some helpful suggestions are listed.

- Build up the experiential background of the child by some of the means suggested in Chapter 12 of this book. Utilize a language experience approach with small groups of children selected on the basis of their interests.
- Develop basic sight vocabularies by means of experience charts followed by VAKT.
- Place greater emphasis upon oral reading with those children whose linguistic skills are poorly developed, for they need to speak and hear ideas expressed in complete sentences.
- Refer the child to a physician when circumstances suggest that physical disabilities may cause or contribute to his reading disability.
- Provide the child with practice in reading thought units by having him underline phrases within sentences.
- Make use of flashcards or a tachistoscope for exposing rapidly phrases which the child is expected to read silently and then express orally in complete sentences.
- Develop a sentence sense by asking *who* and *what* questions. This can help identify subject and predicate.
- Develop meaning of modifiers by *where, when,* and *how* questions.

- Encourage the child to write simple sentences, making certain that he makes use of all the essential elements.
- Help the student to understand, without making him feel inadequate and insecure, that form and preciseness are just as important in sentence construction and reading as in sports, music, art, and other activities requiring skill.
- Show the student how punctuation can facilitate sentence reading. Use simple sentences in beginning this instruction and then go to the more complex.
- Make use of flexible grouping if circumstances in the homeroom permit. This makes it possible for small groups of children to receive specific instruction for short periods of time.

FAULTY PARAGRAPH READING

The main idea of a paragraph is stated in a topic sentence which is frequently at the beginning and sometimes at the end of a paragraph. On other occasions it may be neatly tucked away, difficult for some readers to find. Every sentence in the paragraph should help to develop the main idea expressed by the topic sentence. This is accomplished by adding detail and facts to support the central idea. The main thought of the composition can be supported not only by facts but by arguments, illustrations, and even short anecdotes. Any sentence that departs from the main idea is unnecessary and frequently destroys the unity of the paragraph. The reader should realize that this concept of paragraph organization does not necessarily apply to paragraphs in narrative writing and informal personal essays.

The student's difficulty in determining the central thought of a paragraph may be due to his inability to identify the topic sentence. His limited vocabulary and his inadequate mental content may add further to his difficulty. A lack of interest and an unwillingness to put forth effort can complicate his problem. The following suggestions may facilitate treatment.

- Aid the student in the identification of topic sentences in several paragraphs.
- Have the student express the meaning of these sentences in his own words.

- Have the student analyze the paragraphs to determine how the writer has developed and expanded these central ideas.
- Encourage the student to write a paragraph showing topic sentence along with expanding, amplifying, and supporting sentences. Each paragraph, when completed, should be discussed in detail. The use of each sentence should be justified and those that contribute little should be revised or omitted. This treatment can be utilized with profit from the elementary grades through college. If the student can write a good paragraph, it is assumed that he will be better able to read one.
- Show the student how each paragraph is a unit or step in a sequence of developed concepts leading to a major idea. If the central thought of a paragraph is misunderstood or lost entirely, the major meaning of the larger thought unit will be without significance and not fully appreciated. Paragraph reading and an understanding of the relationship of one paragraph to another in a sequence is difficult for many students chiefly because of an inadequate background in the subject being read. The mental content of these students can be increased by discussion and by reading less difficult material in the field. The responsibility of developing this readiness should be assumed by the student.
- Make use of the *SRA Reading Laboratories* and *The Reader's Digest Skill Builders*[1] for materials varying in reading and interest levels which can reinforce instruction in paragraph reading. Materials should be selected at the student's instructional level or lower.
- Provide praise and commendation to reinforce the student's performance.

FAILURE TO READ FOR A PURPOSE

Effective reading is purposeful and is directed toward the realization of a goal. It is done for fun and enjoyment, and for the purpose of accomplishing a difficult task. Individuals read to get away from the stern realities of everyday life, to identify oneself with others and to enjoy vicariously experiences otherwise unattainable. The student reads to learn what is happening each day; to complete class assign-

[1] Refer to Appendix C.

ments; to gather information; to learn of other people, countries, times and of current happenings; and to discover how to adjust in a changing world. Some individuals, however, read only because they are required to do so and because it is a part of their job.

Some students say they read for *meaning*. This, however, is only a means to an end. Meaning is secured for a purpose and is but a station on the way to the goal. Meaning does not exist by itself, for it is determined and modified by changing experiences and is personal in nature. The value of meaning is dependent upon the use that is made of it. The good reader asks questions of his book and looks for answers. He not only asks *who, what, where,* and *when,* but *why* and *how.* He asks, "What does this sentence say?" He then adds, "Can I accept it or must I reject it?" He identifies the topic sentence in a paragraph and asks, "Did the writer accomplish his purpose? What is the value to me of the concept he has developed?" Such questions provide a purpose for reading and motivate the whole process. In reading a chapter in a textbook, the student can convert major headings into well-designed questions which are actually answered by the text. Obviously, the student who reads for the purpose of answering these questions will obtain more meaning than the student who "just reads." Some authorities in the field of reading believe that purpose affects manner of reading, rate of reading, and the level of thinking achieved by the reader.

In counseling and treating the student who "just reads" it may be well to apply some of the following suggestions.

- Make clear to the student that purposeful reading is most effective and that it is less time-consuming.
- Show him that well-designed questions brought to a sharp focus elicit responses which are meaningful and relevant to the situation under investigation.
- Stress the fact that the form of the question based upon major headings in a textbook requires careful consideration in order to make certain that the question is answered completely by the text. In many instances the reader will find it necessary to construct and then reconstruct his questions. He will need to skim the subject matter under the heading to make sure his question is adequately designed. For some students this activity is difficult to achieve.
- Show the student that after major headings have been restated in

the form of questions, the next act is to read the text in order to secure complete answers. Subheadings can be used as guides in the process.

- Make clear to the student that with *his* purpose clearly in mind, he should read rapidly or skim the material in order to determine whether or not it is of value to him. He should ask himself as he reads, "Does this idea help me to solve my problem? How is this concept related to me and my plans?"

INABILITY TO READ FOR MAIN IDEAS

Many students at various levels of reading attainment have difficulty in reading for main ideas in sentences, paragraphs, and chapters. They frequently become lost in a maze of detail and miss the basic concepts entirely. They fail to identify main ideas in charts, graphs, and tables, for all facts seem of equal importance to them. In the daily paper facts are facts and none seem to stand out. In reading textbooks many students feel guilty unless they follow through a chapter word by word. In the process of such reading they fail to identify main ideas; consequently, some have little to show for their labors. They fail to realize that reading is a thinking process and that they must separate the important from the unimportant, the main ideas from those of lesser significance. In helping individuals read for a purpose, it is advisable for the reading therapist to show the student what he can secure from charts, newspapers, and other major thought units.

Tables and Graphs

The forms of communication generally called charts present information for the purpose of comparison; for the most part such information is statistical in nature and can be expressed numerically. A table is generally the most compact way to present statistical data. Explanatory information is generally given with the title and headings which are shown along the top and left-hand side of the table. There are various forms of graphs designed to portray comparisons and contrasts of data in vivid and graphic form. Line graphs show a continuous curve and indicate that the facts are related. Bar graphs and other spatial figures are employed when the data are not continuous and related. Pictographs and circle graphs are generally used when a comparison of the parts with each other and with the whole is desired by the author.

Securing information from charts necessitates the identification of facts and data that are essential to an understanding of the inferences and conclusions expressed by the author. Not all of the facts shown are of equal importance. The following suggestions for chart reading can prove helpful.

1. Have the student read the legend or title to determine what the writer intends to show.
2. Ask the student to determine what facts are shown vertically and what facts are shown horizontally on the chart.
3. Encourage the student to go from the general to the specific and, when unusual facts, numbers, or peculiarities are presented, to determine what they mean.
4. Have the student record all the facts which he can observe and all the inferences which can be based upon these facts.
5. Encourage the student to read what the author has to say concerning the chart and determine why he has employed this particular means of expression.
6. Have the student compare his inferences with those made by the writer.
7. Ask the student to determine what ideas in the chart are of value to him. Generally use is the best criterion of value.

Newspapers

Generally the major facts in a newspaper story are concentrated in the headlines and the story's introduction, or "lead." Following the lead is the "catch-all," in which minor items are grouped together. The main body of the story which elaborates upon the lead follows the catch-all. The index, generally found on the first page of the newspaper, is apt to show stories and news items of importance and of general interest.

Few readers have time to read completely a whole newspaper; consequently, selective reading is mandatory. It is obvious that what is of importance to one reader is not of equal value to another. Each reader must determine what information he wants and then go after it. The following statements may help the student identify the facts essential to his needs.

- Read the *summaries* and *indexes*, generally found on the first page, for the purpose of discovering and locating articles of importance and interest.
- Scan headlines to determine the news stories related to the interest and purpose of the reader.
- Skim leads to discover the who, what, where, when, and how of the stories.
- Skim the catch-all for minor details.
- Quickly read the main body of the story to make sure that the article has nothing more of importance.
- Evaluate what has been read by answering such questions as: (1) Is this article true? (2) What is the author attempting to do? (3) Are his conclusions justified? (4) How have other papers interpreted this story?
- Encourage the student to increase the range of his reading interests by reading news articles he ordinarily neglects.
- Show the value of reading the editorial page. Newspaper editorials usually state a point of view on a controversial issue. The student should recognize that the writer is trying to influence his thinking and should be aware of the techniques used for persuasion. Encourage the student to draw his own conclusions concerning the controversial issue.

Major Thought Units

To identify main ideas in a major thought unit the student must read selectively. Selective reading is manifest in two forms, *skimming* and *scanning*. Skimming is the process of quickly securing a general impression of a written composition. It is an act of skipping with discretion the unessential and of summarizing that which is judged to be of value. Scanning, on the other hand, is a search for specific facts and detailed information. The reader scans, for example, the dictionary, the telephone directory, and a glossary.

There are five approaches to the identification of the main ideas in an article, major thought unit, and composition. They are the following:

- Skim the introduction to the composition so as to determine what the writer intends to do.
- Skim the summary at the end of the article, if there is one, and discover what the writer says he has accomplished. Generally he has stated his conclusions in brief and concise form. This summary will aid the reader in making a preliminary survey of the article because it provides him with the fundamental and basic concepts of the composition.
- Scan, if present, the large main headings and the various subheadings, for these provide a framework of the unit. Observe carefully the size and kind of type used for major headings, the primary subheadings, and the secondary subheadings. The degree of importance is indicated by the size and kind of type. Centering on the page can indicate concepts of greater importance.
- If there are no headings, scan carefully the topic sentence of each paragraph. Determine its contribution to the main idea being developed by the sequence of paragraphs. The student can then prepare his own headings. He should understand that paragraphs are steps leading to a major idea.
- The mature student should learn to underline and code. He will find it necessary to weigh the importance of facts and make fine discriminations. Some students make use of a felt pen with colored ink for this purpose. They use an asterisk to indicate ideas of particular importance, double lines for key words and phrases which express the main ideas, and a single line to indicate important supporting data.

INABILITY TO MAKE IDEAS ONE'S OWN

Ideas clearly entertained in consciousness work themselves out into action. Concepts are important in everyday thinking and acting. In a changing society new concepts are tools which enable us to adapt our behavior to changing situations. Many readers, however, expose themselves to ideas which apparently fall on sandy and rocky soil. They read, but the ideas do not become their own.

The mature and effective reader can express what he reads in his own words so that his peers can understand and appreciate what he has to say. He does not resort to memorization or to idle verbalization. Instead he identifies, interprets, and evaluates the ideas of the writer and expresses them in his own language. In order to make ideas one's own, they must be integrated and become a part of the reader's mental content. An accumulation of ideas is not sufficient, and concepts cannot exist long in isolation. If a reader perceives no relationship between a new idea and himself, the idea is of no value to him.

The reader who asks questions and reads for answers will "inwardly digest" what he reads. In reading an article, he will convert major headings into questions and read thoughtfully for complete answers. These responses will be stated in his own words and not in those of the author. Some practical suggestions for the student are summarized.

- After adequate questions have been prepared, each should be written on one side of a 3- by 5-in. card.
- The answers to the question stated in the words of the reader should be outlined on the reverse side of the card. Each response should be numbered and worded as briefly as possible. Many students are tempted to write too much.
- To make ideas one's own the following *test* and *study* procedure should be followed. The student should read each question and attempt to answer it without referring to the answer on the reverse side. He should place in one pile the questions that are answered correctly and in another pile the questions that are not answered satisfactorily. It may be necessary for the student to modify his answers as he reinforces his responses. New facts integrated with his previous knowledge produces an ever-expanding understanding of the problem. Discussion with other students provides more mental content and aids in clarification of concepts.

INABILITY TO READ A CHAPTER EFFECTIVELY

Many high school and college students experience difficulty in reading a chapter successfully. Some of these individuals make comparatively high scores on well-known survey tests of reading. When reading a chapter, however, they become lost in a maze of detail and at the conclusion of their reading have little organized information to show for their labor. In this chapter three suggestions have been outlined which, when adequately integrated and applied in the process of chapter reading, can assure the reader of a greater degree of success. These suggestions restated are expressed in the following form. They should be presented to students by teachers and therapists.

1. *Identify main ideas* by skimming introduction and summary. Scan major headings to "spot" again the main ideas of the chapter. This constitutes a preview of the chapter.
2. *Read for the purpose* of converting major headings into questions and for specific answers. The subheadings will help in determining responses to the queries. The use of 3- by 5-in. cards as suggested in this chapter is helpful.
3. *Read to make ideas one's own* by stating answers to questions in one's *own words* and by testing and trying to determine mastery of the concepts expressed in the chapter. The use of the 3- by 5-in. cards with questions on one side and the answers on the other is beneficial to the student.

This integration of reading for main ideas, reading for a purpose, and reading to make ideas one's own has been found helpful by thousands of high school and college students, and many report that after having read a chapter in this manner they have something to show for their effort.

INABILITY TO KNOW WHAT TO ACCEPT AND WHAT TO REJECT

In the changing world of today there are many social, political, and economic theories being proclaimed by the news media, by institutions of higher learning, and by various social agencies. How can one know what to accept and what to reject? Reliable knowledge is required to make valid judgments. Faulty thinking, however, continues to affect the affairs of the home, school, state, and nation. Without doubt every man needs to know how to separate the chaff from the wheat.

Conventional Ideas, Beliefs, and Standards

Many individuals accept without question the fixed ideas, beliefs, and standards of their peers. The preconceived ideas and emotional bias of these readers make it easy for them to select from their reading those facts which substantiate their ideas and to neglect as insignificant those data which fail to verify their belief. Frequently they try to rationalize their behavior by saying, "Everyone knows that, for it has always been true." The effect of customs and social approval upon sound thinking is apparent at all ages and at all levels of academic sophistication.

Some individuals have a "set," or *Einstellung*, which prevents them from accepting new ideas and from applying old ideas in new situations. Their thinking is rigid and lacks flexibility. When reading, these "routine thinkers" withhold and distort facts in order to reconfirm their belief. They snip out from context a sentence or paragraph which, considered by itself, could be interpreted in a way foreign to the writer's original meaning. Rigid and conventional thinkers are apt to oversimplify their conclusions and to demand that their opinions be accepted as facts. They become deeply grounded "in a rut" and see their problems narrowly and attempt to solve them in a rigid manner.

Hasty Rejection of New Ideas

Research in the sciences and social studies are producing new discoveries and new concepts which demand the attention of the thinking individual. The hasty rejection of new ideas can be as unwise as the uncritical acceptance of old ideas and standards. For example, the flight of the Wright brothers at Kitty Hawk in 1903 was discredited by many intelligent readers. These leaders were regarded as "crazy" publicity seekers who were trying to "dupe" the war department. Here again, the "rigid thinkers" had become contaminated with their preconceived ideas and their emotional bias. Objective thinking is not easy.

Propaganda Techniques Used by Writers

Propaganda is rampant on every side. In the market place, in classrooms, in lecture halls, and even in our churches, we are influenced by those who want us to think as they think and do as they do. Some individuals can identify the blatant politician and the silly sing-song salesman on television, but many fail to recognize the more clever and subtle varieties which are far more common. Some of these propaganda techniques are briefly described.

- Use is made of words to create an emotional reaction. Such terms as *communistic* and *reactionary* are used by some writers when they want to create an unfavorable response. These words have a connotation which a writer can use to arouse opposition to a principle, person, or cause. Some words have a halo effect which adds to the ideas with which they are associated. Such words, for example, as *freedom* and *liberty* are accepted by all.

- Testimonials are irresistible to some individuals. The opinions of a famous football coach are valuable when he discusses the forward pass, but his recommendations concerning the merits of a preparation for weight reduction can be worthless.
- Suppression and distortion of truth is a scheme employed by some writers to accentuate the positive and to conceal the negative, even though the importance of the latter far outweighs the former. These writers fail to tell the whole truth.
- The "band wagon" technique is an attempt to influence the reader to accept an idea or a point of view simply because "everybody else" is doing it. "Fifty million Frenchmen cannot be wrong, you know."
- False analogy is used unconsciously and sometimes consciously for propaganda purposes. The argument, for example, that the price of real estate must be reduced because "all that goes up must come down" is false. Fortunately, some readers understand that there is no relationship between the law of gravity and the price of real estate.
- Use of irrelevant associations are frequently made by writers to prove their point by introducing immaterial and inconsequential data. Reference is made in their arguments to Biblical characters, to the common man, and to Abraham Lincoln. Their candidate, for example, is shown leaving a church with his children. All of this is good but quite irrelevant to the issue at hand.

SUGGESTIONS FOR THERAPISTS

- Help the young student to understand that he has a right to disagree with what he reads. He should, however, be expected to state clearly *why* he is unable to accept the writer's statements.
- Point out to the student that conflicting points of view can be helpful. Compromise, however, is generally the desired goal.
- Aid the student in making assumptions concerning the writer's

motives by asking, "Why did he say what he said and what was he trying to accomplish?"

- Show the student that to be objective in his criticism he must determine the writer's purpose and whether or not he was able to accomplish it.
- Encourage the student to read slowly, around and through the writer's words. Some materials should be read again and again. Speed reading is not recommended for critical reading and thinking.
- Provide the child with practice in picking out statements which he thinks are facts and statements which he thinks are inferences.
- Have the child bring magazine articles, pamphlets, and books and encourage him to discuss each in terms of the author's use of personal opinion versus facts, biases, and preconceived ideas.
- Encourage the student to find editorials expressing differing views on a subject and to discuss which are most valid and why.
- Illustrate and discuss with the child or group various propaganda techniques used by writers such as (1) use of words to create an emotional reaction, (2) testimonials, (3) suppression and distortion of truth, (4) the "band wagon," (5) false analogy, and (6) use of irrelevant associations.
- Stimulate an interest in advertisements for the purpose of "spotting" and identifying various propaganda techniques.
- Provide the student with material at his instructional level which is appropriate for critical reading. Have him read the material to identify who the propagandist is, whom he is serving, why he is attempting to sway his readers, and what propaganda techniques he is using.
- Encourage the reader to stop, look, and ponder when an idea expressed by a writer appears *unusual, overdrawn,* and *without support.* Have him refer to other sources for additional points of view.
- Emphasize the value of withholding judgment when facts and experiential background are lacking. Do not permit the student to jump to conclusions.

INEFFECTIVE READING OF MATHEMATICS

In mathematics facts are presented in condensed form and problems are briefly and concisely worded. Details are of great importance and problems must be read carefully so as to understand each symbol, sign, word, and concept. This can only be accomplished by marked concentration and a slow reading rate. The vocabulary in mathematics is technical in nature and requires a high degree of mental content for its appreciation. The reader must generalize and identify principles set forth by the sample problems found in his text. Facts and relevant information must be identified, interpreted, and evaluated. Consequently, the following attainments are required.

- Adequate vocabulary in area of specialization.
- Sufficient knowledge of basic mathematical concepts.
- Flexibility of reading.
- Problem solving.

Some suggestions for the therapist attempting to aid the student who has difficulty reading in the field of mathematics are listed.

- Encourage the student having difficulty in problem solving to read several problems aloud. This will permit the therapist to determine the nature of his reading difficulty and its degree of seriousness. Observe word recognition, understanding of technical terms, ability to interpret thought units, and ability to perceive problems as a whole. Provide treatment for the specific disabilities which are identified.
- Help the student to develop an understanding of the technical terms and the specialized meanings of common words used in mathematics. Some of the suggestions provided in Chapter 12 of this book will be useful in accomplishing this objective. In addition, encourage the student to list in a notebook unfamiliar terms along with their technical meanings. Some students find it advisable to prepare a word file of specialized terms. This can be accomplished by having the student write the term on one side of a 3- by 5-in. card and the definition on the other side. This plan facilitates frequent review.
- Acquaint the student with the symbols and specialized abbreviations which are used in mathematics, such as $+$, $-$, $\times$, $\div$, $=$, $\sqrt{}$, Σ, $>$, and $<$.
- Aid the student in developing an understanding of mathematical concepts. A deficiency of mental content and background is one of the most common causes of disability in mathematics. The develop-

ment of concepts necessitates long-range planning and is not easily achieved. The reading of supplementary texts, participation in classroom discussion, and experience in the concrete application of mathematical principles can prove beneficial.

- Help the student to appreciate the fact that he lives in a world of numbers, signs, figures, and formulas. Encourage him to think in terms of facts, principles, theorems, and mathematical concepts. Help him to understand numbers and their relationship to him and his world.

- Encourage the student to extend his reading of mathematical and scientific materials by intensive work in the library. Show him how to compare the interpretations of different writers in the field and the value of using more than one textbook and one author's point of view.

- Stress the importance of methodical, accurate, and precise reading. Materials in mathematics cannot and should not be read rapidly. Show the student the importance of adjusting his rate of reading to the purpose, nature, and content of the material. In some instances it will be necessary for him to read more slowly.

- Develop the student's ability to read for detail, to draw inferences, to organize facts, to follow directions, and to discriminate between relevant and irrelevant materials by providing him with problems in which data are incomplete, immaterial, or irrelevant—for example, "How long will it take a plane to fly 1,500 miles?" Encourage him to determine why this problem and others like it cannot be solved.

- Develop skill in reading to solve problems by encouraging the student to read for the purpose of answering the following questions and completing the following acts.

  1. What is to be determined?
  2. What facts are known?
  3. What other facts are needed that are not stated in the problem?
  4. Make a picture or illustration of the problem.
  5. Determine the acts that are necessary in solving the problem.
  6. Carry out the computation.
  7. Does the answer seem reasonable?

- Show the student that if he already possesses mental content, learning does not necessarily start at zero. New points of view often develop suddenly when there is familiarity with the problem previously gained by experience.

INABILITY TO READ IN SCIENCE

Students reading in the field of science should know how to add words to their vocabularies, to read a chapter effectively, and to discover for themselves cause-and-effect relationships. In the solution of problems they must be able to determine that which is both relevant and consequential. They must understand *why* and *how* relationships, become acquainted with procedures in scientific study, become familiar with patterns and organization of scientific writing, develop flexibility in reading, and learn to follow directions. These skills are basic and fundamental.

The reading therapist who wishes to aid the student having difficulty in reading scientific materials may find the following suggestions helpful.

- Stimulate the child to observe the phenomena about him, to ask questions, and to consult dictionaries and encyclopedias. For example, the child's question, "Why does rain fall?" should be answered or the child should be referred to an adequate source of information.
- Aid the student to increase his knowledge of scientific terms through the use of context clues, picture clues, structural analysis, and the use of the dictionary or glossary. Encourage him both to prepare a card file of the scientific words which he needs to learn and to review them frequently.
- Stress the importance of reading for main ideas, for the purpose of answering questions, and for the purpose of making ideas one's own.
- Help the student to develop skill in outlining and note taking. It is suggested that the question-outline method rather than the topical outline be utilized by the student.
- Encourage the student to relate pictures and diagrams found in his science books to verbal descriptions of facts and principles.
- Provide the student with practice in reading to follow directions and emphasize the importance of doing so step by step and in the exact order prescribed. In the laboratory this is essential to effective

work. Many intelligent students become overconfident and careless in their reading.

- Aid the student in understanding that the scientist is concerned with both inductive and deductive thinking. Illustrate how inductive reasoning involves going from the parts to the whole or from results to the cause. Show that in deductive reasoning the thinker goes from the whole to the parts or from cause to results. Help the student to understand that, in general, scientists employ inductive reasoning in their investigations and that there are two forms of inductive thinking. One results from the accumulation of data and an attempt to draw inferences from the facts obtained in an investigation. The other involves setting up and testing certain postulates under well-designed and well-controlled conditions. Both of these approaches should be understood and recognized by readers of science.

- Illustrate how the scientist in making an investigation or study utilizes the following four mental processes.

  1. The *problem* is stated accurately and concretely.
  2. Several working *hypotheses* may be set up which later may be accepted or rejected.
  3. A *discovery* of facts and an *explanation* of the relevance of these facts to the problem is made.
  4. A *prediction* of the final outcome and its *verification* is then made.

  An understanding and appreciation of these acts employed by the scientist in his carefully planned research will help the reader to identify, interpret, and evaluate the ideas expressed in science textbooks.

- Acquaint the student with the patterns and organization of scientific writing. The following pattern may aid in the student's orientation.

  1. The purpose of the study is stated definitely and specifically.
  2. Findings of other investigators are summarized briefly.
  3. The procedure and materials employed are described.
  4. The author then summarizes his findings and the treatment of statistical data in order to show their significance.
  5. Finally, the author interprets his facts and states conservatively his inferences and conclusions.

- Encourage the student to adjust his rate of reading to the nature of the material and to the purpose for which he is reading. Scanning should be utilized only when looking for specific information. Skimming can be employed in making a preliminary survey or when attempting to summarize facts for review. In general, scientific material should be read slowly and carefully.
- Demonstrate and explain basic scientific concepts in as concrete a manner as possible. For example, "Why does the wind blow?" "What is the cause of ocean currents?" "How does a barometer work?"
- Stimulate the student to extend his scientific knowledge through wide reading of scientific literature. Suggest that he make use of abstracts in various fields to determine articles of interest to him.
- Plan to use instructional materials with the older disabled reader which are not too difficult and yet which can be used to show him how to get facts, to locate answers to his queries, and to follow directions. Refer to Appendix C.

FAILURE TO READ EFFECTIVELY IN THE SOCIAL STUDIES

In the social studies it is necessary to see how the past has contributed to the present and how a knowledge of previous events can be used in understanding not only the present but the future as well. As in any science, cause-effect relationships must be identified, interpreted, and evaluated. All the student's reading skills are required in this field. Special emphasis, however, will be placed upon his ability

- To read a chapter effectively.
- To secure significant ideas from tables, maps, and graphs.
- To think inductively and deductively.
- To put together information from various sources and to "work it over" so as to bring about a new pattern of ideas through the process of integration.

To the therapist dealing with a student having difficulty in reading in the social studies the following suggestions may prove beneficial.

- Encourage the student to use supplementary materials, such as other textbooks, atlases, encyclopedias, almanacs, and yearbooks. These will provide new ideas from various sources.

- Show the student how to skim a book effectively, for he will generally be required to use several books. He should be taught *why* it is advisable to (1) read the title page; (2) consider the copyright date; (3) read carefully the introduction and preface; (4) scan the table of contents; (5) skim the chapters of importance to the reader, paying special attention to introduction, summary, and main headings; (6) scan the index and the glossary; and (7) skim appendixes to determine if there are materials relevant to the student's problem.
- Evaluate the readability of several textbooks and select one suitable for the student as a supplement to the one he is required to study.
- Encourage the student to list and add to his vocabulary technical words, multisyllabic words, abstract terms, and mathematical terms employed in his text. Use 3- by 5-in. cards with the word used in a sentence on one side and its definition on the other.
- Prepare a thought-provoking question and ask the student to use his textbook in locating answers to the question. Encourage him to skim various parts of the book in his quest. Suggest that he answer the question in his own words.
- Show the advantages and disadvantages of the "buddy system" of study.
- Show the student how to integrate data from various sources—such as textbook, library reading, and lectures—into a new pattern showing cause-effect relationships. The table on page 254 shows this integration.

This table shows the events which led to the invention of the cotton gin and some consequences which grew out of its use. In the social studies cause-effect relationships are important.

INEFFECTIVE READING OF LITERATURE

All forms of literature are to be read for comfort, satisfaction, and pleasure. Some students, however, react with disgust at the mere suggestion that they read a short story, a novel, or a poem. The reading therapist should understand that there is no one way to read literature. Neither does the reading of one form differ greatly from the reading of the others. The effective reader of literature seeks to determine not only *what* has been expressed in words but *why* and *how* it has been asserted and portrayed.

TABLE 13-1 Integration of Information

Event	Causes	Consequences
Invention of cotton gin by Eli Whitney in 1793.	1. Cotton grew well in Georgia and South Carolina. 2. Planters in the South needed a money crop. 3. It was necessary to remove seeds from the cotton bolls. 4. Hand separation was too expensive.	A. Machine could clean 50 lbs. of cotton a day. B. Cotton became money crop in the south. C. United States became largest producer of cotton in the world. D. Economics of south improved. E. More slaves were needed on plantations. F. War Between the States may never have been fought.

Some Significant Elements in the Reading of Literature

Some literary elements common in all types of literature are shown and briefly explained.

Choice of words. The denotation and connotation of well-chosen words adds not only to the clarity of what has been written but to the effectiveness of the writer.

Diction. Diction is the manner of expressing ideas. Often the background, personality, and the intentions of the writer are revealed by his manner of saying what he has to say.

Organization. Organization is the framework of the composition, for it shows how and why the parts fit together. Reading to get a preview of organization can be done by skimming to discover the purpose of the writer, to determine summation of facts or effects, and to find how the writer tried to achieve his goal and the degree of his success.

Form. An analysis of form takes into consideration sentence length and arrangement, sentence rhythm, and paragraph construction. Each of these forms is designed to accomplish a purpose which the mature reader will be able to appreciate.

Tone. Tone is the summation of the intellectual and the emotional effects of writing. It is created by choice of words, diction, organization, and form. Its purpose is to create an effect upon the reader; consequently, it should be understood and appreciated by the well-read individual.

Lack of Appreciation

The appreciation of literature can be taught effectively by one who loves it and is enthusiastic in helping others to enjoy it. As the child learns to hunger for wholesome food, so he can learn to appreciate the short poem, the story, and the drama. His teacher will have him listen for sounds, and look for pictures; the teacher will encourage him to tell what he feels as he hears and sees. Factual information will not be stressed. He will in time be concerned with plot, action, and the emotional quality of the selection. His teacher, however, will help him to make use of delightful imagery and express what he sees, hears, and feels. Oral reading can be for many children a delightful means of expressing to others what they have appreciated in the poem or story. It should be voluntary and seldom required except in private, and then only as a means of identifying significant reading errors or for the purpose of preparing the child to read to his peers in an audience situation.

Treatment of Those Who Have Difficulty in Reading Literature

The teacher and reading therapist in aiding the student to read literature with zest and satisfaction should *stimulate, inform,* and *guide,* with the emphasis upon stimulation and guidance. The therapist himself must have a marked appreciation for and understanding of the literary forms with which the student is having difficulty. Some relevant suggestions and comments may prove helpful.

- Help the child to develop a story sense by telling short anecdotes, and encourage him to follow events and predict what could happen next. Encourage him to relate stories which he improvises as he tells them.

- Assist the child in establishing purposes for reading a story, such as determination of plot, description of setting, and character portrayal.
- Develop desire to read for humor and sparkling jokes. Encourage the child to tell those jokes that he has found most interesting. Help him to emphasize the punch line.
- Ask the child to find stories which can be dramatized. Have him select one whose dramatization he would like to direct. Permit him to select his characters and work out the play on his own.
- Aid the child in finding books at his interest and reading level. Many of the children referred to a reading clinic are reluctant readers to whom books are often a threat. Both teachers and parents want to interest and guide their children into the ways of good reading. The following sources can be helpful: *Teacher's Guide to Children's Books;*[2] *Your Children Want to Read;*[3] *Good Reading for Poor Readers;*[4] *Children and Books.*[5]
- Encourage the student to read widely and in accordance with his personal tastes. The disabled and reluctant reader should not be restricted to prescribed reading lists.
- Read a literary selection of interest aloud to a small group of students. Encourage discussion at the end of each reading, but do not seek detailed analysis.
- Develop background and readiness for reading. Many excellent readers lack the experiential background to interpret and react to a poem, a novel, and even some short stories. Some teachers have encouraged several mature readers to participate in panel discussions of the books they have read. The student lacking background can not only profit from this discussion but may be encouraged to read with zest the same book if it has been appraised highly by someone he admires.

[2] Nancy Larrick, *A Teacher's Guide to Children's Books* (Columbus, Ohio: Charles E. Merrill Books, 1960).

[3] Ruth Tooze, *Your Children Want to Read* (Englewood Cliffs, N.J.: Prentice-Hall, 1957).

[4] George D. Spache, *Good Reading for Poor Readers,* rev. ed. (Champaign, Ill.: The Garrard Press, 1962).

[5] Mary Hill Arbuthnot, *Children and Books,* rev. ed. (Glenview, Ill.: Scott, Foresman, and Company, 1957).

- Demonstrate the use of imagery. The student can learn to make use of imagery, the visual, the auditory, the kinesthetic, the tactual, and all sensory experience. Sensory reactions, however, come only as a result of mental content and previous experiences. To have imagination, one must have the materials with which to imagine and these can come only as a by-product of extensive and intensive living. This mental content can be cultivated and developed by reading, by seeing plays, by listening to good music, and by living and adjusting in our changing society.

- Illustrate the underlying meaning of several selections. The student should look beneath the surface of mere words to discover deeper meanings. He should let his imagination run rampant and actually become involved in the emotional aspects of the selection. He should look, listen, and sense that which the writer has expressed in dramatization, rhythm, metaphors, symbols, allusions, and other forms of tone. What the writer has to express is not as obvious as facts in a textbook. Nevertheless, his subtle meanings can be much more exciting.

- Emphasize the value of reference materials. The dictionary and encyclopedia are helpful in aiding the student with his interpretation of metaphors and allusions. Textbooks in mythology and history are essential in appreciating the latter. Books devoted to the language arts and literature can furnish background for the understanding of the various figures of speech. Literary reviews can provide the older student critical evaluations of contemporary plays and newly published novels. He, however, should read and establish his own judgments and later compare his opinions with those of the professional critics.

- Suggest that the student read leisurely. Literature, like good food, should be taken slowly. Browse, sample, taste, compare so as to stimulate the literary appetite. Relax and be receptive. Skimming and scanning, under some circumstances, can be employed effectively by the mature reader to locate passages of special interest and value to him. He should not hurry.

- Stimulate an interest in short poems and show the student how to read them. Poetry reading can be interesting to people of all degrees of maturity for the poem is a word picture of many sensory experiences. Recordings of poems read by children can not only add interest but can serve as a means of appraising growth. Some suggestions which can be helpful to the reluctant reader are listed.

1. Read the poem as a whole silently so as to obtain the central thought.
2. If some sentences are difficult, determine the subject and the verb and rearrange in conventional order. Determine what the sentence actually says. What did the author accomplish by the unconventional arrangement?
3. Read the poem aloud so as to "catch" the rhythm and be able to express the thought and emotional qualities adequately.
4. Make the poem come to life and avoid an overemphasis on historical background, kinds of meter, and figures of speech. All this can come later.
5. Identify phrases and lines of special interest and determine how the writer has made them effective.
6. Read the poem aloud to a friend and make sure that he too appreciates the excellent qualities of the selection. The student should understand that if the reader appreciates the emotional qualities of the poem, he can express these to others.

• Avoid frustrating the student. The teacher and therapist should consider carefully the advantages and disadvantages of permitting a disabled reader whose performance level in reading is that of an individual in the fourth or fifth grade from enrolling in a class in which, for example, *Hamlet* or *Macbeth* are taught.

SUMMARY

This chapter has endeavored to show the therapist how to treat students having difficulty in reading for meaning. A hierarchy of skills has been discussed ranging from sentence reading to reading in mathematics, science, social studies, and literature. Remediation rather than the teaching of reading has been stressed.

GUIDED ACTIVITY 13

Aim

To provide remediation for students unable to read effectively for meaning.

Materials

1. Chapter 13, *Diagnosis and Treatment of the Disabled Reader.*
2. Materials selected from Appendix C of this book.

Procedure

1. Work out a plan for showing a fourth-grade boy how to identify the central thought of a paragraph.
2. Plan on teaching four sixth-grade boys to read a chapter in a social studies text. Stress reading to find main ideas, how to read for a purpose, and how to make ideas one's own.
3. Outline a plan for showing these boys how to read a chapter without headings.
4. Show a boy in the ninth grade how to read a short poem. Report your observations.
5. Select a child in the sixth grade who has difficulty in reading and solving a problem in arithmetic. Determine by observation and interview why he is having difficulty. Outline the treatment you would suggest.
6. Show how you would teach a child in the fifth grade to write a paragraph.
7. In attempting to reinforce this instruction what materials would you select from Appendix C.
8. Explain why a good reader might have difficulty in reading in the content fields.
9. Show how you would help a small group of sixth-grade children to build experiential background in elementary science. The topic for considera- ation is *Weather and Some Causal Factors.*

QUESTIONS AND REFERENCES

Questions

1. What are some techniques for teaching reading as a thinking process?

2. How can the student learn to concentrate?

References

1. Morton Botel, *How to Teach Reading* (Chicago: Follett Pub- lishing Company, 1959), Chap. II.

2. Homer L. J. Carter and Dorothy J. McGinnis, *Reading, A Key to Academic Success* (Dubuque, Iowa: Wm. C. Brown Company, 1967), Chap. 9.

Questions	References
3. What factors make up an informal reading inventory for high school and college students?	**3.** *Ibid.*, Appendix A.
4. How can students make effective use of books?	**4.** Homer L. J. Carter and Dorothy J. McGinnis, *Teaching Individuals to Read* (Boston: D. C. Heath and Company, 1962), Chap. 8.
5. How can the student in the secondary schools improve his reading?	**5.** M. Jerry Weiss, *Reading in the Secondary Schools* (New York: The Odyssey Press, 1961).
6. What special reading instruction is needed in English, science, and the social studies?	**6.** Ruth Strang, Constance M. McCullough, and Arthur E. Traxler, *The Improvement of Reading*, 4th ed. (New York: McGraw-Hill Book Company, 1967), Chaps. 8, 9, and 10.
7. How can the child be taught to read with understanding?	**7.** John J. DeBoer and Martha Dallmann, *The Teaching of Reading*, rev. ed. (New York: Holt, Rinehart and Winston, 1964), Chaps. 7a and 7b.
8. How can basic comprehension abilities be developed?	**8.** Guy L. Bond and Miles A. Tinker, *Reading Difficulties, Their Diagnosis and Correction*, 2nd ed. (New York: Appleton-Century-Crofts, 1967), Chap. 11.
9. How can reading in the content areas be improved?	**9.** *Ibid.*, Chap. 15.
10. What are some prerequisites to critical reading?	**10.** Arthur W. Heilman, *Principles and Practices of Teaching Reading* (Columbus, Ohio: Charles E. Merrill Books, 1961), Chap. 9.
11. What are some practical suggestions for teaching students to read in industrial arts, music, and homemaking?	**11.** Henry A. Bamman, Ursula Hogan, and Charles E. Greene, *Reading Instruction in the Secondary Schools* (New York:

Questions

References

Longmans, Green and Company, 1961), Chaps. XII and XIII.

12. How can parents, teachers, and community leaders prevent poor readers from becoming school dropouts?

12. Richard L. Watson, "Reading and the Potential Dropout," in Ralph Staiger and David A. Sohn, eds., *New Directions in Reading* (New York: Bantam Books, 1967), pp. 210–213.

Chapter 14

Appraisal of Remediation

After remediation has been provided, the child, his parents, his teacher, and the reading therapist want to know what change has taken place from the time of initiation of treatment to the time of its termination. This chapter will define the nature of progress, set forth some principles of evaluation, and outline some formal and informal methods of appraising change in reading performance which may be due to remediation. Means of evaluating professional skills have been suggested.

WHAT IS PROGRESS IN READING?

Progress in the development of reading skills is the result of growth. In the treatment of the disabled reader it is assumed that factors retarding or preventing growth in reading have been removed or mitigated so as to permit normal development. The assumption is generally made that an increment in performance between the time of initial and final testing is due to effective diagnosis and treatment. This may or may not be true. Only carefully controlled and well-designed experimentation can prove or disprove this assumption.

Growth has many dimensions. As the child grows in his ability to read, he grows physically, mentally, emotionally, and socially. His progress in reading is generally parallel to his progress in other areas. Reading is an act of the total organism and is an inseparable aspect of it. Consequently, in the evaluation of reading achievement many

263

other factors must be considered other than scores resulting from the administration of survey tests in reading.

Progress in reading can be observed. The following questions call attention to several factors which should be considered as points of reference.

Does the student use the library more frequently?

Does the student do more reading at home?

In what way is the student doing better work in the classroom?

Have the student's marks improved in the language arts?

During the study periods has ability to concentrate improved?

Do teachers report that the student's attitude toward reading is better?

Does the student ask for help in reading more or less frequently?

Do the parents report that improvement has been made?

What evidence of growth in reading does the child report?

What evidence of improvement does the teacher report?

Growth in reading, as in any life situation, will be slow. In general, observable change will not take place in less than three to six months, and frequently more time will be required.

AREAS OF APPRAISAL

Reading, as pointed out previously in this book, is a function of the whole individual and is more than an accumulation of specific abilities and skills such as sight vocabularies, word-attack skills, sentence reading, paragraph reading, oral reading, and chapter reading. Instead it is an integration of these abilities and skills into functional acts of living and adjusting. Obviously, all these skills are important as parts and should be evaluated; however, their integration is the chief goal of the teacher's efforts in the classroom and in the life activities of the student. These skills and numerous similar skills must be measured and evaluated, but in doing so the teacher and therapist must not lose sight of the importance of their amalgamation.

Growth is multidimensional and has many facets. Vigorous growth in reading soon becomes apparent not only in an integration of skills as manifested by observable reading performance in the classroom but also in growth in work-study attainments, literary appreciation, personality adjustment, social adjustment, vocational status, and economic status. As the individual grows and matures, reading becomes more and more a way of life and a concomitant of purposeful living. Its appraisal becomes more difficult.

SOME PRINCIPLES OF EVALUATION

Some principles or points of view concerning evaluation may be stated as follows.

Evaluation may be made in terms of usefulness or function. In our society objects and attainments are valued in terms of what can be accomplished with them. The determination of the usefulness of an acquired skill in reading is a generally satisfactory means of evaluation. A teacher, for example, has reported that John has identified the main ideas of a chapter in a social studies text, converted major headings into questions, and answered these questions on cards. This statement is an evaluation of John's ability to *use* effectively his reading skills while studying a chapter. In other words, John was able to identify, interpret, and express certain ideas in words of his own and not those of the writer. He was able to make use of them, and this is an important factor to consider.

Evaluation should be objective. Objective measures are generally effective means of evaluation *if* they measure that which is significant to the teacher. Standardized tests of reading permit statistical treatment which can determine whether or not the results obtained are truly significant. An increment in a score after several months of remediation may or may not indicate a real gain in reading achievement. In well-designed research, measurement is mandatory. Evaluations, however, may be objective without the use of standardized tests. The statement that the student identified the central thought of each of three paragraphs is an objective evaluation if it is made without bias or prejudice.

Evaluation can be subjective. The student's statement, "I have learned to ask questions as I read and to look for answers," is subjective. It is the student's evaluation of his ability to read for a purpose. The value of such statements can be judged in terms of data from other sources. Informal techniques such as oral reading and informal reading inventories can be used to investigate the student's ability to ask questions and then read for answers. Subjective appraisals of reading achievement can be of value to both the student and the therapist.

Evaluation of change in reading performance can be made subjectively by considering the *kind* and *amount* of reading the child does. Furthermore, an appraisal can be made of his *attitude* toward reading. In fact, these evaluations can, in many instances, be of greater importance to the teacher and therapist than age scores, grade scores, and percentiles resulting from the administration of survey tests, for these instruments may not measure those aspects of reading which are necessary to consider in the process of remediation.

Evaluation can be made in terms of goals. Whether or not a student has achieved *his* objective in reading can be significant. Success, even if limited, can be important not only to the student but to the clinician as well. A reading therapist has reported that Lee, who has been working on vocabulary development, has been able to apply successfully five suggestions which she had made to him concerning the study of words required in his biology assignment. This evaluation in terms of a specific goal is objective and has also been made in terms of use.

Evaluation should be an ongoing process. Achievement in reading should be evaluated continuously by both instructor and student. This can be done objectively, subjectively, and in terms of use as well as immediate and ultimate goals. Evaluation, however, is only the beginning of an important process. The disabled reader needs to be shown frequently the progress that he is achieving. If possible, his gains should be shown graphically and actually set forth so as to increase his self-concept. To the student of limited ability in reading, this glimpse of success is of great importance. If insignificant gains have been made, the teacher will want to know why so little has been accomplished and what factors have contributed to the lack of adequate achievement. Deficiencies again must be identified and significant needs must be discovered. Adequate instruction and therapy should be followed.

Results of evaluation must be interpreted. Objective data, judgments, inferences, and opinions need careful interpretation. Even test scores mean nothing aside from the conditions under which they were obtained. The therapist should ask the following questions:

What do these test scores mean?

Are gains the result of remediation or are other factors involved?

Are the Placebo and Hawthorne effects present? In other words, is the treatment really effective or only due to the enthusiasm of the therapist.

What is the opinion of the teacher concerning the child's progress?

To what extent have preconceived ideas and emotional bias affected the teacher's conclusions?

How valuable is the student's report of marked gain?

FORMAL METHODS OF EVALUATION

The standardized test is the most widely used instrument for evaluating reading programs and individual progress in reading. Each test, however, measures only certain aspects of reading; consequently, if only one test is employed, evaluation of reading skills is only partial. Reading is a complex process, and it cannot at this time be adequately evaluated by standardized tests. The teacher and clinician must first determine those aspects of reading that they want to measure and then select the test which can best aid them in accomplishing their purpose.

In the selection of tests the following factors should be considered.

Does the test have educational significance and measure those aspects of reading which have real value to the teacher?

Is it a reliable and valid measure?

Is it easily administered and scored?

Can raw scores be interpreted in terms of grade scores, age scores, or percentiles?

Are equivalent forms available?

How well rated is the test in *Mental Measurements Yearbooks* by Oscar K. Buros?

In attempting to evaluate growth of certain reading skills, an equivalent form of the initial test must be administered. The teacher should follow directions precisely and make no adjustments or changes, however plausible they may seem. Directions for scoring must be followed exactly as given in the manual and if questions arise concerning the statistical significance of scores they should be answered by consulting the manual and by referring to a textbook in statistics. Interpretation of data resulting from tests should be made with care and, if possible, reinforced by facts from other sources for frequently reasonable assumptions can be quite erroneous.

The conversion of raw scores obtained from reading tests into grade scores and age equivalents may lead to faulty interpretations. For many reasons the accuracy of these scores is more apparent than real. Scores interpreted in terms of percentiles can also lead to erroneous conclusions. Teachers are not justified in comparing grade scores, age equivalents, and percentiles obtained on one test with grade scores, age equivalents, and percentiles resulting from administration of another test. This statement, however, does not apply to equivalent forms of the same test.

INFORMAL METHODS OF EVALUATION

Evaluation of change in reading performance can be made by means of interviews, informal inventories, tape recorders, the student's use of the library, and the student's appraisal of his own achievement. In utilizing these informal means of evaluation with children, the attention of the therapist and teacher should be focused upon the child as she *observes* his reactions for *how* the child responds can be more significant than what he actually says in words. In the study of the child, hunches based upon observations should not be neglected.

Interviews: A Means of Evaluation

Interviews with the child, his parents, and his teachers can be a means of estimating the student's progress in reading. After the subject of the interview has been announced and rapport has been established, the interviewee should be encouraged to talk freely concerning the reading program and the progress which may have been made. If necessary, leading questions may be asked concerning what has actually been accomplished. Some typical questions to be asked of teachers are listed.

What evidence have you observed of progress in reading?
How can you support the statement that John is doing better work in the classroom?
What evidence do you have for assuming that this improvement is due to gains in reading performance?

Similar questions can be asked in an interview with parents. Questions which can be answered *yes* or *no* in this investigation will limit the value of the information secured. The attitude of the interviewer should be mildly one of doubt so that the interviewee will find it necessary to prove his point and at the same time not feel compelled to give the interviewer the information which the interviewee assumes the interviewer wants to hear. Data resulting from interviews should be interpreted in terms of information from other sources.

Informal Inventories: A Means of Evaluation

In using informal reading inventories for purposes of evaluation their qualitative rather than their quantitative aspects should be stressed. Obviously, two sets of inventories, one initial and one final, should be employed by the same person and the types of errors made on each set should be compared. Some typical questions to be considered are listed.

What changes occurred in the means of identifying unknown words?
Were contextual clues used more frequently or less frequently on the second inventory?
Were "why" and "how" questions answered with greater ease?
What changes occurred in the child's ability to find answers to factual questions?
What evidence is there for assuming change in the child's attitude toward reading?
How did means of frustration differ on the first and second application of the inventories?

The careful consideration of these and similar questions will be more helpful to the therapist than a comparison of the initial and final capacity, frustration, instructional, and independent reading levels.

The Tape Recorder as a Means of Evaluation

Most students are interested in hearing a reproduction of their own voices. Children should be taught not only to listen but to listen for the purpose of appraising their own achievement. Monroe and Rogers[1]

---

[1] Marion Monroe and Bernice Rogers, *Foundations for Reading* (Glenview, Ill.: Scott, Foresman and Company, 1964), pp. 68–88.

have made several suggestions concerning the characteristics of voice sounds which may be of interest to the therapist. Two recordings of the same selection or of different selections may be compared by the reading therapist and by the child whose reading was reproduced. An analysis of errors may be made by both teacher and child. The qualitative aspects of these studies are more important than the quantitative in the evaluation of achievement. Some illustrative questions to be considered are listed.

Which of the two selections would afford the listener the greater pleasure?

What changes became apparent in the effectiveness of expression of ideas?

What changes in the use of punctuation occurred?

What changes were observed in *intensity* of voice?

What changes were apparent in *quality* of voice?

Were changes in *pitch* of voice observed? (There can be a relationship between pitch and emotional tension.)

Were there more or less substitutions on the second recording?

Were more or less words omitted on the second reading?

In what way did the kinds of mispronunciations differ?

Use of Library: A Means of Evaluation

Good readers make frequent use of the library. The younger children like to browse and select new books. Older students know how to use the card catalogue and the *Reader's Guide* and they are familiar with reference materials and where to find the information they seek. The library is a delightful place for readers who like books, and the extent of its use is an indication of the effectiveness of the entire reading program.

Observations of students in the library are a means of evaluating not only their ability to use reading as a tool but to use it as a way of life and as a source of pleasure and satisfaction. It may be observed that some children, mostly boys, will select books far above their reading level merely for the purpose of impressing their peers and for improving their image in the classroom. These children need remediation.

The following questions suggest factors to be observed in the library.

Does the child enjoy reading?
Does he come frequently?
What section does he visit most frequently?
Does he ask for help?
What titles is he most apt to select?
Is he a "problem child" while in the library?
Does he browse and read alone?
Does he actually read the books he selects?
Can he make effective use of reference materials?
Does he make use of the dictionary?
Does he use the card catalogue?
Does he use the *Reader's Guide?*
What periodicals does he look at or read?
Does he work on his assignments while in the library?
Does he make effective use of his time?

Self-appraisal

The child should be encouraged to make judgments concerning his own performance in reading. He should feel confident in his ability to make both positive and negative appraisals of his reading skills. Children frequently furnish information concerning their interests, abilities, and disabilities which cannot be secured in any other manner. In an interview the child can be made to feel that his opinions concerning his ability are of value to the therapist and that he should express what he really feels concerning his successes and failures in reading. Some areas to be considered in the conference are suggested.

What reading skills does the child think he possesses?
What reading skills does he think he needs to acquire?
How does the child identify unfamiliar words?
What in the opinion of the child can the therapist or teacher do to help?
What does he say that he likes to read best of all?
What does the child say about the reading materials used in the class?
Would the student classify himself as a poor, good, or excellent reader?

Self-appraisal is an act of maturity and is generally manifested by those students who are ready and willing to assume the responsibility of learning to read. It has been observed that superior students have a tendency to underestimate their achievement.

EVALUATION OF PERSONALITY TRAITS

It has been pointed out that therapy is a part of treatment. Consequently, there is a need for evaluating its effectiveness. Objective measures of personality, although of value in making a diagnosis, are of little worth in determining change in personality over a comparatively short period of time. Rating scales in which characteristics to be appraised are defined and illustrated are of value if the rater has actually observed the child in situations where the traits might be revealed. The alert teacher and therapist can, however, utilize an informal inventory to assess personal characteristics or traits which may have been modified by treatment. The following questions based upon observable facts can be used to appraise change that may have occurred following the initiation of remediation. Each item represents an area to be investigated.

Is the child less apt to feel inferior to his friends?

Is he less apt to worry over failure?

Does he find it less difficult to concentrate when reading silently?

Is he less apt to think his friends like to make fun of him?

Is it less difficult for him to forget his troubles?

Is the child less apt to feel sick when he has an unpleasant task to do?

Is he less apt to feel that no one likes him?

Does the child have more confidence in his ability to read?

Does the child appear to like his teacher more than he did?

Does he assume more responsibility for learning to read than he did before treatment?

Is he less apt to exhibit emotional tension such as falling and tripping over things?

While reading silently, is he less apt to move his tongue and lips?

Does he show more zest for reading now?

Does he contribute more to class discussion?

Is he less apt to be tardy?

Is he less apt to laugh for no reason at all?

Is he less sensitive concerning his disability?

Is he more meticulous in his reading?

Does the child have more insight into the nature of his disability?

Is there less difficulty in verbalization?

These items are suggestive of many others which the alert teacher and reading therapist will design to investigate certain personality traits which may have been modified by therapy.

KEEPING RECORDS

The reading therapist comes in contact with many children each day. She is confronted with the problem of interpreting the progress of these boys and girls to their parents and to their homeroom teachers. Consequently, a systematic attempt must be made to record and have available relevant data concerning each child under treatment.

Evaluation of achievement, as previously suggested, should be an ongoing process. The carpenter on the job uses measurements as he works and does not wait until a specified time for an assessment. Appraisal in classroom and laboratory must be continuous; consequently, resulting data should become immediately a part of the child's record. Some therapists have found that a folder for each student can be a locus for a cumulative history of the child's remediation. Anecdotal records, test scores, data from informal inventories, medical records, dated samples of the child's work, statement of the diagnosis, and an outline of treatment are but some of the materials which should be filed and made ready for future reference. Some therapists fold a sheet of typing paper vertically and on the left-hand side of the middle they occasionally write inferences concerning the child and on the right side of the paper they record the supporting data. Each sheet should show the child's name, the date of the comment, and the name of the writer. These generalizations are of real value when reporting the child's progress. Other significant observations made from time to time should be recorded. Care, however, should be taken to distinguish between *facts* and *inferences*. Record keeping should not become a fetish; instead, it should be a means to an end. At the conclusion of the school year the child's folder should be reviewed and all irrelevant materials destroyed.

EFFICIENCY OF CLINICIAN AND THERAPIST

The efficiency of the clinical team should be evaluated in terms of the goals which have been established. In the well-organized clinic or reading laboratory, the following objectives are generally sought.

- Adequate diagnosis.
- Adequate treatment.
- Adequate opportunity for in-service indoctrination of teachers.
- Well-designed and well-controlled research.

It is difficult to determine adequacy of diagnosis, for controls are generally impossible to establish. If growth does take place, it is unwise to assume that gains in reading performance are due entirely to effective diagnosis and treatment. The clinician can always be critical of his approaches, techniques, and judgments. This is especially true if there is a deadly uniformity in his interpretations of children's maladjustments. His attitude must be that of the scientist, and he must always be a doubter. He will hold fast to that which is good, yet always seek that which is new after its worth has been established. Constant evaluation is essential to growth in techniques of diagnosis.

Treatment, instruction, and use of materials are also difficult to appraise adequately, for generally there is a lack of effective controls. It is difficult, indeed, to say that the prescription has accomplished its purpose. One can say, however, that no form of remediation is equally adequate in all instances. The therapist must make sure that he does not administer the same remedy to all his patients. Availability of materials should never determine treatment. Many factors must be given careful consideration in any attempt to evaluate the effectiveness of treatment, instruction, and use of materials.

In appraising results attributable to the clinic, a well-planned follow-up of cases referred to the team can be helpful. Parents and teachers are generally willing to return for a conference in order to discuss adequacy of remediation. Interviews with the child, with his parents, and with his teacher can provide valuable information concerning effectiveness of instruction and therapy. In fact, data secured by interviews may be as significant as objective data provided by tests. Some reading clinics employ well-designed inventories which are completed by the child's teacher and by his parents. Such information can be of marked value in the appraisal of the effectiveness of treatment.

Many clinics achieve success in the indoctrination and in-service training of teachers. It is difficult for school systems and even for institutions of higher learning to secure adequately prepared reading specialists. Some school administrators select from their staff promising young teachers and encourage them to do graduate work in reading. For these young men and women participation in the activities of a reading clinic and laboratory can stimulate their interest and increase their desire for graduate study. Interns from local universities can be attracted, and later there is the possibility of them becoming regular members of the teaching personnel.

There are many opportunities for research in a progressive and growing reading clinic. The staff is generally made up of young psychologists, sociologists, and educators who are research oriented and who desire to make a contribution in their field. Furthermore, these young specialists are aware of the need of well-designed and well-controlled research in the field of reading. In their daily work they focus their attention upon the child and develop hunches which they would like to investigate. In fact, if valid research does not come out of the clinic, the cause should be of concern to the whole staff.

APPRAISAL OF PROFESSIONAL SKILLS

Professional skills increase in kind and degree. The teacher, reading clinician, and therapist are concerned with their development and growth. Each desires to appraise his own attainments and to have these recognized by his associates and adequately evaluated by his superiors. In this professional climate, growth can be stimulated. To accomplish this goal, the writers have suggested the use of the *Clinical Rating Card* and the *Therapist Evaluation Sheet*.

Clinical Rating Card

The purpose of the Clinical Rating Card is to evaluate as effectively as possible the reading specialist in terms of such factors as vitality, general personality, dynamic personality, growth and progressiveness,

Name_____Name of Rater_____Date_____

Quality Groups	Points	Weighted Values of Factors									
		1	2	2	2	2	2	2	4	4	4
		Vital.	Gen. Pers.	Dyn. Pers.	Growth & Prog.	Team Work	Prep.	Control-Manage.	Clinical Tech.	Prob. Solv.	Results
Very Superior	4						✔		✔		
Superior	3		✔			✔		✔		✔	✔
Average	2	✔		✔	✔						
Inferior	1										
Very Inferior	0										

SUMMARY

Values	Points	Products
1	2	2
2	3	6
2	2	4
2	2	4
2	3	6
2	4	8
2	3	6
4	4	16
4	3	12
4	3	12
Total Score		76
Classification		B

DISTRIBUTION OF SCORES   CLASSIFICATION

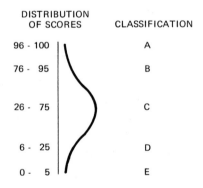

96 - 100	A
76 - 95	B
26 - 75	C
6 - 25	D
0 - 5	E

This rating is the point of view of the rater and represents inferences which are based upon observations made by him. It is his opinion and has been given for the purpose of starting a process of adjustment which may be of mutual benefit both to the reading specialist and the clinic. Consequently, it is urged that these points be discussed freely between the rater and the person rated. In fact, it may be well for the person to rate himself and compare his rating with that of the rater.

Figure 14-1. Clinical rating card.

teamwork, preparation, control and management, clinical techniques, problem solving, and terminal results. The use of this scale is suggested not only to stimulate the growth and development of the individual but to set forth the extent and degree to which the worker possesses, in the opinion of the rater, certain basic and fundamental abilities and traits. It is urged that this scale be discussed freely by the rater and the person rated. In fact, it may be well for an individual to rate himself and compare his rating with that of the rater. The principal purpose of the scale is to start a process of adjustment which will be of mutual benefit to the worker, the clinic, and the school.

In the evaluation of traits and abilities it is essential that consideration be given to (1) the evaluation of a single trait or ability alone and without overlapping with other traits and abilities, (2) a point of reference above and below which variations may be considered, (3) a ranking device of some sort, and (4) conformation of variations above and below the point of reference to a normal curve of distribution. After all factors have been considered and marked on the card, it is then possible to determine a numerical score.

In using the scale it is suggested that the rater read carefully the definitions of the terms used in the procedure of evaluating the effectiveness of the reading specialist. Words and trait names have a way of varying with the background and experience of people who use them. However, such factors as vitality, general personality, dynamic personality, growth and progressiveness, teamwork, and all the others used in this scale may be regarded as "pegs" upon which may be hung a whole series of terms descriptive of the factors used. For example, the factor of vitality is given meaning by the terms *health, endurance,* and *reserve force.* Meaning of terms used in the rating procedure may be stated as follows.

Vitality	Health, endurance, reserve force.
General personality	Sincerity, genuineness, sense of responsibility, dependability, accuracy, discretion, judgment.
Dynamic Personality	Initiative, resourcefulness, enthusiasm, alertness, drive.

Growth and Progressiveness	Professional interest and growth, ability to adjust to new and changing points of view.
Teamwork	Cooperation, individual and group loyalty, attitude toward clinic or reading laboratory.
Preparation	Background, experience, adequate mental content which can be used to solve problems.
Control and Management	Ability to handle children and adults tactfully. Ability to establish rapport. Sensitive.
Clinical Techniques	Skill in observing, interviewing, testing, using informal inventories. Determining relevance of data.
Problem Solving	Ability to recognize a problem, to make an interpretation, and to provide treatment.
Results	Achievement of satisfactory adjustment of child in his environment.

Informal Appraisal of Therapist

The student therapist needs guidance from the classroom teacher, from the supervisor of remedial services, and from the reading clinician. The following evaluation sheet properly used by the individuals responsible for the supervision of the student therapist can provide information, guidance, and encouragement for the therapist preparing herself for work with disabled readers.

Therapist Evaluation Sheet*

Therapist   Child

Date   Age

Supervisor   Grade

Indicate degree of success

	Excellent	Average	Poor
Have each session well planned.			
Arrive before the child and have materials ready.			
Greet the child warmly.			
Establish rapport generally.			
Establish rapport and enthusiasm for specific activities.			
Practice therapeutic techniques:			
a warm smile			
honest praise and commendation			
genuine enthusiasm			
Demonstrate initiative, vigor, and endurance.			
Demonstrate tact, mature judgment and ability in handling the child.			
Have the ability to administer an informal reading inventory effectively.			
Demonstrate knowledge and skill in choosing, administering, and interpreting standardized tests.			
Use tests and informal inventories to guide instruction.			
Let one therapy session help direct the instruction of the succeeding ones.			
Vary the activities and materials.			
Accept suggestions.			
Demonstrate good organization during the teaching session.			
Demonstrate good organization in keeping a log book (lesson plans, written account of conferences, tests).			

* Prepared by Betty Hagberg, Western Michigan University.

Conduct parent conferences tactfully and
effectively.
Demonstrate ability in writing final report
to parent and school.
Show professional growth in therapy.

SUMMARY

This chapter has discussed the nature of progress in reading, some
areas to be appraised, and several principles of evaluation. It has
shown some formal and informal methods of appraising not only
changes in reading performance but modified personality traits of the
individual as well. Some ways of maintaining continuous records have
been included. Furthermore, the writers have suggested means of
assessing the effectiveness of professional workers in their treatment
of disabled readers.

GUIDED ACTIVITY 14

Aim

To secure experience in the evaluation of change in reading performance.

Materials

1. Chapter 14 of *Diagnosis and Treatment of the Disabled Reader*.
2. Tape recorder.
3. The Clinical Rating Card which is found in this chapter.

Procedure

1. Select a child with whom you have worked and for whom you have
   reading test scores. Administer an equivalent form of the test to the
   student. After having scored the test, examine both the initial and final
   tests for the purpose of determining changes which have occurred in
   the interim.
2. Interview the child and investigate some of the areas suggested in
   this chapter.
3. Interview the child's teacher so as to determine the nature of changes
   that may have occurred between the time you began to work with the
   child and the time that you terminated instruction.

4. Interview the child's parents concerning changes in the child's attitude, reading performance, and personality traits that may have occurred during the period of instruction and therapy.

5. Write a brief summary of the facts and inferences resulting from your study of the child's test scores and your interviews with him, his teacher, and his parents.

6. Administer to a child an informal reading inventory and use both oral and silent reading. While the informal oral reading inventory is used, make a tape recording of the child's responses.
   a. Analyze the reading errors that were manifest on these inventories.
   b. Determine those errors on both inventories that in your opinion are significant enough to treat.
   c. Outline the treatment you would recommend for correcting these errors.
   d. Describe the procedure you would follow in appraising the effectiveness of your instruction.

7. Outline a plan for the evaluation of the effectiveness of a school-wide program in reading.

8. Select one of your friends who is a teacher of reading, a reading therapist, or a reading clinician. Ask this individual to make use of the Clinical Rating Card suggested in this chapter in rating you as a therapist. Rate yourself and then compare your rating with that given you by your friend.
   a. How do the two ratings compare?
   b. After you have considered both ratings, what inferences can you draw concerning your strengths and weaknesses as a reading specialist?

QUESTIONS AND REFERENCES

Questions

References

1. How are standardized tests used and misused?

   1. Arthur E. Traxler, "Standardized Tests—What They Are, How They Are Used and Misused," *NEA Journal*, 48:18–20 (November, 1959).

2. How are scores interpreted?

   2. *STEP Manual for Interpreting Scores—Reading* (Princeton, N.J.: Cooperative Test Division, Educational Testing Service, 1959).

3. How can development in and through reading be evaluated?

   3. Ruth Strang, "Evaluation of Development in and Through

Questions	References
	Reading," in Nelson B. Henry, ed., *Development in and Through Reading*, Sixtieth Yearbook of the National Society for the Study of Education (Chicago: The University of Chicago Press, 1961), Chap. 21.
4. How can a reading program be evaluated?	**4.** Robert M. Wilson, *Diagnostic and Remedial Reading* (Columbus, Ohio: Charles E. Merrill Books, 1967), Chap. 9.
5. How effective are programs in reading?	**5.** Emery P. Bliesmer, "Evaluating Progress in Remedial Reading Programs," *The Reading Teacher*, (March, 1962), pp. 344–350.
6. What is the long-term effect of remedial reading instruction?	**6.** Bruce Balow, "The Long-Term Effect of Remedial Reading Instruction," in Leo M. Schell and Paul C. Burns, eds., *Reading: An Anthology of Sources* (Boston: Allyn and Bacon, 1968), pp. 414–420.
7. How can tests be helpful to teachers?	**7.** Henry E. Garrett, *Testing for Teachers* (New York: American Book Company, 1959).
8. What are some appraisal techniques for school and classroom?	**8.** Mary C. Austin, Clifford L. Bush, and Mildred H. Huebner, *Reading Evaluation* (New York: The Ronald Press Company, 1961).
9. How can reading growth be appraised?	**9.** Miles A. Tinker and Constance M. McCullough, *Teaching Elementary Reading*, 3rd ed. (New York: Appleton-Century-Crofts, 1968), Chap. 17.
10. In the analysis of several widely used reading tests, what factors are considered?	**10.** Ruth Strang, *Diagnostic Teaching of Reading* (New York: McGraw-Hill Book Company, 1964), Appendix A.

Chapter 15

Reports, Written and Oral

The assumption is made in this chapter that a comprehensive study of the disabled reader should result in a report of psychological and educational procedures which is meaningful, fundamentally consistent, and communicable to others. To accomplish this objective, the writers have discussed some factors essential to written and oral reports prepared by the reading clinician and therapist.

WRITTEN REPORTS

Written reports are designed to acquaint parents, teachers, and various social agencies with information concerning the individual having difficulty in making satisfactory progress in reading. Their only purpose is to help the maladjusted reader. In providing aid to the disabled reader, two types of reports are essential. The report summarizing a *clinical study* of the child is designed to help the referents as they endeavor to assist him in overcoming his disability in reading and in making a more satisfactory adjustment in the classroom. The second type of report, generally prepared by the reading therapist, summarizes the *results of instruction and therapeutic procedures* over a period of time such as a term or semester.

Each of these reports, written to accomplish a specific purpose, must place the welfare of the child first. His image and self-concept must remain unscathed, and no faulty characterization should be made by the professional workers charged with his diagnosis and treatment. In achieving this goal, it is suggested that reports be evaluated by at least two workers or staff members before being presented in final form.

Both reports of clinical study and reports of progress resulting from instruction and therapy should be meaningful and functional if they are to be helpful to referents, parents, and teachers. In many instances oral communication is unsurpassed as a supplement. Questions can be asked and answered. Ideas can be clarified by discussion, and rapport can be improved by frequent contacts. The activities of both reading clinician and therapist should be summarized in reports which are communicable to parents and teachers. Each specialist should be motivated by his desire to aid the child, his parents, and his teachers. He should have a professional pride in being able to make clear the nature of the problem, his diagnosis, and his suggestions for treatment. Clinicians and therapists should understand that reports live on through the years and that professional status and prestige either can be built up or destroyed by them. Reports are read widely by social agencies, students in training, and by one's colleagues. They should be effective representatives of the clinic and the reading laboratory which produced them.

The Nature of Written Reports

Many reports by both reading clinicians and therapists have limited value because they lack direction and proper focus of detail. Many consist of massed test scores, disintegrated observations, assorted inferences, and disorganized suggestions for treatment.

The report resulting from the clinical study of an individual with a reading disability should be focused upon three major issues:

1. Statement of problem.
2. Brief statement of diagnosis consisting of not more than three or four sentences.
3. Specific suggestions for treatment which are personalized in nature and directly applied to *the child* in *his* classroom, *his* home, and *his* environment.

The report summarizing instructional progress prepared by the reading therapist should be focused upon five major issues:

1. Aims of instruction.
2. Materials employed.
3. Procedures utilized.
4. Evidences of progress.
5. Recommendations for further instruction.

Good reports, written either by reading clinicians or by therapists, should always be brought to a sharp focus, should possess clarity and good organization, and should be tailored to the needs of the child and those who referred him to the reading clinic or laboratory. Test data unless wisely interpreted are a dubious ingredient.

Organization of Content

Organization is a critical problem in report writing. Those who have an inadequate understanding of the physiological, psychological, sociological, and educational factors affecting reading performance frequently organize their reports in a manner which implies that tests and their interpretation are of greater importance in the investigation than the child himself. Test scores can be valuable. They should, however, not become the alpha and omega of the report.

In organizing data resulting from the clinical study of an individual with a reading disability, the following sequence of topics may be found helpful.

1. Brief statement of problem centered around the individual.
2. Summary of relevant data resulting from *histories, interviews,* and *observations.*
3. Summary of relevant *objective data* from various sources.
4. Brief statement of diagnosis.
5. Detailed statements outlining treatment.
6. Brief statement of prognosis.

The main emphasis in this report should be upon statement of problem, diagnosis, and suggested treatment. An illustration of these topics is provided.

Statement of Problem

Ron has been in the public schools for approximately seven years. His grade placement is that of a child five months in the sixth grade; however,

story indicates that his achievement in reading is that of a
child. Parents and teachers report, "Ron is childish and
ut forth and sustain effort unless he is highly motivated.

Ron is not reading according to expectations determined by his grade
placement and in keeping with test scores on the Wechsler Intelligence
Scale for Children chiefly because of emotional immaturity. Inadequate
experiential background and undeveloped language skills are contributing
factors. Furthermore, emotional tension and anxiety having their origin in
the home should not be ignored in this case.

Recommendations

1. It is recommended that Ron and the other children in the home, at
the time of a family conference, be given responsibilities commensurate
with their maturity.

2. Nagging and scolding by the parents should be reduced to a minimum.
Instead, praise and commendation should be given whenever justly deserved.

3. Both father and mother should place a high value upon the importance
of reading, the development of language skills, and the acquiring of experiential background. Means for the implementation of this suggestion
have been discussed with both parents.

4. Ron should learn that he is an intelligent boy who has ability to do
good work in the language arts, especially in reading. Furthermore, he
should realize that the responsibility for growth in reading achievement is
his and not necessarily that of his teachers.

5. It is suggested that in the classroom Ron have an opportunity to
select reading material which has marked interest to him and which is
written at approximately the second-grade level. If wisely selected, these
materials will not be labeled according to grade level. Words unfamiliar
to Ron should be identified by him and their meaning developed from
context. In the study of words, flexibility of approach should be stressed.
Ron should not use only contextual clues but both structural analysis and
phonics as well. Words taught in this manner can be reviewed frequently
in sentences. This procedure was demonstrated in the clinic and observed
by Ron's teacher. It is further recommended that oral reading be reduced
to a minimum. Instead, Ron should be encouraged to read silently for
answers to questions. In reading for detail, *who, what, where,* and *when*
queries should be emphasized.

6. It is suggested that Ron, his parents, and his teacher return to the
clinic after an interim of three months. A brief re-evaluation of his achievement in reading will be made at that time.

The report should be designed to fit the individual who has been studied and not scores of others who may have problems, histories, symptoms, and environments similar in nature. The content of reports should vary so as to fit the patient, the requirements of those making his referral, and the emphasis the writer deems essential. Critics should not be encouraged to say, "If you have read one of the clinic's reports, you have read them all."

The therapist, who is aware of the suggestions made to reading clinicians concerning the organization of reports, can prepare his summary of reading therapy by adjusting the following items so as to individualize his report.

1. Identification of problem.
2. Statement of goals.
3. Outline of materials.
4. Description of procedures.
5. Evaluation of progress.
6. Statement of recommendations.

These items should be treated briefly making use of short, well-constructed sentences. Objectivity is desirable, yet human interest and a friendly tone are essential if rapport is to be maintained. An example of a report written by a therapist to the parents of a young student is included.

Identification of Problem

Joe is a bright fifteen-year-old boy who was referred upon the request of his parents for therapy in reading. He is entering the tenth grade in the fall and has average grades or better in all his classes. He reports that he is a slow and laborious reader who has trouble remembering what he reads in his social studies textbook. Joe was reading as well as an individual six months in the seventh grade when he began his work in the reading laboratory three months ago.

Goals

In working with Joe we have shown him how to add words to his vocabulary, how to read for main ideas, and how to identify supporting detail.

Materials

We have encouraged Joe to use his own textbook, the dictionary, and other social studies texts of lesser difficulty. Several films showing vocabulary development, use of the dictionary, and how to develop reading maturity were utilized.

Procedures

We have shown Joe how to *spot* main ideas in a chapter by use of introduction, summary, major headings, and by sequence of paragraphs. He has been taught how to use the dictionary in order to discover a variety of information. *How* and *why* questions were used to show him the importance of reading for detailed information. He has been shown how to build up a reading and spelling vocabulary by preparing a card file of unfamiliar words encountered in chapter reading. Each word and its definition have been typed on one side of a card and it has been used in a sentence on the other side.

Evaluation of Progress

Joe has made progress in the realization of all the goals he has set up for himself to achieve. His grade score, however, on an equivalent form of the reading test administered at the beginning of the summer term was that of an individual entering the eighth grade. Joe is able now to identify main ideas in a chapter, read for supporting detail, and add words used in his text to his reading and spelling vocabularies. He is proud of his attainment—and so are we.

Recommendations

Our staff has enjoyed working with Joe; we recommend that he be left "on his own" for a six-month period with no further aid in reading. In our opinion he has acquired the essential basic skills and is now ready to apply them in the content areas. Joe must discover this for himself. At the end of this period we suggest that he return to the laboratory for a conference. May we wish Joe the best of good luck.

Style and Language of Reports

Style and language can facilitate or complicate the expression of ideas in report writing. A straight, forward-moving, expository style is recommended. Integration can be secured by an introductory statement, wisely placed headings with subheadings if necessary, and a brief summary. Some principles for effective writing are listed.

- Omit unnecessary words.
- Compress ideas into short effective sentences.
- Avoid the personal pronoun *I*.
- Avoid use of passive voice.
- Use effective language, not "shop talk" known only to specialists.
- Omit unnecessary display of clinical and statistical terms.
- Make reports objective but not necessarily research oriented.
- Do not try to impress.

Most parents and many teachers are dismayed and frustrated when they find in a report such statements as

Bill's potential mental status is considerably higher than his present functioning efficiency. His perceptual training, made necessary by chronic neurological impairment, should consist of tracking and various forms of patterning. There is little evidence of specific behavioral disorders.

Of what value are these statements to parents? What would the teacher do to provide the suggested treatment? The boy's father has asked, "Can Bill ever learn to read?" The teachers who received the report from which these statements were extracted were dissatisfied, for they had expected greater assistance from the clinic. Apparently they wanted practical suggestions and when none were provided they were critical of the whole clinical investigation. These unfortunate reactions occurred because the clinician was unable to communicate effectively with many of his readers. If a clinician really understands what he is attempting to express, technical language is unnecessary. Any concept essential in a report explaining reading maladjustment can be communicated to any literate person of average mentality.

Some reports of clinical studies contain information that is true of almost any person. A child, for example, may be described as "showing at times a high degree of immaturity," "reversal tendencies," "some anxiety," "impairment of self-concept," "dependence upon contextual clues," "some inadequate affective reactions," "some deficiency in mental content," and other universal characterizations. Accompanying these general inferences, which can be characteristic of all individuals at one time or another, supporting evidence should be given. Emotional immaturity, for example, of a ten-year-old boy can be shown by his crying when disappointed and by his refusing to continue in a ball game after striking out. The generalization should also be based upon several observations made in varying situations.

The statements of diagnosis as prepared by many clinicians show a deadly uniformity. Unfortunately, reading centers are known for their "pet interpretations" of the child's maladjustment in reading. Certain geographical areas seem to produce highly systematized theories which too frequently result in a standard diagnosis of reading disabilities. This lack of creativity and sensitivity to the uniqueness of the individual should be of concern to all who prepare reports.

Factors to Be Considered in Preparation

The written report should be *focused* upon the problem of the individual. Its *content* should be relevant, material, and consequential. It should be written in an effective *style* and should manifest a high degree of *clarity*. A thoughtful and honest consideration of the following questions may make it possible to obtain a better understanding of some of the factors affecting report writing. Their perusal can be beneficial to teacher, clinician, and therapist. Each question is designed to call attention to specific criteria underlying effective report writing.

FOCUS

- Is your report child oriented?
- Does your report avoid test by test recording?
- Does the report accomplish its mission?
- Is your report of value as a record for future reference?
- Have you interpreted your data and presented your findings in terms of implications for treatment?
- Have you avoided "shotgun" diagnosis?
- Is your treatment directed to the child under consideration?
- Does your report apply to a specific child and not to all children with a reading problem?
- Do you present the child as a unified whole as opposed to a collection of parts?

CONTENT

- Is nontest information used in your report?
- Does your suggested treatment reflect confidence in the diagnosis?
- Is your report consistent?
- Have you eliminated raw and uninterpreted data from your report?
- Does your report contain only relevant material?
- Are your conclusions adequately supported?
- Is the content of your report based upon, and designed to support, a particular school of thought?
- In your diagnosis have you drawn inferences you are qualified to make?
- Does your report contain only as much detail as necessary?

STYLE

- Does your report avoid irritating the reader?
- Have you used words for effect?
- Have you avoided making the tone of the report defensive?
- Is the report of adequate length?
- Is the tone of your report authoritative?
- Is the tone of your report academic?
- Is the tone of your report oriented to a particular school of thought?
- Is the report written in a simple, matter-of-fact manner?
- Do you vary the form and organization of your reports?
- Is your statement of diagnosis short, simple, and direct?
- Have you avoided writing in the first person?

CLARITY

- Is your report comprehensible?
- Is your report compatible with the background of your readers?
- Have you eliminated all ambiguous words?
- Have you avoided specialized and technical terminology?
- Have you labeled your inferences?
- Have you refrained from using statements likely to be misinterpreted?
- Does your report clearly express your ideas and conclusions?

THE ORAL REPORT

There is no one way to present an oral report to parents, teachers, or reading specialists. The purpose of the report, its nature, the person to whom it is given, and the personality of the reporter are some of the determining factors. The report of a clinical study can be made orally to parents. When this is done, however, only a statement of the problem, diagnosis, and suggested treatment are presented. The classroom teacher and therapist are frequently asked, "How is my son getting along with his reading?" A teacher may ask for a progress report concerning a child referred to the reading therapist. In each instance, an oral report can provide the necessary information perhaps even better than a formal written statement. Several items to be considered in giving an oral report are briefly stated.

Rapport

Rapport is always to be considered in dealing with parents. If the report is requested by them, however, the way is open for free communication. Some parents for various reasons feel inadequate and assume a defensive attitude when discussing educational problems, especially with teachers and therapists who are working with their children. They need assurance and an awareness of the fact that the therapist is primarily concerned with the welfare of their child. In all instances, the reporter must respect the dignity of the parent and clearly suggest, for example, that the mother knows the child better than anyone else and that her aid is being sought.

Immediacy of Report

The oral report implies a sense of immediacy, that is, the information should be imparted at once in order to meet more adequately the new problem which may have developed. In this situation only relevant and material information should be presented. Facts and their interpretation may be requested by the classroom teacher. Information furnished in the report should be focused upon the immediate problem and should be both specific and practical. The listener is not concerned at this time with a long and detailed recital of many facts.

Personalization of Report

The oral report is focused upon the child and his problem and is not generally presented merely for the purpose of giving a report. Pertinent facts related to the child and his problem are expressed and whenever possible concrete examples are given. In many instances information concerning the immediate problem is required, and this should be provided in an objective and concise manner. In general, inferences and opinions should be well supported in terms of facts directly related to the child in his environment.

Opportunity for Reactions

The oral report can bring reactions which can be helpful to the teacher or therapist who is working with the child. A statement to a mother, for example, that her child appears apathetic and tired in the classroom may elicit a response from the mother which suggests impending illness and the need for referral to the family physician. In some instances, an oral report made to a parent can secure a reaction which will explain the child's attitude toward reading and why he feels so inadequate in the classroom.

Danger of Telling Too Much

In giving an oral report there is the danger of telling too much, too soon. In face-to-face situations there is generally the desire to please the person being interviewed, and in achieving this goal it is easy for the therapist to report that which the listener wants to hear. Frequently members of a group will become so deeply involved in the study of a child that they prematurely report information and suggest treatment which later proves to be unwise and unrealistic. Some teachers and therapists have found it advisable to think through carefully what they want to report to parents and other teachers and to outline in detail the relevant and material facts which are actually required.

Language

The oral report should be simple, direct, and informative. It should not be laced with polysyllabic words designed to impress the listener. Psychological and educational phraseology should be avoided. Instead the language can be definite, clear, and understandable even to the unsophisticated. The teacher and therapist, after careful consideration of the child and his progress, should be willing to commit themselves at one level or another and not indulge in hedging and straddling of the issue. Truth or an unpleasant point of view should not be concealed in ambiguous language. Careful observation on the part of the reporter can in times of emotional stress identify "storm signals" which can serve as a warning to plain speaking. An honest and friendly attitude and a willingness to build up the prestige of the listener can alleviate emotional tension and feelings of antagonism. Language can be palliative.

SUMMARY

Reports, whether written by clinician or therapist, should be designed to accomplish specific purposes. To fulfill the needs of the child, his parents, and his teachers, the content should be adequately chosen and well organized. The report should be styled and written in a language which is understandable to any literate individual of average intelligence. Above all, the report, written or oral, should be tailored to fit the problems experienced by the child, shared by his parents, and assumed by his teachers. It should be focused upon the individual and yet prove illuminating and helpful to all who are concerned.

GUIDED ACTIVITY 15

Aim

To acquire some experiences in report writing.

Materials

1. Informal reading inventories.
2. Durrell Analysis of Reading Difficulty.

Procedure

1. Administer an informal reading inventory to a child with a reading disability.
2. Write a brief report of your findings for the child's parents.
3. Write a brief report of your findings for the child's teacher.
4. Observe the same child in his reading class for three twenty-minute periods on three different days.
5. Write a brief report of these observations for the classroom teacher. First summarize your facts and then your inferences. Write an effective concluding sentence.
6. Secure the personnel folder of the same child from the teacher, reading therapist or principal.
7. Summarize those data which you believe to be relevant to the problem of the child. Direct your report to the child's teacher.
8. Observe a mother and child in a supermarket, bus station, or airport. Outline briefly your observation so as to be helpful to the mother in her control and management of her child. How can you establish rapport and really aid her with your suggestions? Assume that your report will be oral.
9. Administer to a child in the fifth grade parts of the Durrell Analysis of Reading Difficulty to discover his weaknesses and faulty reading habits. Prepare a report for the teacher which will emphasize the most significant findings.

QUESTIONS AND REFERENCES

Questions

1. How can reports be edited?

2. What are the factors to be considered in writing a psychological report?

3. How can one review the techniques of writing an interesting, well-organized composition?

References

1. Kenneth R. Hammond and Jeremiah M. Allen, Jr., *Writing Clinical Reports* (Englewood Cliffs, N.J.: Prentice-Hall, 1953), Chap. 8.

2. Walter G. Klopfer, *The Psychological Report* (New York: Grune and Stratton, 1960).

3. John E. Warriner and Francis Griffith, *English Grammar and Composition* (New York: Harcourt, Brace and World, 1963), Chap. 25.

Questions	References
4. How can reports be made to parents?	**4.** Margaret G. McKim and Helen Caskey, *Guiding Growth in Reading,* 2nd ed. (New York: The Macmillan Company, 1963), pp. 408–414.
5. How can interpretation and synthesis of data continue?	**5.** Ruth Strang, *Diagnostic Teaching of Reading* (New York: McGraw-Hill Book Company, 1964), Chap. 14.
6. What do parents want to know about the reading program?	**6.** Mildred A. Dawson and Henry A. Bamman, *Fundamentals of Basic Reading Instruction* (New York: Longmans, Green and Company, 1959), Chap. 15.
7. How can the reading program be interpreted to parents?	**7.** John J. DeBoer and Martha Dallmann, *The Teaching of Reading,* rev. ed. (New York: Holt, Rinehart and Winston, 1964), pp. 397–401.
8. What advice can be given to parents?	**8.** Nila Banton Smith, *Reading Instruction for Today's Children* (Englewood Cliffs, N.J.: Prentice-Hall, 1963), Chap. 20.
9. Should we defend or explain the reading program to parents?	**9.** George D. Spache, *Toward Better Reading* (Champaign, Ill.: Garrard Publishing Company, 1963), Chap. 12.

Chapter 16

Prevention of Reading Maladjustment

Parents, teachers, and administrators in the public schools not only are concerned with remediation of reading disabilities, but also are concerned with what can be done to prevent their development. In the teaching of reading, as in the practice of medicine, a greater emphasis must be placed upon prevention. Success in accomplishing this objective will be unnecessarily limited without parent-teacher cooperation. This chapter sets forth some practical suggestions for parents and school personnel to consider concerning their respective roles in the prevention of reading maladjustment.

PARENTS' ROLE IN PREVENTION

Parents can do more to prevent the development of reading difficulties than anyone else. Before school entrance the child is under the care and supervision of the home. Even after the child has entered school, he spends three fourths of his time under the direction and control of his parents. During these years the parents have an opportunity to stimulate and guide their children so as to develop their language skills. They can produce a favorable environment for learning, develop responsibility, foster emotional stability, and insure both the physical and mental health of their children. In fact, they are the child's first teachers. Some suggestions as to how parents can prevent their children from becoming disabled readers follow.

Parents Can Learn from Research. Studies of parental attitudes related to the reading abilities of children have been discussed in Chapter 4 of this book. A consensus of these investigations shows that children who read and enjoy reading generally come from homes where parents have established a climate conducive to learning by their activities with their children and their attitudes toward the language arts. These parents

- Read to their children, played with them, and visited school with them.
- Took their children on trips and on excursions to visit places of interest and historical significance.
- Were sensitive to their children's feelings and emotions.
- Provided many books for children and encouraged recreational reading and interest in books, stories, poems, words, letters, and numbers.
- Provided a democratic home background which fostered independence, group thinking, and freedom for self-expression.
- Permitted children to be children without attempting to hurry their growth.
- Emphasized the importance of communication and the development of language skills.
- Permitted their children to accept outside influences and various points of view and did not demand total submission to the wishes and desires of the home.
- Encouraged their children to discuss any topic with them without the child's developing fear of ridicule, shame, or reproach.

Parents Can Produce a Favorable Environment. Parents can create an intellectual world in which children can see their parents reading for enjoyment and satisfaction and in which they as junior citizens can ask questions and secure helpful answers. The home can be a comfortable place in which there are books, stories, and parents who stimulate the mental growth of their children. This can be accomplished by making it possible for boys and girls to have new experiences in keeping with their age and desires. Experiential background can be extended, and more mental content can be developed by well-planned trips, excursions, and discussions. Children should be encouraged to express their thoughts and feelings and to tell of their experiences. Parents who enjoy reading generally have children who do what they see their parents do. They acquire early the attitude that learning to read is important and that reading is a source of pleasure and satisfaction. A comfortable and quiet nook for reading and study can be made available for all members of the family. Some parents have a scheduled time for reading when radio and TV programs are put aside for one hour.

Parents Can Develop Responsibility. Learning to read and study can be hard work. Consequently, in the home the child should learn to assume responsibility commensurate with his abilities. He should learn to do the things that need to be done when they need to be done whether he wants to do them or not. Children should understand that they are members of a family group and, like every other member, they have responsibilities to meet and contributions to make. Parents should not do for the child what he is capable of doing for himself. The development of self-discipline on the part of the child is the responsibility of the home and should not be neglected.

Parents Can Develop Emotional Stability. The child should know that his parents love him and should be able to get satisfaction, security, and recognition in the home. He should be able to discuss his problems, his fears, and his worries with his parents without being ashamed or afraid. His unsocial acts should be interpreted as an aspect of his growth and he should be corrected without hurt, confusion, or shame. These suggestions can be more easily accomplished if parents are well oriented in the modern world in which they and their children live.

Parents Can Maintain Health. Many physical disabilities go unnoticed until maladjustment in the classroom becomes acute. A visual and auditory examination prior to school entrance can identify defects which generally can be easily corrected. An annual physical examination for the child can alert the parents to symptoms of physical conditions which can, if ignored, lead to reading disabilities and a lack of academic success. Parents should understand that boys and girls require a substantial breakfast following eight hours of sleep. Some possible visual defects may be shown by the following symptoms.

- Loss of place in reading.
- Letters blurred or run together.
- Manner of holding reading material.

- Coverage of one eye when reading.
- Eyes inflamed.
- Difficulty in seeing at a distance.

Auditory abnormalities may be indicated by the following.

- Reports of inattention.
- Tense facial expressions when listening.
- Listening with one ear turned in direction of sound.
- Failure to respond when back is turned to speaker.
- Adjustment of volume control on television and radio.

Children in the home require guidance in matters of healthful living. Adequate eating and sleeping habits should be developed. Weight and growth patterns, the prevention of accidents, and personal hygiene deserve the attention of parents. Fathers and mothers who are busy earning a living sometimes neglect important health factors.

THE SCHOOL'S ROLE IN PREVENTION

It is the function of the school to help the child to develop physically, mentally, and emotionally and to train him to take his place in a changing world. If this goal is to be achieved, the child must learn to read effectively and continue to read throughout his life. Specific reading objectives must be set forth and materials must be selected to accomplish these goals. Approaches, methods, and techniques must be adjusted to the particular needs and interests of the child. Several suggestions for the prevention of reading disabilities follow.

Need for Adequate Educational Philosophy

There is great confusion in the minds of both parents and teachers concerning the aims and content of modern education. Several conflicting philosophies are briefly stated.

- Education is chiefly the training of the intellect.
- Education is adjustment.
- Education should be centered around the interests of the growing child.
- Education is to facilitate social change.

Many educators and some parents are concerned with whether or not learning to read or social adjustment should receive the emphasis in the public schools. Should children be taught to accept each other in the classroom regardless of their color or religion even when their parents do not hold such tolerant points of view? Should money be spent for classes in second- and third-year German or for a driver's training course instead? A unified educational philosophy, accepted by a majority of parents and teachers, is essential if the problems of our society are to be resolved.

Readiness

Elementary teachers should not expect a child to read until he is sufficiently mature. This maturity can be appraised fairly well by observation. The mentally mature child is alert, notices likenesses and differences, and can tell of his experiences. He makes use of language, tells and recites stories and poems. He memorizes easily and pays attention for longer periods of time. He can generalize and make inferences.

The emotionally mature child can easily make home-to-school adjustments, can accept change in routine quietly and calmly, and can experience opposition and defeat without being emotionally upset. He plans and does things on time and assumes responsibility. He takes care of his clothing and materials and meets and talks to strangers without shyness or undue boldness.

Readiness for reading is a by-product of purposeful living and can be developed early in the home and later in the school by group activity and group planning. Teachers who stimulate and guide their students and who encourage creativity contribute much to the mental and emotional maturity of their children and their readiness for books.

Importance of Teaching Methods

Adequate teaching methods in small classes can reduce the number of children with reading disabilities. No one method can be expected to work equally well with all students. In some instances trial-and-error procedures may be necessary. Instead of shopping around for a "best method" of teaching reading to a group, the teacher should seek a workable method for *the child*. Teaching methods are more effective if, in preparation for a class or group activity, the teacher focuses her attention upon objectives to be accomplished, materials to be employed, and definite procedures to be followed. It is unwise for teachers to discard a method of teaching reading and accept another approach without careful study and systematic investigation of research which has been well designed and well controlled. Members of other professions and parents are becoming distrustful of educators who jump from one "band wagon" to another.

The school can prevent reading disabilities by increased attention to individual differences. Flexible grouping plans make it possible to group children tentatively in order to accomplish specific objectives. Aims, materials, and procedures can vary with each group; consequently, individual needs can be adequately met. A knowledge of each child is essential to the operation of this plan.

Materials

Reading materials should be so selected that every child in the class is reading at his own level and not necessarily at the grade level in which he is enrolled. Each child should be assured of his share of success in reading and should have the opportunity to select materials and supplementary texts which harmonize with his interests and experiential background. The school should provide ample supplies of books at various grade levels which will afford the child an opportunity to apply his reading skills in subject matter fields such as social studies, science, and literature. The creative teacher with the aid of her pupils can construct materials which are of interest to her students and which are designed to accomplish a specific purpose. Experience charts and records, for example, can be used successfully at various grade levels.

Reading consultants and clinicians, in cooperation with teachers of reading, should be given an opportunity to select and purchase various diagnostic instruments and remedial materials from publishers and manufacturers of equipment of value in developmental and corrective reading.

Functional Reading Program

The school can make reading a part of the student's daily living. In the elementary grades the child can be given an opportunity to talk, listen, write, and read in areas of interest to him. He can be given a variety of interesting experiences designed to develop experiential background and mental content. Later he can be shown how to use reading as a tool and as a means of developing work-study skills. He can be taught how to identify main ideas, how to read for a purpose, and how to make ideas his own. Children have personal problems and they can be shown how reading can be used to solve them. Students can be taught how to make effective use of books and how to concentrate as they read and study. They can be shown how to read a newspaper, maps, time tables, and other materials so essential in our society. A functional reading program, carefully planned, can help to reduce reading disabilities and prevent school dropouts.

Reluctant readers and the so-called culturally deprived children cannot, at the present time, be expected to read the classics. The main reason for this is their lack of experiential background. Consequently, these students should be encouraged to read material of value and interest to them. Young Puerto Rican, Indian, and Negro children want to read real stories about real children "just like us." They want more than integrated picture books with the same old stories which seem so "foolish" to them. They do not require a "low" vocabulary, for this threatens their self-concept. Materials which they appreciate are direct and to the point. Short sentences, well-developed paragraphs, large print, and small units of thought are qualities of effective writing which these boys and girls require. They want "content" about their people, their homes, and their ways of life. Books for them must be functional.

COOPERATION OF HOME AND SCHOOL

Parents are not generally prepared to teach their children to read. They are, however, deeply concerned with the progress their children are making. Some typical questions frequently asked by mothers and fathers are listed.

Should I teach my child the alphabet?
Will phonics help my son to read?
Can I use i.t.a. at home?
How can I interest my son in books?
Where can I get special help in reading for my child?

The teacher says my son is "brain-damaged." Where can we secure treatment?

Where can I find books of interest to my son that he can actually read?

My child has a perceptual difficulty. Where can I get help?

Why is there so little agreement among reading specialists?

My son is in the seventh grade and his teacher says he is reading only as well as a child in the third grade. Why was he promoted from grade to grade?

These are but a few of the many questions teachers are expected to answer. Adequate replies are difficult, and in some instances impossible, to make.

Teachers want to assist parents and to discuss with them the problems of their children. Time and opportunity, however, are difficult to arrange. Here are some suggestions which may be helpful.

- Arrange each year a reading conference for parents to be held in the evening from seven to nine. Invite parents to bring relevant questions to be answered by a group of reading specialists. Provide opportunity for discussion.
- Organize a reading seminar designed for parents of children with reading problems. Questions and answers with free discussion rather than lectures should make up each evening program. It is suggested that these seminars be held each month during the school year.
- Make available at the school library a reading bibliography of professional books for parents.
- Invite parents to visit the school to see demonstrations of various reading activities and special approaches to the study of reading problems.
- Avoid, under school sanction, giving publicity to unorthodox methods and materials designed to pressure parents into spending large sums of money for the treatment of disabled readers.
- Plan for the organization of a local chapter of the International Reading Association.

NEED FOR SPECIALIZED SERVICES

If the school is to do its share in preventing reading disabilities, provision must be made to add to the staff a *reading consultant* who will advise, counsel, and guide classroom teachers. Larger school systems will recognize the need for a *reading clinician* whose primary function will be that of diagnosis and the clinical study of the disabled reader. By participating in these studies teachers, as members of a team, have an opportunity for in-service training and professional growth. The *reading therapist* in her contact with teachers and parents can contribute to the prevention of reading difficulties.

SUMMARY

Prevention of reading disabilities should be stressed before treatment. In this chapter suggestions have been made to both parents and teachers which can be considered in the prevention of reading maladjustment. Cooperation between the home and school is emphasized in dealing successfully with the problem for when parents are actively involved in understanding the reading program of their school, teachers are encouraged and children are benefited.

GUIDED ACTIVITY 16

Aim

To explore means of preventing reading disabilities.

Materials

1. Chapter 16, *Diagnosis and Treatment of the Disabled Reader.*
2. The reading curriculum of your school system.

Procedure

1. Select with the aid of the school personnel a disabled reader twelve years or more of age and with the permission of his parents investigate some of the causes of his disability.
2. List the measures the home could have taken to prevent these disabilities.
3. Examine the child's school history and determine what preventive measures the school could have taken.
4. After you have studied the curriculum of your school system, work out a program for the prevention of reading maladjustment in your school.

5. Outline a talk to parents on the topic "Prevention of Reading Disabilities in the Home" which you could present at a PTA meeting.

6. Prepare an outline of a talk to eighteen teachers of an elementary school which you, a reading consultant, have been asked to give. The topic for discussion is, "How Can the Home and School Cooperate in Meeting the Needs of Disabled Readers?"

7. Plan a reading seminar for parents which will meet once each week for six weeks. Prepare a list of topics which parents may want to discuss.

8. What changes would you suggest in the philosophy underlying the reading curriculum of your school?

QUESTIONS AND REFERENCES

Questions

1. What are some recommendations for improving the preparation of teachers?

2. What are the responsibilities of the whole staff for teaching reading?

3. How can a reading program be developed?

4. How can one advise and work with parents?

5. Why prevention before remediation?

References

1. Mary C. Austin et al., *The Torch Lighters: Tomorrow's Teachers of Reading* (Cambridge, Mass.: Harvard University Press, 1961).

2. Ruth Strang and Dorothy Kendall Bracken, *Making Better Readers* (Boston: D. C. Heath and Company, 1957), Chap. 4.

3. Roma Gans, *Common Sense in Teaching Reading* (Indianapolis: The Bobbs Merrill Company, 1963), Chap. XX.
H. Alan Robinson and Sidney J. Rauch, *Guiding the Reading Program* (Chicago: Science Research Associates, 1965).

4. Nila Banton Smith, *Reading Instruction for Today's Children* (Englewood Cliffs, N.J.: Prentice-Hall, 1963), Chaps. 19 and 20.

5. Mildred A. Dawson, "Prevention Before Remediation," in Ralph Staiger and David A. Sohn, eds., *New Directions in Read-*

Questions	References
	ing (New York: Bantam Books, 1967), pp. 205–210.
6. What are the necessary preschool experiences for comprehending reading?	**6.** Marion Monroe, "Necessary Preschool Experiences for Comprehending Reading," in Ralph Staiger and David A. Sohn, eds., *New Directions in Reading* (New York: Bantam Books, 1967), pp. 9–18.
7. What are parental roles in diagnosis, remediation, and prevention?	**7.** Robert M. Wilson, *Diagnostic and Remedial Reading* (Columbus, Ohio: Charles E. Merrill Books, 1967), Chap. 10.
8. How is reading ability related to high school dropouts?	**8.** Ruth C. Penty, *Reading Ability and High School Drop Outs* (New York: Bureau of Publications, Teachers College, Columbia University, 1956).
9. When is a child ready to read?	**9.** John J. DeBoer and Martha Dallmann, *The Teaching of Reading*, rev. ed. (New York: Holt, Rinehart and Winston, 1964), Chap. 5a.
10. What are the characteristics and experiences of children who learn to read successfully?	**10.** Jerry G. Keshian, "The Characteristics and Experiences of Children Who Learn to Read Successfully," in Virgil M. Howes and Helen Fisher Darrow, eds., *Reading and the Elementary School Child* (New York: The Macmillan Company, 1968), pp. 416–419.

GLOSSARY

This glossary is provided to help the reader become acquainted immediately with some of the terms used in this text. For more complete definitions consult a dictionary and, in some instances, a medical dictionary.

ability grouping — Practice of subdividing a group of pupils into smaller groups of relatively equal ability, either in some one subject or in general ability. This practice is not to be confused with flexible grouping.

accommodation — The act of adjusting the lens of the eye to keep a sharply focused image on the retina.

achievement age — Level of ability, especially in school, measured in terms of the average for a given life-age group.

achievement test — Device for measuring level of ability or performance actually reached in a given field.

acuity — Sharpness or keenness.

age norm — A standard in respect to any quality or characteristic (including especially ability as measured by some standard test) based on the average of a large, unselected group of children of a given age.

alexia — Loss of memory for process of reading, caused by a pathological condition.

alternating vision — Visual sensations alternating between the two eyes but not simultaneously.

ambidexterity — Equal facility in using both hands. Sometimes used to include equal facility in using both feet.

amblyopia — Dimness of vision for which no organic defect in the eye can be discovered.

ametropia — An error of refraction, such as farsightedness, nearsightedness, or astigmatism.

anecdotal record — A record of facts which can be used in establishing inferences.

aniseikonia — Ocular images of different sizes and shapes.

anthropometrics — Measurement of human body and its parts.

aphasia — Impairment of ability to use language, believed to be due to lesions in the brain.

astigmatism — A defect of vision caused by irregularly shaped refractive media. A term applied to the condition of an eye whose refraction is not the same in all parts.

audile — Ear-minded.

audiogram — A record of a test of an individual's hearing. Generally in graphic form.

audiometer — Instrument for measuring the sensitivity of hearing.

auditory acuity — Keenness of hearing.

auditory discrimination — Ability to discriminate between sounds.

auditory memory — Memory for what is heard. The term is used chiefly in connection with tests of memory span.

basic-reader approach — The development of basic reading abilities and skills by means of special textbooks; the development of initial reading skills and abilities by means of basic readers.

Binet test — A measure of language intelligence. From the test a mental age and an intelligence quotient are obtained.

binocular — Two-eyed.

binocular regression — Right-to-left return of both eyes during reading.

blend — The fusion of two (or more) sounds in a word without loss of identity of either sound.

Buddy system — Two students studying together.

carpal age — Age obtained by measuring anatomical growth.

catharsis — A release of emotional tension brought about by free discussion of problem.

causation — Factor or factors that are found to be responsible for the reading disability.

centile — A division obtained by arranging all the cases in order of merit and dividing them into 100 groups or ranks.

choral reading — Reading in a group or chorus. Sometimes called *choric speaking* or *group speaking*.

chronological age — Calendar age or age since birth.

clinic — An organization or team of workers to which an individual is referred for remediation.

concentration — Exclusive attention to an object or aspect of an object.

configuration — Pattern, general form, or shape of a word.

configuration clue — An element in a word form which aids in the recognition of an unfamiliar word. For example *mill*, a new word, resembles the familiar word *fill*.

connotation — Meaning suggested by a word apart from its explicit and recognized meaning.

consequential — Bringing about or responsible for significant changes or results. Directly related to effect.

constitutional cause — A cause which resides within the body and is not local.

context clue — A means of identifying a new reading word by anticipation of the meaning or through the words and ideas adjacent to the new word.

convergence — The act or power of turning the eyes inward from their normal position of rest so that the image of a near object will fall on corresponding parts of the retina in each eye.

corrective reading — Teaching in which a particular effort is made to improve reading abilities and skills.

correlation — Relationship between two variables.

cross dominance — Control that is right-handed and left-eyed or left-handed and right-eyed.

cursive writing — Longhand or script writing commonly used above the primary grades.

decibel — A unit of hearing or audition.

denotation — Specific meaning as distinct from connotation.

developmental reading — Reading activity during which a group is given directed instruction in vocabulary development, silent-reading preparation, oral reading, rereading, and supplementary reading for the purpose of increasing reading achievement at the instructional level.

dextral — Right-handed and right-eyed.

diagnosis — Identification of abnormality from symptoms presented and from a study of its origin. Any classification of an individual on the basis of observed characteristics. An explanation of difficulty.

diction — Manner of expressing ideas.

directed reading activity — A reading lesson based on basic-reader material; a developmental activity in which provision is made for orientation, silent reading for survey purposes, vocabulary and comprehension development, silent or oral rereading, and follow-up.

dominance — Control of the actions of another. *Ocular dominance:* Preferential use of one eye so that objects are usually fixated by that eye only, the other eye remaining a little off from exact fixation. *Manual dominance:* Preferential use of one hand.

dyslexia — A disturbance of the ability to read.

dyspituitarism — A faulty functioning of the pituitary body.

educational age — A pupil's average accomplishment in school subjects stated in terms of the average accomplishment of those of that life age in school.

educational guidance — Assisting pupils to select the best program of studies in the light of their capacities, interests, plans, and general circumstances. Remedial instruction is occasionally included.

educational measurement — Method of determining school attainments by means of standardized tests or new types of examinations, and the use of this method to determine the effectiveness of various educational procedures.

einstellung — Mental set or rigid opinion.

emotion — A disorganized response.

emotional blocking — Inhibition of thinking or of other forms of adjustive response due to excessive emotions, usually of the fear group.

emotional maturity — Extent to which an individual is able to control impulses and emotions.

emotional stability — Consistent and dependable emotional reactions.

endocrine dysfunction — Faulty functioning of the endocrine glands.

endogenous — Produced within the organism.

enuresis — Involuntary discharge of urine.

epiphysis — Bone process attached to another by cartilage which later becomes ossified.

error — A mistake, a departure from correctness. Belief in that which is untrue.

esophoria — Condition of the eyes in which the visual axes tend to deviate inward when the extrinsic muscles are in a state of rest.

etiology — Causative factors of disabilities.

exciting cause — A cause which leads directly to maladjustment.

exophoria — Condition of the eyes in which the visual axes tend to deviate outward when the extrinsic muscles are in a state of rest.

experience approach — The development of basic reading skills and abilities through experience; the use of language and reading of experience records to develop initial reading skills and abilities.

experience chart or record — Individual-, group-, or class-dictated composition.

eye movement — Change in position of the eyeball.

eye pause — Brief moment during which the eyeball is at rest. Only during such a moment is it possible to make visual discriminations. Points of fixation.

feedback — Partial reversion of the effects of a given process to its source so as to reinforce or modify it.

fixation — The turning or holding of the eyeball in such a position that an object or fixation point lies along the fixation line, which is the line drawn from the fovea through the pupil.

fixation pause — The length of time required for the eyes to fix on a given part of a line in reading.

flexible grouping — Practice of grouping individuals temporarily in order to accomplish a specific purpose.

free reading — Independent reading for information or pleasure.

Frohlich syndrome — Group of symptoms associated with insufficient pituitary activity: delay in skeletal development, obesity, infantilism, or childishness of bodily appearance.

frustration — The result of conflict between two or more goals or between a goal and actual attainment.

frustration level — The level at which the individual is thwarted or baffled by the difficulty of the reading material.

fusion — The mental blending of the right and left eye images into one composite image.

Gestalt — A structure of psychological phenomena so integrated as to make up a functional unit with properties not derivable from an accumulation of its parts.

Gestalt psychology — A branch of psychology which teaches that the student should study the whole pattern of behavior instead of trying to understand it by studying its elements, because the whole is more than the sum of its parts.

grade placement — Grade in which child is actually placed.

grade score — Average achievement for a given grade level. For example, a grade score of 3.2 means that the performance level of an individual is two months in the third grade.

guiding question — Question used by the teacher to lead a beginner through the thought of a unit. In the initial stages of learning to read, the guiding question may focus the attention on the reading of a single sentence. As the pupil grows in reading power, the guiding questions will focus attention on paragraphs, pages, and larger thought units.

Hawthorne effect — A reaction to treatment which is due to the enthusiasm of the therapist and not to the effectiveness of medication.

homogeneous grouping — Grouping according to capacity or ability. Should not be confused with flexible grouping.

hyperopia — Farsightedness.

hypopituitarism — Underfunctioning of the pituitary gland.

image — A mental reconstruction of sensory experiences.

imagery — Collective mental images: Visual, auditory, kinesthetic, gustatory, olfactory, pain, and thermal.

increment — Amount of increase in a quantity; or, more general, increase or decrease (the latter is negative increment, or decrement).

infantilism — Manifestation by an adult or adolescent of infantile traits, physical or mental. Many symptoms of mental disorder are held to be infantilisms.

inference — A logical conclusion from given data.

inhibition — Mental condition in which a person finds it difficult to begin or continue a course of action; there is a peculiar hesitancy and a feeling as if restrained by outside agency. Sometimes equals suppression or repression.

input — The act, process, or instance of putting in (facts, information, experiences).

intelligence quotient — Mental age in years and fractions of years divided by chronological or life age; i.e., by number of years and fraction of years one has lived.

intelligence scale — A series of tests so arranged that varying degrees of intelligence may be indicated by more or less equal steps.

intelligence test — A device for measuring the intelligence of individuals.

kinesthesis — The sense which yields knowledge of the movements of the body or its several members.

kinetic reversals — Confusion of directional sequence, such as *left* for *felt*.

language-rhythm clue — A word which suggests a relationship or opposite, such as *one, two, three; up, down; high, low.*

lateral imbalance — A tendency of one or both eyes to deviate inward or outward from their normal position.

lead — A short summary, an introduction to a news story.

linguistics — Science of language.

maladjustment — State in which a person falls short of being able to do what is expected of him by others or by himself.

manuscript writing — "Printing" or lettering by a free-hand process in which the letters are not connected as in common longhand or script writing. Recommended for use in the primary grades by both teachers and pupils.

material — That which is essential to case at hand and which cannot be dispensed with without serious alteration of the problem.

maturation — Growing up plus training.

mental age — Level of development in intelligence expressed in terms of the age at which the average child attains that level.

mental content — The result of experience.

mental deficiency or defect — Term for all degrees of lack in intelligence.

mental maturity — Mental capacity.

mental set — An attitude.

mental test — Standardized procedure applied to an individual to ascertain his ability in comparison with others.

metabolism — Summation of the processes concerned in the building up of protoplasm and its destruction incidental to life.

metacarpal — Pertaining to the part of the hand between the carpus and the phalanges.

mirror writing — A tendency to write mirrored forms of words, letters, and numbers; writing read in a mirror.

mixed dextral — Right-handed and left-eyed.

mixed sinistral — Left-handed and right-eyed.

modality — A group of sensory qualities having certain rather ill-defined similarities; e.g., all visual qualities belong to visual mode, all sounds to the auditory.

monocular regression — Right-to-left movement of one eye during reading.

motile — Motor-minded.

myopia — Nearsightedness.

neurology — Science dealing with the nervous system.

neurosis — Mental disorder generally of milder character than a psychosis. The terms *nervousness* and *nervous breakdown* usually mean *neurosis*.

nystagmus — Short, jerky movements of the eye.

objective test — A test completed by checking a number or letter.

ophthalmologist — A physician trained in the study of the eye.

ophthalmology — The science which treats of the structure, functions, and diseases of the eye.

otologist — A physician trained in the study of the ear.

otology — The sum of what is known concerning the ear.

overcompensation — An extreme form of compensation.

overlearn — To continue to study or practice after reaching a generally accepted level of performance.

pathological — Pertaining to disease.

pediatrician — A specialist in the treatment of children's diseases.

pediatrics — Medical science dealing with treatment of children.

percentile — A point in a distribution of scores so selected that a certain number of cases are above it and a certain number of cases are below it.

perception — Mental awareness and integration of sensations.

personality test — A test designed to appraise an individual's personal and social behaviors.

phalanges — The digital bones of hand or foot. Plural of phalanx.

phonetic analysis — The analysis of a word into its phonetic elements for pronunciation purposes; commonly used as a synonym for phonics.

phonetics — The science of speech sounds.

phonics — The science of speech sounds as applied to reading.

phonogram — A letter or group of letters forming a speech sound.

phoria — Tendency.

picture clue — An element in a picture which provides meaning.

picture dictionary — A dictionary of commonly used words with corresponding pictures illustrating each word.

placebo effect — A phenomenon resulting from the administration of treatment having no therapeutic value.

pluriglandular — Concerning more than two glands.

predisposing cause — Anything which renders a person liable to maladjustment without actually producing it.

primary cause — The principal or original cause of maladjustment.

primary reading disability — A disability experienced by a child who is not aware of his deficiency and is not penalized because of it.

projective techniques — Devices for studying personality through the use of inkblots, pictures, and designs.

psychogenic — Originating in the mind.

psychology — Science of human behavior.

psychometrics — Mental testing.

pubes — The pubic region.

range — Distance from highest to lowest score or value in a distribution.

rapport — Unconstrained, intimate, and friendly relationship between two persons.

readiness — A physical, mental, and emotional preparedness for a given learning activity.

reading clinician — A reading specialist with training in psychology, sociology, and education. Primarily concerned with diagnosis and treatment of reading disabilities.

reading consultant — A reading specialist with training in education with emphasis upon supervision of teaching methods.

reading laboratory — A workroom in which treatment in reading is provided.

reading maladjustment — Inability to adjust to the requirements of effective reading.

reading therapist — A reading specialist with training in psychology and education who actually works with disabled readers either individually or in groups.

refractive mechanism — Any mechanism having power to refract.

regressive eye movement — Right-to-left return of one or both eyes during reading.

relevance — A logical connection with matter under consideration, related to problem at hand.

reliability — Extent to which a measurement is uninfluenced by variable factors.

remedial reading — Clinical procedures in which particular effort is made to discover the exact cause or causes of deficiency and means of removing or mitigating causal factors.

remediation — The acts of providing both diagnosis and treatment.

response — Activity of an organism resulting from stimulation. Such activity or inhibition existing in a covariant relationship with drive, cue, and reinforcement.

retina — Nervous and sensitive layer of the eye.

reversal tendency — The tendency of an individual to reverse letters or words while reading, writing, or speaking.

root — An original word form from which words have been developed by addition of prefixes, suffixes, and inflectional endings.

scanning — The act of reading for specific information such materials as telephone directory, dictionary, or glossary.

score — Credit or value given to a specific response to a test item. Sum of the credits obtained on all the items of a single test.

secondary cause — A cause which helps to bring on maladjustment.

secondary reading disability — A disability experienced by an individual who is aware of his maladjustment and is penalized because of it.

sella turcica — A bony box containing the pituitary gland.

sensation — Impression received by the sense organs.

sibilant sound — A hissing speech sound. The sibilants in English are *s, z, sh, zh,* and *ch.*

sibling — One of two or more offspring born at different times from the same parent.

sight word — A word that is memorized or recognized as a whole.

significant difference — A difference between two measures not due to chance.

sinistral — Left-handed and left-eyed.

skimming — The act of reading rapidly to secure the gist, central thought, or summary.

sociology — Science of the origin and evolution of society.

somatic — Having to do with the body.

span of attention — Number of objects which can be unified in a single act or "moment" of apprehension.

stem — A word form from which words have been developed by the addition of prefixes, suffixes, and inflectional endings.

stereopsis — Depth perception.

stimulus — Something that produces a temporary increase of activity in an organism. An agent exciting a sensory end organ.

strabismus — An incoordinate condition of the eye.

strephosymbolia — Twisted symbols; a special type of reading disability. For example, the reading of *saw* for *was* or *left* for *felt.*

structural analysis — The process of studying an unknown word for the purpose of identifying the root or base.

subjective — Perceptible to the individual.

suppression — Psychological blocking of vision in one eye. Involuntary exclusion of anything from awareness.

syndrome — Collection of symptoms which characterize a particular disorder or disease.

table — An arrangement of scores which displays their relations to each other.

tachistoscope — Instrument for providing a brief exposure of visual material.

tactile, tactual — Having to do with touch.

therapy — Treatment intended to cure or alleviate a disordered condition.

tic — Twitching.

tone — Summation of intellectual and emotional effects of writing or speaking.

tool subject — School subject thought of as valuable merely because of service to other subjects or to practical pursuits.

topic sentence — The sentence in a paragraph which states the subject to be discussed and developed in the paragraph by various means.

trait — A characteristic of behavior. A distinguishing quality of personality.

VAKT — A visual, auditory, kinesthetic, tactual method of word study.

validity — State of being valid or trustworthy.

verification — The use of objective data to establish a hypothesis.

vertical imbalance — A tendency of one eye to deviate upward.

visual acuity — Keenness of vision.

visual discrimination — Adeptness at seeing likenesses and differences in geometrical figures, pictures, and word elements.

vocabulary test — A random sample of the words in a complete general dictionary presented for definition; the score is an index of the examinee's total vocabulary.

vocalization — Movement of lips, tongue, or vocal apparatus of the throat.

volition — A state of decision or choice, the end condition of voluntary activity.

Wechsler Intelligence Scale for Children — A measure of mental maturity called the WISC. Five subtests make up the verbal scale and five subtests make up the performance scale. The WISC provides three IQs, a verbal, a performance, and a full scale.

whole-word method — Word analysis without the physical separation of the word into its phonetic or structural elements.

word analysis — The analyzing of an unfamiliar word into known elements for the purpose of identification.

word pattern clue — See configuration clue.

Appendix A

Tests are tools which can be employed for both survey and diagnostic purposes. Each test has its advantages and disadvantages. Those suggested in Appendix A are only a few of many worthy of consideration. Like all tools they should be selected and used with care. For detailed information concerning these tests the reader is referred to *Mental Measurements Yearbooks* by Oscar Krisen Buros.[1]

[1] Published by The Gryphon Press, Highland Park, New Jersey.

Survey Tests in Reading

Name of Test	Grade Level	Description	Publisher
California Reading Tests	1–2 3–4.5 4–6 7–9 9–14	Reading vocabulary and comprehension.	California Test Bureau Del Monte Research Park Monterey, Calif. 93940
Durrell-Sullivan Reading Capacity and Achievement Tests	2.5–6.0	Reveal discrepancies between understanding of spoken language and understanding of the printed word.	Harcourt, Brace and World, Inc. 757 Third Avenue New York 10017
Gates-MacGinitie Reading Tests—Primary	1–3	Vocabulary and comprehension. A supplementary test CS may be used to measure reading speed.	Teachers College Press Columbia University New York 10027
Gates-MacGinitie Reading Tests—Survey	4–6 7–9	Vocabulary, comprehension, and rate of reading.	Teachers College Press Columbia University New York 10027

Test	Grade Levels	Description	Publisher
Iowa Every-Pupil Tests of Basic Skills Reading Comprehension Work-Study Skills	3–5, 5–9 3–5, 5–9	Vocabulary, reading, spelling, capitalization, punctuation and usage, map reading, interpretation of graphs and tables, and use of reference materials.	Houghton Mifflin Co. 110 Tremont St. Boston, Mass. 02107
Iowa Silent Reading Tests—New Edition	4–8 9–12 and college	Rate and comprehension, directed reading, word meaning, paragraph comprehension, sentence meaning, and location of information.	Harcourt, Brace and World, Inc. 757 Third Avenue New York 10017
Sequential Tests of Educational Progress: Reading	4–6 7–9 10–12 13–14	Tests the student's abilities to read a variety of materials with understanding.	Cooperative Test Division Educational Testing Service Princeton, New Jersey 08540
Stanford Reading Tests	1.5–2.4 2.5–3.9 4.0–5.4 5.5–6.9 7–9.9	Word and paragraph meaning.	Harcourt, Brace and World, Inc. 757 Third Avenue New York 10017
Survey of Reading Achievement	7–9 9–12	Measures vocabulary, ability to follow directions, reference skills, and comprehension.	California Test Bureau Del Monte Research Park Monterey, Calif. 93940

Diagnostic Reading Tests

Name of Test	Grade Level	Description	Publisher
Diagnostic Reading Tests	K–4 4–8 7–13	Word attack and comprehension, oral and silent reading, vocabulary, and rate of reading.	Committee on Diagnostic Reading Tests, Inc. Mountain Home, N.C. 28758
Durrell Analysis of Reading Difficulty	1–6	Oral reading, silent reading, listening comprehension, word recognition and analysis, visual memory, auditory analysis, spelling, and handwriting.	Harcourt, Brace and World, Inc. 757 Third Avenue New York 10017
Gates-McKillop Reading Diagnostic Test	1–12	Oral reading, timed and untimed presentation of words and phrases, knowledge of word parts, recognition of the visual form of sounds, auditory blending, and supplementary tests of spelling, oral vocabulary, syllabication, and auditory discrimination.	Teachers College Press Columbia University New York 10027

Test	Grade	Description	Publisher
Gilmore Oral Reading Test: New Edition	1–8	Individual test, oral reading, accuracy, comprehension, and rate.	Harcourt, Brace and World, Inc. 757 Third Avenue New York 10017
Gray Oral Reading Test	1–12	13 paragraphs of increasing difficulty; word attack skills, oral reading efficiency.	Bobbs-Merrill Company 4300 West 62nd St. Indianapolis, Ind. 46268
Monroe Diagnostic Examination	1–6	Specific reading errors: Reversals; addition and omission of sounds; and substitution, repetition, addition, and omission of words.	C. H. Stoelting Co. 424 N. Homan Ave. Chicago, Ill. 60624
Primary Reading Profiles	1–3	Aptitude for reading, auditory association, word recognition, word attack, and reading comprehension.	Houghton Mifflin Co. 110 Tremont St. Boston, Mass. 02107
Spache Diagnostic Reading Scales	1–8	Three word recognition lists, twenty-two reading passages, and six supplementary phonics tests.	California Test Bureau Del Monte Research Park Monterey, Calif. 93940
Stanford Diagnostic Reading Test	2.5–8.5	Identifies specific strengths and weaknesses in reading comprehension, vocabulary, syllabication, auditory skills, phonetic analysis, and rate of reading.	Harcourt, Brace and World, Inc. 757 Third Avenue New York 10017

Measures of Intelligence

Name of Test	Age Level	Description	Publisher
Arthur Point Scale of Performance Tests, Revised Form II	5–15	An individual test of non-language ability.	Psychological Corp. 304 East 45th St. New York, 10017
Illinois Test of Psycholinguistic Abilities	2–10	An individually administered diagnostic test designed to investigate the child's ability in auditory-vocal communication, visual-motor communication, as well as certain receptive, organizing, and expressive processes.	The University of Illinois Press Urbana, Ill. 61801
Lorge-Thorndike Intelligence Tests	Grade Level K–1 2–3 4–6 7–9 10–12	Nonverbal and verbal measure of intelligence.	Houghton Mifflin Co. 110 Tremont Street Boston, Mass. 02107

Peabody Picture Vocabulary Test	2½–18	Measures verbal intelligence.	American Guidance Service, Inc. Publishers' Building Circle Pines, Minn. 55014
Stanford Binet Intelligence Scale	2–Adult	Individual test of intelligence.	Houghton Mifflin Co. 110 Tremont Street Boston, Mass. 02107
Wechsler Intelligence Scale for Children	5–15	Five verbal tests and five performance tests. Yields verbal IQ, performance IQ, and full scale IQ.	Psychological Corp. 304 East 45th St. New York 10017

Screening Tests

Name of Test	Age Level	Description	Publisher
Audition:			
Audiometer	3–Adult	Measures auditory acuity.	Maico Electronics Inc. Minneapolis, Minn. 55408
Wepman Auditory Discrimination Test	5–10	Individual test of auditory discrimination.	Joseph M. Wepman, Ph.D. 950 E. 59th St. Chicago, Ill. 60650
Dominance:			
Harris Tests for Lateral Dominance	7–Adult	A series of easy-to-administer tests of lateral dominance.	Psychological Corp. 304 East 45th St. New York 10017
Vision:			
Keystone Visual Survey Telebinocular	5–Adult	Measures such aspects of vision as vertical posture, lateral posture, fusion, visual acuity, and stereopsis at both far and near points.	Keystone View Company Meadville, Pa. 16335
Ortho-Rater	5–Adult	Measures near and far acuity, depth perception, lateral and vertical phorias.	Bausch and Lomb Rochester, N.Y. 14601

| Sight-Screener | 5–Adult | Measures near and far acuity, depth perception, lateral and vertical phorias. | American Optical Co. Box 1 Southbridge, Mass. 01551 |

Appendix B

The value of the clinical history and school data blanks shown in Appendix B is dependent upon the thoroughness and accuracy with which they are completed. These means of organizing personal data should be employed by an experienced interviewer and should not be treated as a questionnaire. The rights of privacy of each individual involved in the study of the child should be respected. *All data are confidential.*

Psycho-Educational Clinic
Western Michigan University
Kalamazoo, Michigan 49001

Clinical History

The following data are to be regarded as suggestive of the many facts to be obtained in the study of a child's behavior. These data should be summarized by an experienced interviewer and should not be regarded as a questionnaire.

Name ———————————————— School ————————————

Age ————————— Date of birth ——————— Grade ————
        Yrs.   Mos.

Birthplace ——————————— Nationality or Race ——— Sex ——

Parents ————————————————— Address ————

Referred by ————————————————————————

Brought by ————————————————————————

Problem ———————————————————————————

————————————————————————————————

Send report to ————————————— Address ————

Person giving information ——————————————————

Date when this blank was completed ———————————————

Family History

	Name	Age	Occupation	Education	Living with Family	Remarks
Father						
Mother						
1.						
2.						
3.						
4.						
5.						
6.						
7.						
8.						

(Include children in order of birth. Give some account of grandparents et al. Write below.)

HOME CONDITIONS: (Neighborhood; home itself; general home atmosphere; religion; income, thrift, and culture levels; care and control of children; attitude of parents: (a) to children (b) to each other (c) to problem, etc.; attitude of child: (a) to other children in the home (b) to parents. Who is the dominant member of the household? Family friction? What language is spoken at home?)

Development History

Age of mother ———— and father at time of birth ———— Weight of child at birth ———— Health of mother during pregnancy ————————

Shocks or accidents during pregnancy ————————————

Was baby delivered feet first, head first, breech first, or by Caesarean operation? ———————————————————————

Were instruments used? ———— Were there any injuries or marks of malformations? ——————————————————————

Did baby nurse easily? ———— Any convulsions or bleeding? ————

Was there difficulty in starting breathing? ——————————————

Was baby breast or bottle fed? ————————————————

Was the rate of growth normal? ———— Give age in months at which following took place: First tooth ———— Full set of second teeth ————

Creeping on all fours ———— Sitting alone ———— Walking alone ————

Feeding self ———— Said mama or dada ———— Got voluntary control of urination ———— Have there been any serious diseases, accidents, convulsions, or operations? ——————————————————————

Does child have any physical deformities? ——————————————

Is child very ————, fairly ————, or not very energetic? ————

In what activities is child very awkward? ——————————————

Very well coordinated? ————————————————————

Is the child right or left handed? ———— Did anyone attempt to change the child's handedness? ———— Has the child ever written backwards? ———— Are there many activities which he can do better with the usually nonpreferred hand? ————————————————

Is there any lefthandedness in the family? ——————————————

Personal and Social Behavior

A. *Personal Habits*
1. Eating? (control, fastidiousness)
2. Dressing? (fussy, neat)
3. Cleanliness? (washing, handkerchief, things out of mouth)
4. Sleep? (quickly, soundly, dreams)
5. Toilet? (regularity, soil or wet bed)
6. Sex behavior?
7. Speech? (articulation, stuttering)
8. To what extent has this individual acquired a sense of responsibility?

B. *Social Behavior*
1. Like to play? (hard, alone, with others, age)
2. Like pets?
3. Favorite pastime?
4. Sociable with other children?
5. Get along? (quarrelsome)
6. Affectionate with parents?
7. Sociable with strangers?
8. Adjusts well outside of home? (party, picnic, doctors, Sunday School, etc.)
9. Obedient?
10. Obstinate?
11. Deceptive?
12. Sensitive?
13. Jealous?
14. Nervous?
15. Need any special discipline? (What?)
16. Responds to discipline?
17. Is he sensible, reasonable about things? (sense of value)
18. Sense of humor?
19. Cry easily?
20. Tantrums?
21. Moody?
22. Babyish?
23. Timidity or fears?

C. *Independence and Self-Reliance*
1. Can he play contentedly by himself? How long?
2. Does he lead other children?
3. Stand up for his rights? For his possessions?
4. Can he take responsibilities at home? If so, what are they?
5. Errands?
6. Money?
7. Very selfish or self-centered?
8. Lack self-confidence?
9. Suggestible?
10. Show initiative, originality, imagination, concentration?

D. *Special Traits*
(Note any special achievements, excellences, or distinctive characteristics.

Also any peculiarities, habits, or weaknesses that need guidance or correction.)

General School History

1. Grade now in? _____ Years in school? _____

2. Grade or grades "skipped"? _____ Why? _____

3. Did pupil ever fail to be promoted? _____ Why? _____

Grade	School Attended	Age Entering	No. of Yrs. in Grade	Descriptive Statements concerning quality of work
Kindergarten				
First				
Second				
Third				
Fourth				
Fifth				
Sixth				
Seventh				
Eighth				
Ninth				
Tenth				
Eleventh				
Twelfth				

ADDITIONAL REMARKS:

4. Average mark received (during the past year) in each subject taken by the pupil.

Subjects	Grade	Subjects	Grade
Reading		Mathematics	
Spelling		Science	
Language			
Writing			
Social Studies			

5. Is slow progress in any subject due to difficulties in reading? (Comment in detail.)

6. Has attendance been regular?   Causes of irregularity and amount?

7. Attitude of pupil to (last) teachers?   Attitude of pupil to school?

8. Does pupil use library?   How much?

9. What are the child's special interests?

Report of Medical Examiner

No case should be presented to the Psycho-Educational Clinic without the concurrence or recommendation of the family physician.

Child's name ——————————————————— Age ——— years

Parent's name ————————————— Address ——————

Medical examination made by ————————————— M.D.

Address _____ Date _____

Vision: R _____ L _____ Hearing: R _____ L _____

General Condition: (Physical growth and development, nutrition, nervous stability, teeth, nasopharynx, heart, lungs, glands, spine, etc.)

Abnormalities: (Of growth, development, or function; gait, posture, speech, etc.)

General Impressions:

Other findings negative except as follows:

Recommendations:

Date of this report _____

Reported by _____
(Physician)

Additional Information:

Psycho-Educational Clinic
Western Michigan University
Kalamazoo, Michigan 49001

School Data

Dear Co-worker:

In order to obtain the necessary data for a comprehensive and clinical study of the disabled reader, the cooperation of the teacher is essential in the gathering of information concerning the personality, emotional make-up, and behavior traits of the individual referred to the clinic. We shall greatly appreciate it if you will carefully answer the queries in the following questionnaire concerning ———————————————— who is or has been

(Child's Name)

a pupil under your supervision. Before you complete this questionnaire, please sign your name.

_____
(Your Name)

_____
(Name of School)

_____
(Address)

_____   _____
(Date)   (Telephone Number)

All information furnished to the clinic will be considered confidential and will not be made available to unauthorized persons.

1. As you see it, is this pupil maladjusted? If so, is the maladjustment of a social, emotional, or scholastic nature, or is it a combination of two or more of these factors?

2. When and in what capacity have you known this pupil?

3. How long has this individual had difficulty in reading and what do you think might have precipitated it?

4. Is the student aware that he has a reading problem? If so, do you think he wishes to improve his reading and is willing to put forth effort to do so?

5. What is the student's attitude toward reading?

6. What kind of a reading program has he experienced in the past?

7. What kind of a reading program is he having now?

8. Have you ever given this pupil special attention in relation to his reading difficulty? What was the nature of the special attention which was given?

9. Did he seem to realize that he needed help and did he cooperate with you in trying to remedy his difficulty?

10. Do you think that you have gained his confidence? If so, what problems does he discuss with you?

11. How well adjusted is the child in the classroom?

12. Does he get along well with other children? Does he have one particular friend?

13. Do any of his associates ever come to you with any disparaging remarks about him? If so, what kind of remarks are made?

14. Do any of his associates make any exceptionally commendable remarks about him to you? If so, what kind are they?

15. What is your personal reaction to this pupil, that is, do you like or dislike him and why?

16. What has the child been successful in doing?

17. What are his extracurricular activities?

18. Is the child a member of Boy Scouts, Girl Scouts, Four-H Club, or other organizations?

19. What is his attitude toward you? Does he seem to like you and want to please you or does he tend to be defiant and disobedient?

20. How regular is the pupil's attendance?

21. Is the pupil shy, quiet, self-conscious, introverted, easily offended?

22. Is the child impulsive, hot tempered, irritable, excitable, nervous, over-active? (Underline your response.)

23. Is he cheerful, humorous, distractible, depressed, indifferent, coopera-tive? (Underline your response.)

24. Does he show self-confidence?

25. Does he make any antisocial attempts to gain recognition such as trying to be funny, acting "smarty" or babyish?

26. What special disciplinary measures does he require?

27. Has this pupil ever shown any unusual aptitude or interest in any one subject and if so, has he shown a tendency to neglect other subjects in the interest of this particular one?

28. Does he ever say that he hates this or that subject?

29. Are there any unusual animosities between this pupil and any other boys or girls which you would consider of any possible causal influence in his present difficulty?

30. In your opinion does the home provide a climate which would stimulate an interest in reading?

31. Does he appear to have good relationships with his parents?

32. What are the parents' expectations for this child?

33. Have his parents ever come to you to discuss his problems? To what extent do they seem concerned?

34. Would you say his parents are either strict or overprotective?

35. Do you think he is expected to accept responsibility at home?

36. Is he able to keep at a task until it is finished or is he easily distracted?

37. Can he follow directions, work independently, and assume responsibility or does he require individual help?

38. What can you say of the quality of work which he is doing in school?

39. Do you consider the presence of this pupil in the school a deterrent to the healthful, normal development of others?

40. Do you think there is anything in his home or community environment which might be upsetting to him?

41. Do you think that his trouble is the unfortunate result of conditions over which he has no control and that an alteration of such conditions would markedly improve his behavior?

42. Do you think that he is mentally incapable of doing the work, that he is lazy, that he is distracted by outside interests, or that he is suffering from some emotional trouble?

43. As far as you know, is this pupil suffering from any physical disorder or abnormality of any kind? If so, state what it is. If he is exceptionally tall or short, fat or thin, please mention it.

44. What do you think is the probable cause or causes of this pupil's difficulty?

Test Data

I. *Intelligence Tests*

Name of Test	Date	Score
a.		
b.		
c.		
d.		

II. *Reading Tests*

Name of Test	Date	Score
a.		
b.		
c.		
d.		

III. *Other Tests*

Has he ever been referred to the school diagnostician for a psychological evaluation or to the visiting teacher for study? If so and if you know the results of the findings, please summarize them briefly below. Also, please note the date these services were rendered.

We wish to thank you for your consideration in this matter.

Appendix C

The materials listed in Appendix C have been helpful to teachers and therapists working with disabled readers. They may be employed in many ways and at various age and grade levels. Their use will be determined both by the needs and the interests of the child. The manuals accompanying these materials will be beneficial for purposes of selection and for ascertaining means of application.

Books and Workbooks

Name of Materials	Grade Level	Description	Publisher
Basic Reading Skills	7–9 and 9–12	Workbook providing a refresher program on reading skills for students not reading up to their grade level.	Scott, Foresman and Company 433 East Erie St. Chicago, Ill. 60611
Be a Better Reader	6–12	Develops common skills needed in reading all types of materials and the special skills needed in reading in content areas.	Prentice-Hall, Inc. Englewood Cliffs, N.J. 07632
Better Reading Books	4–12	Designed to develop reading speed with comprehension. Available in a series of three volumes, each at a different reading level. Each volume includes twenty reading selections accompanied by comprehension and vocabulary tests.	Science Research Associates 259 E. Erie St. Chicago, Ill. 60611

Title	Grade	Description	Publisher
Developing Your Vocabulary	9–12	Offers techniques for learning new words, use of the dictionary and thesaurus, and discusses homonyms, figurative language, meanings and connotations of words.	Science Research Associates 259 E. Erie St. Chicago, Ill. 60611
Diagnostic Reading Workbooks	K–6	Designed to develop the ability to read for main ideas and word-attack skills.	Charles E. Merrill Books, Inc. Columbus, Ohio 43216
Language Experiences in Reading Program	1–3	Provides guidance for the teacher to follow in teaching reading through a language-experience approach.	Encyclopaedia Britannica Educational Corporation 425 North Michigan Ave. Chicago, Ill. 60611
Let's Read	1–2	A linguistic approach to the teaching of reading.	Clarence L. Barnhart, Inc. P.O. Box 250 Bronxville, N.Y. 10708
Merrill Linguistic Readers	1–2	Designed to develop letter discrimination, spelling ability, and reading for meaning.	Charles E. Merrill Books, Inc. Columbus, Ohio 43216
New Phonics Skilltexts Series	1–6	Emphasizes phonics, structural analysis, comprehension, and listening skills.	Charles E. Merrill Books, Inc. Columbus, Ohio 43216

Name of Materials	Grade Level	Description	Publisher
New Reading Skilltext Series	K–6	Designed to develop skill in getting information, understanding ideas, organizing ideas, making judgments, and studying words.	Charles E. Merrill Books, Inc. Columbus, Ohio 43216
New Rochester Occupational Reading Series	9–12 and Adult	Provides both reading instruction and information about the attitudes and skills that lead to success on the job and in society. Level 1—Reading Level 2 Level 2—Reading Level 3–4 Level 3—Reading Level 4–5	Science Research Associates 259 E. Erie St. Chicago, Ill. 60611
Phonics We Use	1–6	Develops word-attack skills.	Lyons and Carnahan 407 E. 25th St. Chicago, Ill. 60616
Phonovisual	K–2	Emphasizes auditory discrimination and a phonetic approach to word study.	Phonovisual Products, Inc. Box 5625 Washington, D.C. 20016
Reading, A Key to Academic Success	9–14	Shows students how to make effective use of their books. Emphasizes reading in the content areas.	Wm. C. Brown Co., Publishers Dubuque, Iowa 52001

Title	Grade	Description	Publisher
Reading for Meaning	4–12	Designed to improve vocabulary, rate of reading, identification of central thought, and reading for detail.	J. B. Lippincott Company East Washington Square Philadelphia, Pa. 19105
Scope	8–12	Weekly periodical developed for the student with mature interests but below normal academic abilities written at fourth- through sixth-grade reading level.	Scholastic Magazines, Inc. 902 Sylvan Ave. Englewood Cliffs, N.J. 07632
Specific Skill Series	1–6	Practice exercises designed to develop skill in reading to follow directions, to locate answers, to get facts, and to use the context.	Barnell Loft, Ltd. Rockville Centre, N.Y. 11571
Standard Test Lessons in Reading	2–12	Designed to develop rate of reading and comprehension.	Teachers College Press Columbia University New York 10027
The Reading Skill Builders	1–14	Designed to aid students in developing sight vocabulary, word attack skills, and reading for meaning.	Reader's Digest Services, Inc. Pleasantville, N.Y. 10570

Kits and Packaged Materials

Name of Materials	Grade Level	Description	Publisher
Dolch Teaching Aids:			
Match Games	K–1	The ninety-five most common nouns. Emphasizes picture clues.	The Garrard Press Champaign, Ill. 61820
Picture Word Cards	K–1	The ninety-five most common nouns. Develops the beginning of a basic sight vocabulary through picture clues.	
Basic Sight Cards	1–6	Designed to develop a sight vocabulary of 220 basic words.	
Group Word Teaching Game	2–6	Bingo-type game to develop a basic sight vocabulary.	
Sight Phrase Cards	2–6	140 sight phrase cards to help in teaching phrase perception.	
What the Letters Say	K–1	Teaches the beginner to realize that every letter has a name and a sound.	
Consonant Lotto	1–4	Provides practice in listening for consonant sounds.	

Vowel Lotto	2–6	Provides practice in hearing and learning short vowels, long vowels, vowel digraphs, and diphthongs.	
The Syllable Game	3–6	Develops word attack skills.	
Picture Readiness Game	K–1	Lotto-type game to develop visual discrimination.	
Frostig Program for Individualized Training and Remediation in Visual Perception	K–3	Provides remedial exercises in five visual perceptual areas: (1) Eye-motor co-ordination, (2) figure-ground, (3) constancy of shape, (4) position in space, and (5) spatial relationships.	Consulting Psychologists Press 577 College Ave. Palo Alto, Calif. 94306
Non-Oral Reading Series	1–3	Sequence of lesson plans and materials for teaching writing, spelling, colors, numbers, oral language, and speech simultaneously.	Primary Educational Service 1243 West 79th St. Chicago, Ill. 60620
Peabody Language Development Kits	K–3	Stresses the development of overall oral language skills through reception, expression, and the cognitive processes.	American Guidance Service, Inc. Publishers' Building Circle Pines, Minn. 55014

Name of Materials	Grade Level	Description	Publisher
Phonics We Use Learning Games Kit	1–6	A word-recognition program which emphasizes phonics.	Lyons and Carnahan 407 East 25th St. Chicago, Ill. 60616
Pilot Library 2a 2c 3b	4–5 6–7 8–9	Bridges the gap between reading training and independent reading with short excerpts from noted literature.	Science Research Associates 259 E. Erie St. Chicago, Ill. 60611
Reading for Understanding Junior Edition Senior Edition General Edition	3–8 8–12 5–College	An individualized reading program to develop skill in reading to analyze a sequence of ideas and to make logical conclusions.	Science Research Associates 259 E. Erie St. Chicago, Ill. 60611
Reading Laboratory 1: Word Games	1–3	Reading laboratory 1 is the phonics portion of the Reading Laboratory program. It is a separate laboratory designed to supplement Laboratories 1a, 1b, and 1c.	Science Research Associates 259 E. Erie St. Chicago, Ill. 60611

Title	Levels	Description	Publisher
Reading Laboratory Series 1a 1b 1c 2a 2b 2c 3a 3b 4a	 1 2 3 4 5 6 7–9 8–10 9–12	Reading selections and exercises are grouped at the reading levels normally found in a class. Created to develop vocabulary, comprehension, and word-attack skills.	Science Research Associates 259 E. Erie St. Chicago, Ill. 60611
Speech-to-Print Phonics	1	Contains fifty-five lessons in relating phonemes in words to their printed form and ten lessons for teaching letter names and forms.	Harcourt, Brace and World 757 Third Ave. New York 10017
Steps to Mastery of Words	1–6	Method of teaching spelling built on all phases of word analysis.	Educational Service, Inc. P.O. Box 219 Stevensville, Mich. 49127
Tactics in Reading	9–11	High-interest selections for the development of specific reading skills: Word-attack, dictionary use, sentence and paragraph meaning, and reading to understand figurative language and relationships.	Scott, Foresman and Company 433 East Erie St. Chicago, Ill. 60611

Name of Materials	Grade Level	Description	Publisher
The Macmillan Reading Spectrum	4–10	Eighteen colorful booklets that give pupils sequential instruction in word analysis, vocabulary development, and comprehension.	The Macmillan Co. 866 Third Ave. New York 10022
Webster Classroom Reading Clinic	4–9	Contains materials, varying in reading difficulty, designed to develop a basic sight vocabulary, word attack skills, and ability to read for meaning.	Webster Division McGraw-Hill Book Company Manchester Road Manchester, Mo. 63011

Machine-Type Aids

Name of Materials	Description	Publisher
Controlled Reader	Can be employed at various levels to deal with orientation, word attack, and meaning disabilities.	Educational Developmental Laboratories Huntington, N.Y. 11743
Dolch Sight Words and Phrase Slides	Recommended for use with tachistoscope to develop sight vocabularies.	Keystone View Company Meadville, Pa. 16335
Flash-X	Can be helpful in increasing accuracy of perception.	Educational Developmental Laboratories Huntington, N.Y. 11743
Leavell Language Development Service	Provides hand-eye coordination training.	Keystone View Company Meadville, Pa. 16335
Reading Accelerator	Uses student's own reading materials. Adjustable to wide range of reading rates.	Science Research Associates, Inc. 259 E. Erie St. Chicago, Ill. 60611
Tachistoscope and Tachistoslide Units	Can be used at various levels for many purposes.	Keystone View Company Meadville, Pa. 16335

Index

ability grouping, 309
Abrams, Jules C., 90
academic history, 21
accommodation, 49, 309
achievement age, 309
achievement test, 309
acuity, 309
administrator, role in treatment, 183–184
age norm, 309
alexia, 309
Allen, Jeremiah M., 295
Allen, R. V., 231
Almy, Millie Corinne, 63
alternating vision, 309
ambidexterity, 309
amblyopia, 309
American Psychological Association, 13
ametropia, 309
Anastasi, Anne, 17, 128
anecdotal records, 79–80, 309
  illustration of, 80
  use of, 79–80
aniseikonia, 49, 309
anthropometrics, 161–162, 309
aphasia, 309
appraisal, areas of, 264–265
  of factors affecting reading performance (formal), 106–126
  of factors affecting reading performance (informal), 134–148
  methods of, 267–273

principles of, 265–267
  of professional skills, 275–280
  of remediation, 263–273
Arbuthnot, Mary Hill, 256
Arthur Point Scale of Performance Tests, Revised Form II, 326
Artley, A. Sterl, 191
association cards, 142–145
association, difficulties of, 213–215
associative skills, informal measures of, 141–145
astigmatism, 49, 309
attitudes, 61–65, 122–124, 132, 145–146, 298–299
audile, 309
audiogram, 309
audiometer, 111–112, 309, 328
audition, 111–112
  measures of, 111–112, 328
auditory acuity, 51, 111–112, 310
auditory defects, symptoms of, 112, 300
auditory discrimination, 51–52, 217, 310
  informal measures of, 137–138
auditory factors related to reading, 51–52
auditory memory, 51–52, 310
  informal measures of, 138–139
Austin, Mary C., 16, 68, 69, 167, 282, 306
Ausubel, David P., 67
Ausubel, Pearl, 67